# Corporate and White-collar Crime

John Minkes and Leonard Minkes

Los Angeles • London • New Delhi • Singapore

First published 2008

SAGE Publications Ltd
1 Oliver's Yard
55 City Road
London EC1Y 1SP

SAGE Publications Inc.
2455 Teller Road
Thousand Oaks, California 91320

SAGE Publications India Pvt Ltd
B 1/I 1 Mohan Cooperative Industrial Area
Mathura Road,
New Delhi 110 044

SAGE Publications Asia-Pacific Pte Ltd
33 Pekin Street #02-01
Far East Square
Singapore 048763

Library of Congress Control Number: 2007942661

British Library Cataloguing in Publication data

A catalogue record for this book is available from the
British Library

ISBN 978-1-4129-3457-2
ISBN 978-1-4129-3458-9 (pbk)

Typeset by C&M Digitals (P) Ltd., Chennai, India
Printed in Great Britain by TJ International, Padstow, Cornwall
Printed on paper from sustainable resources

This book is dedicated to the memory of Ruth Minkes who did so much to support the careers of the two editors.

# Contents

Terms which are included in the Glossary are printed in **bold** on the first occasion on which they appear in the text.

# Notes on Contributors

**Robert Elliott Allinson** is Professor of Philosophy and Director of Humanities at Soka University of America. He was previously Professor in the Department of Philosophy at the Chinese University of Hong Kong and has been invited to hold senior visiting appointments internationally, including Yale, Oxford, Cambridge and Copenhagen. His numerous books and papers, notably on cross-cultural and business ethics, include *Saving Human Lives: Lessons in Management Ethics* (Springer, 2005) and *Understanding the Chinese Mind* (OUP, 2000).

**James Gobert** has been a Professor of Law at the University of Essex since 1988, including a three-year term as Dean of the Law School. Before coming to Essex, he was a Professor of Law in the US for 15 years, with appointments at the University of Tennessee, Vanderbilt University and the University of Michigan. Over the past decade, his research has focused primarily on corporate crime, and he has written several books and articles on this topic, including, most significantly, *Rethinking Corporate Crime* (with M. Punch) (Butterworths, 2003).

**Omi Hatashin**, LLB (Tokyo), MA, PhD, is a barrister of the Inner Temple, a member of the Academic Society of Comparative Law, Tokyo, an occasional associate member of the Nissan Institute of Japanese Studies of the University of Oxford (2004–7) and a visiting fellow at the Institute of European and Comparative Law, Oxford (2008–9). His interests centre on comparative legal studies in a socio-cultural dimension with particular reference to Japan.

**Brian J. Loasby** is Honorary and Emeritus Professor of Economics at the University of Stirling. He has written five books and over a hundred journal articles and chapters in multi-author books. His interests centre on the relationships between knowledge and organization, conceiving both as selective connections, and extend to human cognition, firms and inter-firm relationships, decision processes, the history of economics and economic methodology.

Gerald Mars, an applied anthropologist, is Honorary Professor at University College London and Visiting Professor at Liverpool Hope and London Metropolitan Universities. He is Joint General Editor of The International Library of Criminology, has published eleven books and over sixty papers and in 2003 was awarded the Royal Anthropological Institute's Lucy Mair medal 'for consistent excellence in applied anthropology'.

John Minkes is a Lecturer in Criminology and Criminal Justice at the Centre for Criminal Justice and Criminology, Swansea University. He was previously a probation officer, a researcher at Cardiff and Bristol Universities and a social worker. His primary research interests are corporate crime, the history of criminal justice and probation and youth justice.

Leonard Minkes is Emeritus Professor of Business Organisation, University of Birmingham. He has had an extensive academic career in Britain and overseas, as well as in advisory and consulting work in business and public sector organizations. He also had a period in the United Nations in Geneva early in his career. His primary interest and numerous publications are in corporate strategy and management.

Nicole Leeper Piquero is an Associate Professor of Criminal Justice in the Wilder School of Government Affairs at Virginia Commonwealth University.

Maurice Punch has worked at universities in the UK, the USA and the Netherlands where he has lived since 1975; he has researched corporate crime and police corruption and published widely; after twenty years in Dutch universities he became an independent researcher and is currently Visiting Professor at the London School of Economics.

Laureen Snider is Professor of Sociology at Queen's University, in Kingston, Ontario, Canada. Her most recent publications on corporate crime include 'This Time We Really Mean It! Cracking Down on Stockmarket Fraud', in H. Pontell and G. Geis (eds), *International Handbook of White-Collar Crime* (Kluwer, 2006); 'From Manslaughter to Preventable Accident: Shaping Corporate Criminal Liability', *Journal of Law & Policy*, 2006 (with Steve Bittle), and 'The Criminological Lens: Understanding Criminal Law and Corporate Governance', in J. O'Brien (ed.), *Governing the Corporation: Regulation and Corporate Governance in an Age of Scandal and Global Markets* (Wiley, 2005).

Steve Tombs is Professor of Sociology at Liverpool John Moores University and Chair of the Centre for Corporate Accountability (www.corporateaccountability.org/), a human rights charity. His most recent publication is *Safety Crimes* with Dave Whyte (Willan, 2007). He co-authored *Corporate Crime* (Longman,

1999) with Gary Slapper, and *Toxic Capitalism* (Ashgate, 1998; Canadian Scholars' Press, 1999) with Frank Pearce, and co-edited *Beyond Criminology? Taking Harm Seriously* (Pluto Press, 2004), *Criminal Obsessions* (Crime and Society Foundation, 2005), and *Unmasking the Crimes of the Powerful: Scrutinising States and Corporations* with Dave Whyte (Peter Lang, 2003).

**Elin Waring** is Professor of Sociology at Lehman College, City University of New York. She has published extensively in the areas of white-collar crime, organized crime and co-offending. Her major works include *Russian Mafia in America: Crime, Immigration and Culture; White Collar Crime and Criminal Careers*, and *Crimes of the Middle Classes*.

**David Weisburd** is Walter E. Meyer Professor of Law and Criminal Justice and Director of the Institute of Criminology at the Hebrew University Faculty of Law in Jerusalem, and Distinguished Professor of Administration of Justice at George Mason University in Virginia. He has authored or edited with colleagues a number of books on white-collar crime including *Crimes of the Middle Classes* (Yale Press, 1991), *White-Collar Crime Reconsidered* (Northeastern University Press, 1992) and *White-Collar Crime and Criminal Careers* (Cambridge University Press, 2002). He is also co-editor (with Sally Simpson) of a forthcoming book entitled *The Criminology of White-Collar Crime* (Springer Verlaag).

# Introduction

*John Minkes and Leonard Minkes*

Many academic disciplines are interested in the behaviour of corporations. Management scholars, of course, are concerned with understanding the behaviour of large organizations and the factors which govern their effectiveness. Lawyers contemplate the questions raised by the emergence of the corporation as the main vehicle of economic production and the challenges this presents to legislators and regulators. Business ethicists discuss the moral, ethical and philosophical questions posed by the everyday activities of corporations and their shareholders, directors and employees. Anthropologists describe the organization of structures and roles within large institutions. And criminologists document and analyse the damage caused by corporations which break the law.

On the whole, though, these enquiries are carried out separately. With few exceptions (e.g. Vaughan, 1983, and Punch, 1996, and this volume), those interested in corporate conduct, or more specifically, misconduct, remain within their own disciplines. The contention of this book is that the study of corporate and white-collar crime should become a transdisciplinary field. Thus, it brings together contributions from each of the subject areas mentioned. That is not to say that each of the chapters is itself transdisciplinary; each is designed to give an insight into different approaches to and aspects of corporate and white-collar crime. We have referred elsewhere to the need for scholars from different disciplines to engage in a learning process about what we termed 'the criminology of the corporation' (Minkes and Minkes, 2000). Therefore, the aim of the book as a whole is to encourage students, academics and researchers to investigate all these fields, and to show how each is essential to a full understanding of the complexities of this major social issue. It will be especially appropriate for postgraduate and advanced undergraduate students of criminology generally, for specific courses or modules on corporate crime, and in business and management studies.

In this introductory chapter, we set out the chain of ideas about criminology and the behaviour of organizations and the individuals within them which led to a book which is concerned with both subjects, and thus provide an overview of the book as a whole. We preface this by emphasizing that the subject is one about which there are differing opinions and although there are many points of convergence among the authors, neither this nor the other nine chapters are designed to present a single view about the nature of corporate crime. Each chapter presents the approach of the author concerned: the aim of the book is not to present a uniform editorial view, but rather to initiate debate on the connections between the subjects.

## Related disciplines

In what ways, therefore, do or should the disciplines come together? The concern of criminologists with the question of corporate misconduct has its parallel in the study by management scholars of the twin problems of accountability and responsibility in organizations, especially in large businesses and public bodies within which there are decentralized groupings. Thus, the problem of attributing liability to corporations as such, which exercises the minds of criminologists and lawyers, has its counterpart in the studies of decision-making in organizations by economists and organization analysts such as Simon, Cyert and March, Bass and many others in the United States, or Alford, Hannah, Child and others in Britain, to name but a few.

This is reflected in the present book, in fact, in the extent to which authors writing from different perspectives have raised related questions in related language. For example, in Chapter 3, James Gobert contrasts the approach of methodological individualism with the concept of corporate identity, while Brian J. Loasby, in Chapter 6, is concerned with the question of the implications for decision-making of the existence of organizations. In Chapter 5 by Maurice Punch, which bridges criminology and organizational sociology, attention is focused on malpractice which is systemic rather than strictly individual. This is what Punch described elsewhere as more than failures by 'rotten apples'; rather, he suggests we turn our attention to the orchard (Punch, 2003).

In another context, in Chapter 1, Steve Tombs expresses an underlying interest in moral standards in his critique of corporate behaviour, while in Chapter 2 Laureen Snider is explicit about business ethics. Robert Elliott Allinson, in his sharp critique as an ethicist and philosopher, describes the term 'business ethics' as an **oxymoron** in Chapter 4. He argues that there is a question of ethical or unethical behaviour in general and that it is in those terms that business behaviour should be assessed.

There is a further general point which precedes our discussion of organizational decision-making. In a number of cases which are discussed in the book, for example, Enron and Barings Bank, there was specifically fraudulent, illegal activity which led to legal action and conviction in the courts. In other instances, such as the *Challenger* Space Shuttle disaster in 1986, there was clearly no malicious intent but there are significant questions about responsibility and, as Allinson (1993) has remarked, ethical queries.

We do not intend to rehearse in advance all the ideas which the reader will find in the chapters of this book, but rather to set out some of the questions with which we, as editors, had become concerned from our different perspectives. We have, nevertheless, to take up some questions with which several of our contributors are explicitly concerned, for example, what is an organization, and does it have an identity over and above the identities of its individual members? Associated with these questions, there has been considerable research on the idea of organizational learning: economists and management scholars have discussed the idea that an organization can be said to learn.

## On organizations

Why do organizations, and specifically, business corporations, exist at all? Why does the world not consist only of individuals producing and trading independently of one another? This does happen, after all, in a number of service trades – plumbing, electrical work, household decorating, for example – in which one person deals with numbers of customers by making individual arrangements. In effect, the service provider makes a series of contracts with clients. An immediate answer to this question was given by the American economist, Kenneth Arrow: he wrote (1974: 33) that:

> The purpose of organisations is to exploit the fact that many (virtually all) decisions require the participation of many individuals for their effectiveness. In particular ... organisations are a means of achieving the benefits of collective action in situations in which the price system fails.

We do not need, here, to enter into detailed discussion of the meaning of 'price system' but we do have to observe that in a market economy the co-ordination between buyer and seller is affected by prices. In the examples we have given, the plumber or decorator specifies a price quotation for a defined task and the client accepts or refuses. The lines of responsibility are clear as between individuals. Moreover, if the task also requires a particular skill which the plumber, etc. does not have, he or she may strike a deal or price with another individual who can contribute that skill.

This seems, no doubt, elementary enough and there are substantial areas of the market economy which work in just that way. And to cast a glance towards criminology, we can say that if any party to the transaction is dishonest or unethical, it is possible (though not always easy) to point the finger of responsibility. But there are very large parts of the modern economy which are not a bit like that; the dominant characteristic is the corporation, and the large corporation at that (though this is not to deny the importance of small and medium-sized enterprises).

Economists and management scholars have gone on, consequently, to give various explanations of why these corporations have come into being and why they grow, e.g. by utilizing **economies of scale**. We do not need to examine them exhaustively in this Introduction, bearing in mind the factors set out in Loasby's chapter. But we do need to examine some characteristics which have a special bearing on the link with criminology.

The real world of decision-making is characterized by uncertainty and ambiguity, incomplete information, dispersal of information and different access to information by different persons involved in any decision-making situation. Furthermore, there are costs of securing information and evaluating it: these are examples of what the economist Ronald Coase (1937) refers to, in a notable paper, as transactions costs of using the market. Consider, for example, a firm which is considering whether to manufacture a particular component which it requires for its main product, or to buy it from an external supplier. If it buys it, it faces costs of acquiring knowledge of available suppliers and of assuring quality. If it decides to do the job itself, it will of course incur production costs but within in its own control, and it will hope to reduce uncertainty.

The reduction of risk and uncertainty is a significant question in the decision to expand an organization and it is given here as an important feature in the growth of firms. A related feature is that the ability of individuals to acquire and evaluate information is limited and here, again, there can be gains from organizational structures which can accumulate and evaluate information, including specialist information. These structures may be formal, with rules and regulations, departments and divisions. They may also be informal understandings, which have been described as 'conventions of governance'; together with the formal organization, they constitute the organizational culture.

We emphasize these aspects because they lead to an understanding that when individuals become members of an organization, as managers, for example, they become committed in some measure to its goals and values; hence: 'Social scientists cannot hope to understand decision-making if they do not analyse the organisational contexts and institutional frameworks in which there are conflicts of interest and the group and inter-group processes by which decisions are made' (Zey, 1992: 22).

This argument can be extended to the nature of information flows within organizations. It is true that organizations are means of dealing with the uncertainties of the real world within which information is dispersed and specialized. The same phenomenon applies within organizations; as we have pointed out elsewhere (Minkes and Minkes, 2005), information inside a corporation is diffused throughout it, among different individuals and business units. Some of it consists of hard data e.g. of past sales, some of it may be best guesses e.g. anticipated future sales or the likely behaviour of competitors. The information which is received by the upper echelons of a corporation will have been assembled at lower levels and sifted before transmission to top decision-makers. Some will not, therefore, have been transmitted either because it is not thought to be sufficiently important or for reasons related to power. It is also understood, of course, that there are differences in the kinds of information to which there is access at different levels in the hierarchy.

The consequences of these lines of argument are:

- Organizations are not repositories of perfect knowledge; they exist as a means of handling uncertainty and they do so by establishing decision structures, formal and informal, to make the world manageable.
- Within organizations, knowledge is dispersed. Even in a corporation headed by a powerful individual, as in the case of, say, Robert Maxwell, that individual does not have all the information – he or she is in some measure dependent on the information-gathering and transmitting by subordinates.
- Decisions are made at various levels in an organization. Hence, consequences are the outcome of a complex of decisions. Since there is multi-causality, there must be multi-responsibility. This does not, of course, absolve the top echelons of the organization of their overall responsibility for leadership.
- The existence of formal rules and informal conventions in an organization makes it appropriate to speak of organizational culture. This may also be influenced by national cultural characteristics, as may be seen in Omi Hatashin's contribution to this book (Chapter 7).

## Responsibility and motivation

We have so far discussed organizations and given some picture of the ideas which interest economists and management scholars. This led to a brief statement of the multi-character of the decision process in large organizations and of the practical problems which arise in the large decentralized corporation. Alfred Sloan, who was head of General Motors, was one industrialist who drew attention to this aspect when he wrote that the company had never ceased to grapple with the problem of reconciling decentralization with central control (Sloan, 1965). We may argue from this, that the old aphorism that 'the buck stops here' should be enlarged to say that 'the buck stops here and everyplace else too' (Allinson and Minkes, 1990).

The relevance of these propositions to the assignment of responsibility is evident and this applies to criminological and ethical matters as to other decisions. There is then the question of what organizations exist to achieve: the question of the goals of the corporation. Economists and many others who are interested in firms have typically adopted what might be described as a rational actor approach or **rational choice theory**. That is, they have assumed that there is a decision-maker or unit such as the firm, which behaves rationally; in the case of the firm, seeking to maximize profits and knowing how to do so. As we note below, this model is readily adopted by some criminologists who accuse corporations of placing profit above any competing considerations such as the health and safety of employees or customers.

This view of the world has its virtues from the point of view of analysing economic choices and it has been argued by many scholars (Milton Friedman, for example) that the value of a theory depends not on the reality of its assumptions but on its predictive effectiveness. We do not enter into this argument in detail because we are more concerned with understanding actual behaviour. Consequently, and this has a particular significance in the context of this book, we observe, first of all, that the business corporation, in common with other organizations, cannot make absolutely optimal, perfect choices because this would require an extent of knowledge beyond the capacity of human beings. Loasby refers to this in his chapter and to the idea of **satisficing** behaviour, but for specific reasons puts it aside. Our point here is not to dispute that a corporation tries to do the 'best' it can, but that limits to human knowledge mean that it cannot know the 'best best'.

A fundamental proposition which follows from our description of organization is that it is not realistic to argue as if there were only a single goal for any system. Profitability is clearly a major goal, whether we see it as a motivating factor or a necessary condition of survival. The American management writer Peter Drucker (1977) regarded it as a necessary condition, the test of validity: if the Board of Directors consisted of archangels, he held, they would still need to make a profit. There are also other goals or conditions which play a part: expansion of market, growth in scale and power are examples. To these should be added the goals of the various departments and other units which make up the totality of the organization. Last but most certainly not least are the goals of individual members of organizations – their career ambitions, for example.

The complexity which is implicit in this multiplicity of goals has led some writers to comment that rather than envisaging organizations as existing to satisfy a common purpose, they should be seen as satisfying the joint purposes of their members. It should be noted, however, that this does not mean that all purposes are of equal weight, nor does it underrate the significance of profit as a necessary condition in a market economy.

The picture we have given of the organization as a network of persons and groups and a pattern of decision-making by individuals and more or less separate units may appear at first sight to make it unacceptable to speak of organizations as such having decided or been responsible for anything. Yet we customarily refer to NASA policy with respect to space exploration, or the Government or the University of … or ICI or Mitsubishi, and we seem to do so without difficulty in understanding what these shorthand terms mean. Moreover, although we have emphasized the diffusion of information, ambiguity and the compartmentalization of decision-making, and the function of the individual as decision-maker, this does not mean that it is inappropriate to ascribe liability to the organization as such.[1]

There are formal, interconnected reasons for this. The first is that decision-makers in an organizational context differ in an important respect from those made in a wholly individual matter. This was put succinctly by Simon (1957) when he commented that the executive makes his decisions with one eye on the matter in hand and the other on the organizational context. The second aspect is that the very existence of organizations gives rise to rules and systems: also, decisions are made within assumptions and procedures, analogous to fixed capital equipment (see Loasby, 1976). The design of decision processes and how efficiently they are managed can reasonably be judged in situations in which failures or malpractice occur.

## On business ethics

A major consequence of the existence of organizations is that there may be tensions between the individual and the organization. This is of particular relevance when we consider the subject of business ethics, on which there is a substantial body of literature (for an overview of this literature, see, for example, Treviño and Nelson, 1999). It deals with how corporations, private and public, do or should behave and embraces questions about what is termed corporate social responsibility. It is concerned with internal behaviour towards employees, external behaviour towards consumers and obligations to the wider community. In the present context, it might be thought that only those actions contrary to law merit consideration, but, in fact, underlying conceptions of what is acceptable behaviour are clearly relevant to an understanding of important questions of trust and accountability which arise in the large, decentralized organization.

Such matters may arise at the individual as well as the organizational level. Is it unethical behaviour on the part of an individual employee to work in the marketing department of a cigarette manufacturer if he or she believes that tobacco is dangerous to health? And does that extend to the employees whom one of the editors saw sorting tobacco leaf in a factory in Sri Lanka? Or consider a dilemma of the kind described by Provis (2004) in which a female member of staff asks for help from a more senior colleague, also female, because she is being harassed by a male supervisor. What does the senior colleague do, if she herself fears that bringing the problem into the open may have consequences for her own position and progress in the organization?

Such conflicts raise questions about the legitimacy of the demands made by an organization on individual members and also about the extent to which an individual, by working in an organization, can be held to have given consent to its behaviour. We have referred elsewhere (Minkes, 2005) to an interesting example of a BBC executive who resigned because he disapproved of the decision to televise *Jerry Springer: The Opera*. As far as we are aware, the executive had no part in that decision; he just did not wish to belong to the organization that had made it.

Such individual instances are by no means trivial. They reflect the implications for individuals of dilemmas arising from organizational life, raising also the question of the whistle blower and how this relates to the proposition that 'the fact of obedience is perhaps the dominant fact of behaviour in organisations' (Bradley and Wilkie, 1974: 70). Together with the topic of ethics of the corporation, they underline the observation that while something criminal may be unethical, it certainly does not follow that something which is not criminal is necessarily ethical.[2] When Allinson (1993) in his chapter on the *Challenger* disaster asserted that the astronauts had a right to be fully informed of the risks they were running, he was referring to a moral right, whether or not it was enshrined in law or organizational regulation.

We can extend the argument to the ethical climate of the organization as a whole, which is composed of formal and informal arrangements. In the case of Enron, which is discussed in this volume by Laureen Snider and Maurice Punch, there was criminal fraud, but part of the problem arose from the fact that auditors from Arthur Andersen also acted as consultants. The conflict of interests implicit in such an arrangement renders it morally dubious. Bazerman and Watkins (2004) consider that problems of that kind cannot be resolved simply by codes of ethics but also require improved training of accountants and auditors. It can hardly be denied, however, that the moral climate was a relevant factor in the Enron case.

We have argued that in the modern corporation, especially when it is large, divisionalized and departmentalized, there are major problems of informational dispersal. There is also a problem of information overload which may lead to efficiency loss because of 'the tendency in that situation to filter information in accordance with one's preconceptions' (Arrow, 1974: 75). An example Arrow gives is: 'when the *Titanic* began to broadcast for help, the captain of a nearby ship decided that the messages must be a mistake or a hoax. It was well known that the *Titanic* was unsinkable.' The characteristics and problems of decision-making as a whole in organizations spill over, so to speak, into the realm of ethics and organizational culture. To what extent are the members of a corporation implicitly or explicitly responsible for its failings or misdemeanours? In many instances, employees will not be fully informed. Of course, there are instances in which they are responsible, as in the kind of workplace deviance with which Gerald Mars is concerned, but there are others in which they are not.

Several of the contributors to this book have written sceptically about the possibility of ethical behaviour in a world of rational profit maximization and the probability that corporate behaviour inevitably extends to crime. Sutherland, the pioneer in the study of corporate crime, was not radical in his politics and believed in competition, but he also thought that crime was endemic in the corporation (Geis and Goff, 1983). Even Adam Smith (1863: 116), thinking, it is true, of monopolistic collusion, commented that: 'People of the same trade seldom meet together even for merriment and diversion but the conversation ends in a conspiracy against the public, or some contrivance to raise prices.' It is in this context, we might perhaps say to this challenge, that the extensive literature on business ethics and corporate social responsibility has to respond. Bowie (1991: 17), while writing that 'its legitimacy as a subject is suspect' added, 'Unless business ethics is part of the business curriculum, the legitimacy of the business curriculum is suspect.'

Or again, Kuhn and Shriver (1991: 12) remark that:

> The quantitative differences between the world of the Smithian producer and that of today's managers are vast. Modern economic environments have created qualitative – and ethical – differences large enough to encourage all of us re-examine the economy's provision of the quality and ethics of economic life.

Those two quotations make large claims: they are important and they have to be seen as elements both in the structure of business ethics and in the extent to which study of business ethics carries over effectively to management behaviour. They have to be seen also in the wider framework of ethics and the corporate economy which has been drawn in several chapters of this book.

## Criminology and the corporation

The core concern of criminology, naturally enough, is the study of crime and its causation, but, as with the law (cf. Gobert in this volume), the focus has usually been on the actions of individuals. More than that, it has been on certain types of crime committed by certain types of individual. This was the starting point for Sutherland (1940): in his presidential address to the American Sociological Association, he made it clear that his purpose in investigating the criminality of commercial corporations was not to criticize the mode of economic production in the United States but to challenge criminology. Criminologists, he argued, were purporting to build general theories of the causation of crime on the basis of a very partial picture of its prevalence, informed by a criminal justice system which prosecuted the poor and disadvantaged while the wealthy and powerful used their influence to avoid prosecution. His survey of criminal, civil and administrative findings against the largest corporations in the USA showed that many of them were offenders and some of them confirmed recidivists (Sutherland, [1949] 1983).

The study of corporate and white-collar crime has nevertheless remained a minority interest in criminology. Thirty years ago, Wheeler (1976) informed the American Society for the Study of Social Problems that only 2.5 per cent of the books and articles listed in the *Criminological Index* for 1945 to 1972 dealt with corporate or white-collar criminality (and half of those were studies of organized crime). A glance now at the list of research studies published by the Home Office in Great Britain, one of the major funders of criminological research in the United Kingdom, reveals a total absence of titles on corporate crime and few references to any form of white-collar offending. Modern criminology textbooks usually include at least one chapter on these topics (e.g. Tombs, 2005; Nelken, 2007) but the fact remains that, on the whole, academic criminologists concern themselves with what may be termed 'conventional' crime; in common with politicians and the media, they focus mainly on burglary, street robbery, drugs and serious physical and sexual violence.

## Perspectives on corporate crime

Those criminologists who have written about corporate crime have done so from a variety of perspectives. Sutherland's objective, as we have already noted, was to change criminology. Theories which blamed crime on poverty, poor education, bad housing or conflicting value systems could not be sufficient if wealthy, successful and powerful people were also shown to break the law. His answer was the theory of differential association: people committed crimes if the balance of definitions available to them favoured crime. In other words, they would break the law if those around them did so (and were willing to initiate them into the necessary techniques). This theory, he claimed, could be applied to all forms of crime.

Sutherland was an enthusiastic supporter of competition and the capitalist mode of production; his argument was with the major corporations that did everything they could to subvert it by, for example, advertising false claims for their products or forming illegal price-fixing cartels. Similarly, Braithwaite in his many writings on the subject (e.g Fisse and Braithwaite, 1994) and Punch (1996, 2000, and this volume) have catalogued at considerable length the misconduct of corporations all around the world without expressing opposition to the concept of capitalism itself. They may regard features of corporate organization as criminogenic but the solutions they propose involve better regulation or self-regulation.

Other criminologists have approached corporate wrongdoing from a more radical perspective, as part of a wider critique of capitalism. Pearce (1976) and Box (1983) make no bones about their belief that corporations in capitalist economies will always put profit before obedience to the law, risking the health and safety and financial security of their employees and customers if the company's interests demand it. Slapper and Tombs describe themselves as engaged in 'a partisan scholarship', in their contribution, 'in the struggle for a more equitable social order' (1999: 233). While the collapse of the Soviet bloc has made it less likely that radical writers will look to Eastern Europe for a model economy, their scepticism about the possibility of improving the behaviour of corporations in a capitalist society is apparent.

One idea that is common to all who write about corporate misconduct is that corporations and their owners and directors use their power to influence legislators and enforcement agencies. This can be clearly illustrated by two examples, the Ford Pinto and British legislation on corporate killing. In the 1970s, Ford marketed a small sports car named the Pinto in the USA, despite apparently knowing that an easily (and cheaply) correctable design fault caused it to burst into flames in low speed rear-end collisions (Dowie, 1977). Faced with claims that they were responsible for hundreds of deaths and serious injuries in the resulting fires, Ford protested that the car met all the relevant safety standards. They neglected to mention, however, that they had campaigned for eight years against the introduction of more stringent standards. In Britain, twenty years later, the Law Commission recommended new legislation on corporate killing (Law Commission, 1996) in the wake of the collapse of the *Herald of Free Enterprise* prosecution, among others, but the government were so careful to ensure that the legislation was acceptable to business that it took no less than 11 years for a restricted statute to be enacted (see Gobert, this volume).

This is by no means an exhaustive list of those criminologists who have striven to establish the prevalence of corporate crime and the threat it poses to its victims and, some would argue, to society as a whole. In turn, the study of corporate misconduct has contributed to debate about the nature of crime and criminology itself.

Sutherland's challenge was not only to criminological theory but to the very concept of crime. He courted controversy in his work when he included breaches of regulations and administrative rules in his definition of crime. This not only meant that he had to remove the names of the companies from the first (1949) edition of *White Collar Crime* for fear of libel suits, but also led to a fierce debate with Tappan (1947) over the nature of crime. In contrast to Sutherland's broad concept, Tappan argued that the term 'crime' could only refer to actions defined as such by law and for which the law prescribed punishment – the so-called 'black letter law' definition – and this definition should also set the boundaries of the discipline of criminology. Tappan's position is meaningful, of course, if one is dealing with the operation of the law as it stands. However, it ignores the role of power in forming the law and determining, for example, which forms of wrongdoing will be the subject of criminal prosecution and which will be subject instead to administrative and civil sanctions. Thus, his narrow definition would preclude criminologists from studying a wide range of behaviours that cause harm. In contrast, corporate wrongdoing is one of the areas which has inspired Hillyard et al. (2004), among others, to argue that the term 'criminology' is too narrow for a subject that seeks to understand a broad range of misconduct, leading to the development of the concept of 'social harm'.

Nelken emphasizes the value of this debate to criminology as a whole: 'The topic of white collar crime ... illustrates the possibility of divergence between legal, social and political definitions of criminality – but in so doing it reminds us of the artificiality of all definitions of crime' (2007: 742). The study of corporate crime, therefore, has helped to show that crime is a contested concept; that is, it is not a category or label which can be taken for granted, but one which reflects societal values and often those of particular sections of society.

It is important to acknowledge that there has been confusion in the terminology used by criminologists; although the term 'corporate crime' is widely used to describe offences which benefit the corporation, Sutherland's book on this topic was entitled *White Collar Crime*. Here, we follow the former practice, using the term white-collar crime as it is used by Weisburd et al. (this volume; Weisburd and Waring, 2001) to refer to non-violent property offences, usually involving some element of fraud or deception. For crimes committed by people in the course of their work but for their own benefit, we follow Mars in favouring the term 'occupational deviance'. However, our use of corporate and white-collar crimes as umbrella terms should not be taken to indicate that we regard them as monolithic categories, capable of simple and singular explanation. Sutherland's concept of differential association, despite its resonance with, for example, some biographical accounts of corporate offending, has long been abandoned as a potential general theory of white-collar crime, let alone all crime, and not simply because of the lack of clarity in his definition of the term. Indeed, most criminologists have ceased to search for a single explanation of crime in the face of the diversity of behaviours defined as such, and the debates, noted above, about the very nature of the term. In addition, it is the one of the purposes of this volume to broaden the discussion still further. Criminology has been memorably described by Garland as a 'rendezvous subject', bringing together a number of academic disciplines and this is as true in the fields of corporate and white-collar crime as it is in criminology's traditional concerns.

## Corporate and white-collar crime

It will have been noted that much of the discussion in this Introduction, and the majority of the chapters in the book as a whole, deal with corporate crime, defined as offences which benefit the organization and for which responsibility may be assigned to the organization as a whole, rather than (or possibly as well as) individual offenders. The last two chapters, however, deal with two different topics: occupational deviance – offences committed in the course of employment but for the benefit of the individual not the employer – and the careers of white-collar criminals, non-violent property offenders whose offences are generally unconnected with their employment. This is because one of our objectives in this book is to take the study of crime beyond the usual categories which are generally termed 'conventional crime'. Given the scale of the physical and economic harm caused by corporate crimes, we think it is appropriate that most of the chapters are concerned with corporate crime and the business organization. But we also think it important to include chapters on other types of crime which are too often ignored.

In fact, these topics challenge us not only to broaden our concepts of the nature of crime and its perpetrators, but also to reconsider the very idea of crime as something abnormal. If white-collar crime is widespread and is committed by people who are no different to the rest of us, if up to 92 per cent of employees admit in self-report studies to pilfering and stealing from their employers (Henry, 1981), then what is normal? This argument is taken even further in the recent work of Karstedt and Farrall (2006; 2007) who refer to the 'everyday crimes' committed by people who regard themselves as law-abiding, such as inflating insurance claims or requesting payments in cash in order to avoid tax. They suggest that the prevalence of this sort of dishonesty is a better measure of the moral state of a society than official statistics on violent crime, and their work certainly underlines the value of focusing on the process of criminalization: why is it that only certain types of misconduct are stigmatized as 'real crime'?

## Identifying transdisciplinary issues

The essential focus of the book is, of course, on corporate malfeasance and hence, on the relevance to crime, of the managerial processes by which the organization and its individual employees are governed. For the criminologist, therefore, there is a need to understand the complex of decisions and internal relationships within the corporation. It also raises the question of how wide is membership to be defined – if, indeed, the term membership is appropriate. If we follow Gobert's critique of methodological individualism, and if responsibility is associated with legal sanction, are shareholders to be regarded as members? Yet if ownership and control are separated in a managerial world, is it reasonable that penalties should be borne by shareholders who are not involved in running the corporation?

This further touches on the question of how to punish a corporation which has been found guilty of an offence, in particular, a criminal offence as in corporate manslaughter. Corporations are commonly fined; in some jurisdictions, they can be subjected to periods of official supervision or ordered to carry out work for the benefit of the community, just as individual offenders may be. They can also be ordered to make amends and to correct management failings.

Some of these penalties are aimed at sanctioning past behaviour, others at influencing future conduct, which raises the question of the purpose of sentencing and the effectiveness of different measures. In truth, though, responses to corporate and white-collar crimes are often based not on coercion but on persuasion and non-prosecution. Some have argued, on the basis of the view mentioned above of corporations as rational actors, that a harsher regime would deter them from offending, a view supported by Davis (2004) in her review of research findings. On the other hand, if one accepts the complexity and imperfection in decision-making processes revealed by management studies, a more varied approach may be appropriate (see Simpson, 2002).

Experience with conventional offenders, however, suggests that the impact of sentencing and prosecution policies on general levels of offending is very limited; for one thing, the vast majority of offences, be they conventional, corporate or white-collar, never come to the notice of any authorities (Maguire, 2007). What, then, do the transdisciplinary perspective and the roots of organization as, say, Loasby describes them, suggest as solutions to the problem of reducing or preventing corporate and white-collar crime? One possible route is that of business ethics and the idea of corporate responsibility and the development of norms of acceptable behaviour. In this context, it would surely be significant to look beyond accounts of malpractice and focus attention on the management practices of firms whose behaviour meets good standards – this is a largely neglected area of research.

The contribution of ethical standards as that term is used in business ethics is probably not a complete answer to the problems, even if we take a less critical view than those criminologists who are sceptical of their significance. But Punch's experiences of discussing business ethics with students and broader concerns about the limited space given to ethics teaching in management training, suggest that there is scope for greater emphasis to be placed in such training on the need to assess potential negative consequences of management decisions, and not just in terms of the consequences for business. Criminologists need to learn from management scholars about the behaviour of organizations and the individuals within them, but management studies can also benefit from criminological analyses of corporate and white-collar misconduct.

## Conclusion

This book was conceived not only as a collection of knowledge from different disciplines but also as a stimulus to future research and theoretical development. The interrelatedness among different disciplines is reflected in the extent to which individual authors have referred, from their varying perspectives, to similar topics. The critical feature of corporate identity, for example, is explicitly considered in several chapters, from legal and organizational points of view; so are some distinctive cases which have occurred in different countries. Enron is such an example, as are the railway disasters in the UK and Japan.

This Introduction has presented ideas mainly from the two disciplines represented by the editors but has also sought some measure of synthesis of all the fields represented in the book by identifying, albeit briefly, issues that would benefit from interdisciplinary analysis. These would include the question of assigning responsibility, the effectiveness of regulation and sentencing in prevention and the role of business ethics.

## Notes

1 For example, in matters where there is a statutory obligation as in health and safety, but also in more general matters such as corporate manslaughter.
2 We have used the term 'may be unethical' because there may be laws which can be regarded as unjust: law and justice are not necessarily identical.

## References

Allinson, R.E. (1993) *Global Disasters: Inquiries into Management Ethics*. Singapore: Prentice Hall/Simon and Schuster (Asia) Pte Ltd.

Allinson, R.E. and Minkes, A.L. (1990) 'Principles, proverbs and shibboleths of administration', *International Journal of Technology Management*, 5(2): 179–87.

Arrow, K. (1974) *The Limits of Organization*. New York: W.W. Norton.

Bazerman, M.H. and Watkins, M.D. (2004) *Predictable Surprises*. Boston: Harvard Business School Press.

Bowie, N.E. (1991) 'Business ethics as a discipline: the search for legitimacy', in R.E. Freeman (ed.), *Business Ethics: The State of the Art*. Oxford: Oxford University Press.

Box, S. (1983) *Power, Crime and Mystification*. London: Tavistock.

Bradley, D. and Wilkie, R. (1974) *The Concept of Organization*. Glasgow: Blackie.

Coase, R.H. (1937) 'The nature of the firm', *Economica*, iv (November): 386–405.

Davis, C. (2004) *Making Companies Safe: What Works?* London: Centre for Corporate Accountability.

Dowie, M. (1977) 'Pinto madness', *Mother Jones*, September–October, (2), pp. 17–19.

Drucker, P. (1977) *Management*. New York: Harpers College Press.

Fisse, B. and Braithwaite, J. (1994) *Corporations, Crime and Accountability*. Cambridge: Cambridge University Press.

Geis, G. and Goff. C. (1983) 'Introduction', in E. Sutherland, *White Collar Crime*. New Haven, CT: Yale University Press.

Henry, S. (1981) 'Introduction', in S. Henry (ed.), *Can I Have It in Cash?: A Study of Informal Institutions and Unorthodox Ways of Doing Things*. London: Astragal Books.

Hillyard, P., Pantazis, C., Tombs, S. and Gordon, D. (2004) *Beyond Criminology: Taking Harm Seriously*. London: Pluto Press.

Karstedt, S. and Farrall, S. (2006) 'The moral economy of everyday crime: markets, consumers and citizens', *British Journal of Criminology*, 46(6): 1011–36.

Karstedt, S. and Farrall, S. (2007) 'Law-abiding majority? The everyday crimes of the middle classes'. Available at: www.crimeandsociety.org.uk/briefings/lawabiding majority.html

Kuhn, J.K. and Shriver, D.W. Jr. (1991) *Beyond Success: Corporations and their Critics in the 1990s.* New York: Oxford University Press.

Law Commission (1996) *Legislating the Criminal Code: Involuntary Manslaughter.* London: HMSO.

Loasby, D. (1976) *Choice, Complexity and Ignorance.* Cambridge: Cambridge University Press.

Maguire, M. (2007) 'Crime data and statistics', in M. Maguire, R. Morgan and R. Reiner (eds), *Oxford Handbook of Criminology.* Oxford: Oxford University Press.

Minkes, A.L. (2005) 'Review of C. Provis', *Ethics and Organisational Politics, Philosophy of Management,* 5(3): 128–9.

Minkes, J.P. and Minkes, A.L. (2000) 'The criminology of the corporation', *Journal of General Management,* 26(2): 17–33.

Minkes, J.P. and Minkes, A.L. (2005) 'Decentralisation, responsibility and ethical dilemmas', *Social Responsibility,* 1(1/2): 16–20.

Nelken, D. (2007) 'White-collar and corporate crime', in M. Maguire, R. Morgan and R. Reiner (eds), *Oxford Handbook of Criminology.* Oxford: Oxford University Press.

Pearce, F. (1976) *Crimes of the Powerful.* London: Pluto Press.

Provis, C. (2004) *Ethics and Organisational Politics.* Cheltenham: Edward Elgar.

Punch, M. (1996) *Dirty Business: Exploring Corporate Misconduct.* London: Sage.

Punch, M. (2000) 'Suite violence: why managers murder and corporations kill', *Crime, Law and Social Change,* 33: 243–80.

Punch, M. (2003) 'Rotten orchards: "pestilence", police misconduct and system failure', *Policing and Society,* 13(2): 171–96.

Simon, H.A. (1957) *Administrative Behavior,* 2nd edn. New York/London: Free Press/Collier Macmillan.

Simpson, S. (2002) *Corporate Crime, Law and Social Control.* Cambridge: Cambridge University Press.

Slapper, G. and Tombs, S. (1999) *Corporate Crime.* London: Longman.

Sloan, A.P. (1965) *My Years with General Motors.* London: Sidgwick & Jackson.

Smith, A. (1863) *An Inquiry into the Nature and Causes of the Wealth of Nations.* London: Ward, Lock & Co.

Sutherland, E. (1940) 'White Collar Criminality', *American Sociological Review,* 5(1): 1–12.

Sutherland, E. (1949) *White Collar Crime* revised and reprinted (1983) as *White Collar Crime: The Uncut Version.* New Haven, CT: Yale University Press.

Tappan, P.W. (1947) 'Who is the criminal?', *American Sociological Review,* 12: 96–102.

Tombs, S. (2005) 'Corporate crime', in C. Hale, K. Hayward, A. Wahidin and E. Wincup (eds), *Criminology.* Oxford: Oxford University Press.

Treviño, L.K. and Nelson, K.A. (1999) *Managing Business Ethics: Straight Talk about How to Do It Right,* 2nd edn. New York: John Wiley & Sons, Ltd.

Vaughan, D. (1983) *Controlling Unlawful Organizational Behavior: Social Structure and Corporate Misconduct.* Chicago: The University of Chicago Press.

Weisburd, D. and Waring, E. (2001) *White-Collar Crime and Criminal Careers.* Cambridge: Cambridge University Press.

Wheeler, S. (1976) 'Trends and problems in the sociological study of crime', *Social Problems,* 23(5): 525–34.

Zey, M. (1992) 'Part 1: Critiques of rational choice models', in M. Zey (ed.), *Decision-Making: Alternatives to Rational Choice Models.* Newbury Park, CA: Sage.

## Suggestions for further reading

Cannon, T. (1992) *Corporate Social Responsibility*. London: Pitman.

Jackall, R. (1988) *Moral Mazes: The World of Corporate Managers*. New York: Oxford University Press.

Minkes A.L. (1987) *The Entrepreneurial Manager: Decisions, Goals and Business Ideas*. Harmondsworth: Penguin.

*Philosophy of Management* (2005) Vol. 5, Number 3; Special Issue on Business, Legitimacy and Community.

Pontell, H. and Geis, G. (eds) (2007) *International Handbook of White-Collar and Corporate Crime*. New York: Springer.

Vaughan, D. (1983) *Controlling Unlawful Organizational Behavior: Social Structure and Corporate Misconduct*. Chicago: The University of Chicago Press.

# ONE

## Corporations and Health and Safety

### Steve Tombs

## Introduction

Corporations affect – or, as this chapter will begin by indicating, *infect* – every area of our lives. And if the ubiquity of the corporation is, it must be remembered, a relatively recent phenomenon, in the past 30 years or so, the influence of corporations over and within our daily lives has grown exponentially. Swept along on the international tidal wave of neo-liberalism, governments across the world have, in that 30-year period, relinquished ownership and control of whole swathes of economic activity and services provision. Transportation systems, the provision of basic utilities such as electricity, gas, water, telecommunications, health care and social services, pensions provision, even the conduct of war, state security and intelligence, and criminal justice are now arenas in which corporations play increasingly significant roles. If the mixed economy still exists in some states, the private sector has gained political, economic and *moral* (Tombs, 2001) ground during this period.

If there are benefits of this activity, the rise of the corporation, coupled with the states' very recent handing over of activities to them at the same time as softening regulatory regimes, has increased our exposure, as citizens, workers, consumers, and so on, to the inherent downsides of corporate activity. Some of these, those harmful and illegal activities of corporations which detrimentally affect human health and safety, are the subject of this chapter.

## Corporate crimes against health and safety

Corporate crime is a wide-ranging term, and has been subject to enormous, and in many respects unhelpful, definitional controversy. For the purposes of this chapter, such crimes are as 'illegal acts or omissions, punishable by the state under administrative, civil or criminal law, which are the result of deliberate decision-making or culpable negligence within a legitimate formal organization' (Pearce and Tombs, 1998; 107–10, following Box, 1983, Schrager and Short, 1977). Even this relatively simple definition encompasses a vast range of offences of omission and commission with differing types of *modus operandi*, perpetrators, effects, and victims – and many of these offences impact directly, or vicariously, upon people's health, safety and well-being.

One general area of corporate crimes are those committed directly against consumers, many of which affect their health and safety. Examples include: the sale of unfit goods (such as the drug Thalidomide); the provision of unfit services (trains which crash, aircraft in which we breathe polluted air or suffer illness as a result of inadequate leg room); false/illegal labelling or information (endangering health when household cleaning products are improperly used, for example); and the fraudulent safety testing of products (as in the development of the contraceptive device, the Dalkon Shield). A classic example of a crime directly against consumers, routine in its commission but perhaps unique in its consequences, was the outbreak of E-Coli among Lanarkshire residents in November 1996, resulting in 18 deaths and almost 500 people ill. The poisoning was traced back to a local butchers, eventually fined £2,500 for failing to ensure equipment was kept clean and that food was protected against contamination. More generally, food poisoning, although with generally far less significant consequences, is widespread. For example, the 2001 FSA Consumer Attitudes to Food survey recorded 12 per cent of UK consumers – equivalent to 5.5 million people – stating they had experienced food poisoning in the last year. Almost three-quarters of them – approximately 4.2 million – believed their food-borne illness was caused by food prepared out of the home.[1] By the fourth survey, self-reported incidence of food poisoning was at 16 per cent of the sample population, 82 per cent of them claiming the source was outside the home (TNS, 2004: 61). Only 2–3 per cent reported these cases of food poisoning to their local council or an environmental health officer; of this percentage, just 11 per cent were aware of any action being taken against the outlet in question (TNS, 2004: 65). According to the Food Standards Agency, 365,356 establishments were inspected in the UK in 2005/06; 160,158 uncovered infringements which led to formal action by the enforcement authorities.[2]

We can also identify crimes arising out of the employment relationship. One area that has been subject to study more than most, and which falls into this category, are crimes against worker health and safety. And even a cursory scrutiny of this one sub-category indicates the heterogeneity of the offences under consideration in this chapter. Such offences may, for example, produce large-scale disaster – such as the gas leak at Bhopal, India, which killed tens of thousands (see Pearce and Tombs, 1998: 194–219); or a multiple fatality train crash (Wolmar, 2001: 155–79); more often, the consequences of such an offence are very localized, if often tragic (such as the death of Simon Jones, a

24-year-old student who died within hours of his first day at work at Shoreham docks).[3] Even more likely is the creation of an illegal and unsafe state of affairs which may produce no death or injury. That said, being a victim of a work-related fatality in the UK is much more likely than being a victim of homicide. And even if not all of these deaths are formally processed as crimes – of the 1,600–1,700 deaths per annum, only about 200 are ever investigated – there is good evidence from the regulator, the Health and Safety Executive, to believe that some two-thirds to three-quarters are the result of offences (Tombs and Whyte, 2007). Offences producing death – and the same goes for injuries – are widespread.

A final category of offence, crimes against the environment, includes illegal emissions to air, water, and land; the failure to provide, or the provision of false information; hazardous waste dumping; and illegal manufacturing practices. Thus, as citizens we may breathe illegally polluted air, ingest toxins from waterways, and suffer exposures from poorly maintained HGVs (Heavy Goods Vehicles), taxis and buses. The vast majority of such exposures are never recognized, let alone processed as crimes. For example, a 2001 Greenpeace report calculated that between 1999 and 2001 there were 533 *known* breaches of licences by the ten municipal waste incinerators operating in England. Most were likely to be emissions of dioxins, highly toxic, known cancer-causing substances – but only one of these breaches had been prosecuted (Brown, 2001; Whyte, 2004). More recently, the Government's latest Corporate Environmental Crime[4] report notes that

[The] number of substantiated environmental incidents reported to the Agency remains relatively constant at about 29,000 pa ... Of this number, approximately 1,300 are of the most serious category 1 and category 2 types where major or significant environmental harm has been caused. (House of Commons Environmental Audit Committee, 2005: Evidence Ev1).

The Environment Agency currently conducts about 700 prosecutions per annum (ibid.). The Report further noted that 'SMEs [Small and Medium Enterprises] are responsible for up to 80% of all pollution incidents and more than 60% of the commercial and industrial waste produced in England and Wales.' '[Environment Agency] ... research shows that, 70% ... or 75% of SMEs are not actually aware of their environmental obligations', and 'the majority of these businesses are also not aware of environmental legislation' (ibid.: 14). There are 3.7 million SMEs registered in the UK; it is clear that the scale of environmental offending is vastly under-recorded.

Even this brief overview of the range of offences that fall within the general rubric of 'corporate crime' indicates that such crimes have enormous physical costs – deaths, injuries, ill-health – arising out of dangerous workplaces, polluted environments, unsafe goods and services, and so on. Corporations impact upon our health and safety in a myriad of direct ways. Yet corporate crimes also have corrosive social effects. The physical costs in general fall upon those in society who are already relatively disadvantaged: low paid workers are most likely to work in dangerous workplaces; poorer people are least able to relocate from polluted neighbourhoods; those on the tightest budgets are most vulnerable to purchasing unfit goods, such as the cheaper cuts of 'fresh' or processed meat. A further social cost of corporate crime is a diminution of social trust in the corporations upon whom we rely for employment, the food we eat, the services we use, and, by implication, the lack of trust in governments for their failure to regulate effectively the activities of these corporations.

## Corporate crimes, law and order

Given their ubiquity and significant consequences, why are corporate crimes against health and safety almost entirely absent from 'crime, law and order' agendas? To address this question we need to recognize that there is an array of social processes that contribute to removing such offences from dominant definitions of 'crime, law and order' (Slapper and Tombs, 1999).

For example, both formal politics and the law play crucial roles in the production and maintenance of definitions of 'real' crime that exclude corporate crimes against health and safety. At the political level, both in particular policy decisions – such as resource allocations for various enforcement agencies – and in the political rhetoric of crime, law and order, corporate crimes are largely marginalized. As political parties ratchet up the stakes to sound tougher on crime, the crimes to which they refer, so 'natural' that this never needs definition, refers to those conventional offences, mostly committed by marginalized, lower-class young men. Turning to the application of law and legal regulation, we find that, at every stage of the legal process, law tends to operate quite differently with respect to corporate crimes than in the context of 'conventional' crimes. Thus, in the very framing of the substance and parameters of legal regulation, its enforcement, the ways in which potential offences and offenders are investigated, the prosecution of offences, and the use of sanctions following successful prosecution, most forms of corporate and organizational offences are relatively decriminalized. As indicated above, if just 200 of the 1,600-plus fatal work-related injuries that occur in the UK each year are investigated, then the prosecution, conviction and sanctioning levels are similarly low – most recent figures show 22 prosecutions following a work-related fatality, with 18 convictions resulting in an average fine of £27,876.

Related to the political and legal invisibility afforded to corporate crime is the poverty and paucity of official corporate crime data. Measures used to indicate the scale of the crime problem do not include corporate offences. Quite simply, we lack basic, utilizable data on the scale of victimization to corporate crimes against health and safety. Even official measurements of deaths at work – irrespective of whether or not these were the result of crimes – is unreliable. Thus, while the Health and Safety Executive (HSE) claims there is a headline figure of around 250 such deaths in any one year, the more accurate total is some 1600–1700 (Tombs and Whyte, 2007). Deaths from occupationally caused illness are even less reliably measured. The example of one category of deaths in one country – deaths from asbestos exposures in Britain – is instructive here. HSE has noted that in 2004, there were 1,969 deaths from mesothelioma, an asbestos-related cancer, and 'around as many asbestos related lung cancer deaths in Great Britain' in the same year, along with 100 deaths where 'asbestosis is described as being the underlying cause'.[5] In fact, as the HSE itself recognizes, the actual numbers of deaths related to asbestos exposure are far, far higher than this 4,000 per annum total. Asbestos-related deaths continue to rise in this country (not to peak until around 2025, according to the British government), years after the apparent demise of the industry, and over 100 years after the first record of death related to asbestosis in this country (Tweedale, 2000: vii). Thus:

> Excess deaths in Britain from asbestos-related diseases could eventually reach 100,000 ... One study projected that in western Europe 250,000 men would die of mesothelioma [just *one* asbestos-caused cancer] between 1995 and 2029; with half a million as the corresponding figure for the total number of West European deaths from asbestos. (Ibid.: 276)

Even these estimates can be questioned if one examines attempts to uncover much more localized estimates. For example, through the use of novel sources of data, the Merseyside Asbestos Victims Support Group has been able to compile indications of the sheer scale of victimization in Liverpool and surrounding areas. It uncovered a letter sent by a consultant pathologist working in Liverpool Broadgreen Hospital in 1976 to the Asbestos Information Committee, an asbestos industry-supported body. Part of that letter notes:

> At present I am assessing the asbestos fibre lung content of the adult population of Liverpool, from post-mortem tissues and surgical tissues, in people who had no known asbestos contact. By the method I use most urban adults have between 2,000 and 7,000 asbestos fibres of dried lung. Only 8% of the population studied so far had a total absence of asbestos.[6]

Similarly, as the Group also reports, an occupational health project interviewed 2,601 men in doctors' waiting rooms in Liverpool between April and October 1992 and found 335 cases of exposure to asbestos. Thirteen per cent – or one in eight – men were found to have been exposed to asbestos at work. And even these figures are under-estimates. They do not capture those people who remain unaware of their exposure to asbestos, and this would include many groups of workers, DIY-ers, women who washed the clothes of men working with the stuff, those working in deteriorating or refurbished buildings where asbestos is present, and those in local communities where the substance is illegally dumped following the introduction of regulations designed to ensure its safe removal.

If we have little useful data on the scale of corporate offending, this is partially related to the fact that representations of business create significant difficulties for naming corporations as (potential) offenders (see Lacey, 1995: 21). Corporations are viewed differently to the objects of 'traditional' crime concerns; 'conventional criminals' tend to be represented as a burden upon society in a way that corporations will not be. Further, where business organizations engage in criminal activity, this is represented as an aberration from their routine, legitimate activities, while such offending tends to be cast as involving technical infringements of law, rather than real crimes. Corporate offenders are rarely, if ever, cast as 'pathological' in the same ways as individual, low-level offenders are so routinely.

These assumptions, and the general contrast with 'real' crime and 'real' criminals', are reflected in and reinforced by the media. Whether we survey fictional or documentary-style treatments of crime on TV, or newspaper and other print media coverage of the issues, we find that while there may be some attention to corporate crime, representations of crime converge to produce 'blanket' conceptualizations regarding 'law-and-order' that reinforce dominant stereotypes of crime and the criminal (Chibnall, 1977). Thus, where corporate crime is covered, its presence is vastly outweighed by treatments of conventional crime, it is treated in lesser profile outlets or formats, and is often represented in rather sanitizing language as food scares, drugs scandals, accidents at work, rail disasters, tragedies at sea, rather than in the language of crimes and criminals (Tombs and Whyte, 2001).

None of the various mechanisms whereby corporate crimes are rendered relatively invisible are particularly remarkable in isolation. What is crucial, however, is *their mutually reinforcing nature* – that is, they all work in the same direction and to the same effect, removing corporate crime from 'crime', law and order agendas.

## Victims of corporate crimes

In a series of recent reviews, Croall has demonstrated how individuals and communities fall victim to corporate crime in the home, their local neighbourhoods, at work, as consumers, when travelling, using health and welfare services, or at leisure (1995, 1998, 1999, 2001). However, a further, significant contributory factor to the relative invisibility of crimes against health and safety is the fact that this everyday, every-place victimization is so mundane, so routine, that the vast majority of victimization is either actually, or effectively, obscured; it is simply not recognized or, if identified, not acted upon. There are several dimensions to this claim.

First, many victims of corporate crimes are unlikely even to be aware of any crime, let alone their victimization to it (Grant Stitt and Giacopassi, 1993; Meier and Short, 1995). For example, it is unlikely when buying chocolate that we stop to wonder whether it is free from salmonella, or when choosing meat products in the well-known high street stores, we do not expect labels to mislead by understating the percentage of water added to the product, or that it may have been illegally imported from continental Europe; or when driving on a motorway that we may fall victim to an 'accident' caused, ultimately, by a poorly maintained lorry or impossibly tight timescales set by the company upon its driver.

Somewhat different, but related, is an awareness of some unfavourable personal circumstance or outcome, but a lack of any awareness that we have been the victim of any type of legal offence. For example, most of us are unlikely to think of our workplace as a causal site when suffering some form of illness, and even less likely to consider unhealthy conditions in terms of illegality on the part of our employer. In the event of 'accidents' – be these major or minor – ideologies of the accident-prone worker are so prevalent that workers often routinely place blame upon themselves, as a result of their carelessness or bad luck (Tombs and Whyte, 2007). Where our child suffers from breathing difficulties, we may think in some generalized way about the state of our local environment (for example, poor air quality), but are unlikely to consider concretely ourselves as possible victims of illegal emissions from a local factory.

Finally, a key element in relation to corporate victimization is the ability, or most people's perceptions of their abilities, to seek redress. That is, where victims of corporate harms *are* aware of their status as victims, actually acting upon this awareness is often extremely difficult. Indeed, an informed understanding of the extent of these difficulties may act as a disincentive against reporting or acting. This might be manifest in rationalizations invoking bad luck or being more careful in the future, and uttering platitudes such as 'win some, lose some' or 'once bitten, twice shy', and so on. Yet even where victims might seek redress, either independently (via civil law, for example) or through an enforcement agency, then distances in time and space between victim and offender(s), and consequent difficulties of proving an offence has occurred even where – as is often the case – the offender is identified, are likely to prove overwhelming obstacles.

Many of these problems of both awareness and then seeking redress can again be illustrated concretely through the case of asbestos in the UK. In the case of asbestos exposure, knowledge and regulation are such that at least some financial compensation is available to victims and their families – still rare in the case of occupational disease in this country. Yet even here, it is hard to come by, since such claims are 'very complex':

> The nature of asbestos civil claims makes it very difficult for victims to claim; in 95% of the cases they are referring to asbestos exposure some 30 to 40 years ago. However, a case cannot proceed without proof of employment at a place of work where the claimant was exposed to asbestos. The claimant also has to produce witnesses to that exposure. This may mean a 60-year-old building worker who may have worked with asbestos in the 1950's

on a small maintenance job, will have to produce eye witness accounts to his asbestos exposure from as long as 30 or 40 years ago. This makes it extremely difficult for claims to proceed.[7]

And even this litany of obstacles does not account for both ignorance and recalcitrance on the part of legal and medical professions, for each of which occupational health issues are low down on their agendas, if present at all. Given these observations, it is not surprising that, as the Hazards movement[8] has recently determined, only half of the almost 2,000 people officially recognized as

dying each year of the asbestos cancer mesothelioma receive industrial injuries benefit payments – despite the condition being accepted as caused by work, devastating and a guarantee of an excruciating death. Scarcely anyone suffering the even more common asbestos related lung cancers – fewer than 100 a year – receive compensation.[9]

## Criminology, the corporation, and crimes against health and safety

If corporate crimes against health and safety are at least potentially a significant crime problem, then, as we have indicated briefly, there are a range of social processes through which political, social, legal and regulatory processes combine to obscure their nature, extent, scale and consequences. This social construction of corporate crimes against our health and safety as something other than a crime problem extends to the discipline of criminology which, through its definitions of 'crime', 'violence' and 'policing', further marginalizes phenomena. Thus we should consider the extent to which, theoretically and empirically, health and safety crimes might be placed upon the criminological agenda.

One of the most famous claims regarding corporate crime in general was that of Sutherland, who argued that corporations, as large capitalist organizations, have particular key characteristics:

The corporation probably comes closer to the 'economic man' and to 'pure reason' than any person or any other organization. The executives and directors not only have explicit and consistent objectives of maximum pecuniary gain but also have research and accountancy departments by which precise determination of results is facilitated ...

The rationalistic, amoral, and nonsentimental behaviour of the corporation was aimed in earlier days at technological efficiency; in later days more than previously it has been aimed at the manipulation of people by advertising, salesmanship, propaganda and lobbies ... [T]he corporation selects crimes which involve the smallest danger of detection and identification and against which victims are least likely to fight ... The corporation attempts to prevent the implementation of the law and to create general goodwill. (Sutherland, 1983: 236–8)

Now, to attribute rationality to the corporation is to recognize that this is its *raison d'être*, rather than a description of how actual companies actually operate at all times; managements often manage poorly, so that calculations are either not made or, if they are made, are in fact erroneous. Yet, as we have argued elsewhere (Alvesalo et al., 2006), the corporate aims of rationality and calculability indicate that there are good theoretical and empirical reasons for at least considering the application of classicist or 'rational choice' forms of reasoning to the area of corporate crime control. While the rational choice perspective pre-dates modern criminology, it has made an indelible mark upon the development of deterrence perspectives. To argue that rational choice theory is more applicable to corporate crimes than to the types of crimes to which it is normally applied, is to accept that corporate crimes are the result of the functioning of rational, profit-maximizing entities.

In for-profit organizations, the claim that accumulation (to sustain or expand profitability) ultimately takes priority over issues of health and safety – indeed, any other goal – within a corporation seems incontrovertible. Thus it would be ludicrous to ignore the dynamic tendency to accumulate within a capitalist system, since this provides the *raison d'être* of the private corporation. However, the primacy of accumulation does not mean that there cannot be some congruence between worker and public health and safety, on the one hand, and efficiency/profitability, on the other, within a given organization. While there is an ultimate and inevitable 'truth' to the argument that profit maximisation within capitalist economies is the most fundamental cause of crimes against health and safety, we need to move beyond this level of analysis if we are to explore fully how safety crimes are produced. It is to the use – the potential and limitations – of criminological theory (beyond the rational choice perspective) in furthering this understanding, that we now turn.

To what extent, then, can crimes by corporations against health and safety be captured through the lens of criminology? This can only be addressed schematically here, yet the short answer is that this enterprise is rarely undertaken, and in practice would have limited utility.

Various forms of individual positivism that emerged after the heyday of the eighteenth- and nineteenth- century classicist theorists sought to identify the 'abnormalities' that either propelled individuals into crime, or ensured that they were more predisposed to committing crime than the general population. Now, there have been some attempts to apply an individual positivist type analysis to corporate crime, though these have been marginal to criminology, conducted mostly within business or management studies. These have tended to seek to identify those 'personality' factors associated with people who succeed in private companies, and tend to highlight features such as being innovative, ambitious, shrewd, aggressive, impatient, and possessing a 'moral flexibility' (see Snider, 1993). More recently, however, and squarely within a 'criminal justice' framework, Babiak and Hare (2006) have examined the role of the 'psychopath' in corporations. As Hare has claimed:

> The world of unfeeling psychopaths is not limited to the popular images of monsters who steal people's children or kill without remorse. After all, if you are bright, you have been brought up with good social skills, and you don't want to end up in prison, you probably won't turn to a life of violence. Rather, you'll recognise that you can use your psychopathic tendencies more legitimately by getting into positions of power and control. What better place than a corporation? (Hare, cited in Hilpern, 2004)

Now, we do not need to accept pseudo-scientific categories such as 'psychopath', nor the theoretical framework of individual **positivism**, to see how certain qualities are likely to be both valued within the corporate world, while at the same time individuals possessing such characteristics may also be more likely to be involved in corporate illegalities, either as leading figures or as individuals prepared to turn a blind eye to organizational illegality.[10] If corporations seek to recruit particular types of people, and if it is the case that the higher one goes up the corporate hierarchy, the more likely are certain characteristics to be present, valued and accentuated, then we need to know something about the culture and functioning of the corporation itself, as well as the environments within which it operates, to understand how its employees, from the most senior downwards, act, think, rationalize, and so on. For example, to understand how Bhopal was produced requires more than understanding the actions and omissions of Warren Anderson; on the other hand, Anderson clearly typified many of the qualities valorized by corporate America, and thus requires some place in an overall story of the production of thousands of deaths. In this context, it is important to bear in mind that very often there is an almost total lack of meaningful differences between corporate offenders and corporate non-offenders (Snider 1993: 61; see also Virta 1999; Weisburd and Waring, 2001).

If a myopia towards corporate offenders has been the hallmark of individual positivisms, so too has this been the case with the vast range of sociological positivisms that have come to dominate criminological theorizing since the 1930s. Here, however, we come to some notable exceptions. Sutherland himself attempted to develop a general, sociological, theory of crime causation, claiming that 'differential association' could explain both upper-class and lower-class crimes: crime arises from an excess of definitions favourable to law violation over definitions unfavourable to law violation. Criminal activity – motivations, *post-hoc* rationalizations and actual techniques of commission – is, like all behaviour, learnt. This learning, and exposure to different definitions regarding the appropriateness or otherwise of certain behaviours, emerge out of our various associations – and these associations vary by frequency, duration, priority and intensity.

Moreover, we know, on the basis of documented evidence, insider accounts, and, indeed, reasonable inference, that within certain corporations or even industries, certain forms of activity are prevalent, both in terms of knowing how to engage in them and knowing why one must engage in them. So presumably if this holds for legal activity, it holds for illegal activity too. For example, in the cockling industry off the North-western coast of England, one must assume that 'everyone knows' that there is available a pool of illegal labour, and how to draw upon this, just as in the construction industries of many of our regenerating urban centres it is common knowledge that there are armies of migrant labour, where the pick-up points and times to collect these each day are, and how these should be treated to conceal them from any external authority, and so on. Further, and crucially, there may also be generalized knowledge within a particular sector that 'everyone is doing it' – which not only provides a motivation, since not to do it is to place one's own shop or company at a competitive disadvantage, but also that to do it is so generalized that it is acceptable, not really criminal.[11]

**Differential association** is a problematic concept, and has been subjected to stringent criticism (Taylor et al., 1973: 125–30). It is of interest, however, precisely because it attempted to incorporate corporate crime within a general theory of crime. Other variants of sociological positivism have not sought to do so in such an explicit manner, yet there still remain elements or forms of these modes of explanation that can be or have been utilized by subsequent theorists to explain incidences of corporate crime. Notable here is Mertonian **strain theory** and its central concept, anomie. For example, Passas (1990) has linked deviant behaviour to the disjunction between institutionalized aspirations and the accessibility to legitimate opportunity structures. Although Merton saw these phenomena in terms of the lower classes, Passas argues that there is no compelling reason why anomie theory cannot be applied to high-class and corporate deviance:

> As the meaning and content of success goals vary from one part of the social structure to another, similar difficulties in attaining diversely defined goals may be faced by people in the upper social reaches too; they are, therefore, far from immune to pressures towards deviance. (1990: 158)

Of course, the pressures to succeed exist for business and organizations in terms of maximization of profit, growth and efficiency. These goals may have to be obtained *by all* or *any means*, particularly when the continuation of the corporation is at stake and key actors have come to equate the furthering of their own ends as largely dependent on the prosperity of the firm, an attitude underpinned by the system of financial rewards which apply to senior management, not least bonus and share schemes linked to stock market performance. Structural pressures and strains may be applied both to those at the top as well as to employees, and the employment of deviant methods may be the only possible way of dealing with problematic situations, or, may be perceived as such (see Box, 1983).

Finally, various forms of critical and radical criminologies – including Marxisms and feminisms – have made important contributions to our body of knowledge regarding corporate crime causation. Since Frank Pearce's *Crimes of the Powerful* (1976), where he argued that corporations act systematically to control the markets within which they operate, often criminally, and frequently with the connivance of the state, there has been a vibrant tradition of using critical theoretical frameworks within which to expose and analyse corporate crimes against health and safety. Particularly of note in the context of this chapter are two texts. One is Szockyi and Fox's (1996) anthology of analyses of the myriad ways in which corporations exploit constructions of gender to victimize female consumers, workers and recipients of health care – not least in terms of a range of assaults upon their health and safety. A second is Stuart Hills's edited collection on *Corporate Violence* (Hills, 1987a), precisely because it consists of a series of empirical and theoretical case studies of the ways in which injury and death are produced systematically by the drive for profit. Indeed, the most important aspect of this text is in its very naming of a phenomenon – corporate *violence*.

## Corporate violence?

In Hills's (1987a) use of the term 'corporate violence' – so accurate, yet so jarring in the light of the ways in which the term violence is predominately used in criminology – we have further, stark illustrations of the possible incompatibilities between criminology and the study of corporate crimes against health and safety. Let us consider in a little more detail the dominant constructions of violence which pervade the discipline.

Across criminology, studies of violence are in many respects heterogeneous – yet if there are enormous epistemological, theoretical and political differences between a variety of approaches to and studies of violence, these overwhelmingly share certain characteristics and, indeed, two central assumptions: first, a primacy granted to intention; and, second, a focus upon individual as opposed to collective sources of violence, and thus the centrality of violence as interpersonal as opposed to structural.

Now, intent enjoys significant legal status – while, relatedly, for some it is a key distinguishing criterion between conventional ('real') crime and corporate crime (merely technical offences) (see Pearce and Tombs, 1998: 231). However, it is worth noting here that the notion of intent presupposes, and then concretizes, a moral hierarchy which, once examined, is counter common-sensical. Reiman has contrasted the motives (and moral culpability) of intentional murder with what he calls the indirect harms on the part of absentee killers, such as deaths which result where employers refuse to invest in safe plant or working methods, where manufacturers falsify safety data for new products, where illegal discharges are made of toxic substances into our environment, and so on. Reiman notes that intentional killings generally result from acts directed explicitly at one (or, rarely, more than one) specific individual;[12] in such cases, the perpetrator – who in many respects fits our archetypal portrait of a criminal – 'does not show general disdain for the lives of her fellows' (Reiman, 1998: 67). These intentional killings are contrasted with deaths that result from 'indirect' harms; locating these different types of offenders on a *moral* hierarchy arguably inverts, or at least collapses, the hierarchy of culpability around which criminal law operates. Thus the mine executive

> wanted to harm to no-one in particular, but he *knew his acts were likely to harm someone* – and once someone is harmed, the victim is someone in particular. There is no moral basis for treating *one-on-one harm* as criminal and *indirect harm* as merely regulatory (Reiman, 1998: 67–70, original emphases)

Thus, Reiman concludes, offenders of intentional, one-on-one harm are less likely to represent some generalized threat to others than the mine executive. The reasoning is convincing, and points to indifference or 'indirect' harm as at least, if not more, culpable than intention and 'direct' harms – with implications for how these are treated by any criminal justice system (see Pemberton, 2004). Yet the greater moral culpability that is attached both legally and popularly to acts of intention can also allow those implicated in corporate crimes to rationalize away the consequences of their actions – **techniques of neutralization** made possible through, and supported by, key institutions such as the media, or formal political debate (see Slapper and Tombs, 1999: 105–7, 118–22).

If intent is central to dominant legal and academic understandings of violence, also significant is the primacy attached to explanations at the level of the individual. As Salmi has written, the 'usual treatment of violence' is infected with '[e]xcessive individualisation', 'attributing solely to individual factors actions that cannot in reality be accounted for in individual terms. By so doing, the possibility of a causal link between the violence observed and the surrounding social structure is systematically dismissed' (Salmi, 1993: 8). Rather, focus remains upon 'the individual and the eradication of such deplorable behaviour' (Catley, 2003: 4; Tombs, 2006). This is unsurprising in advanced capitalist societies, since analysis at this level coheres entirely with the ethos of individualism upon which such societies are maintained.[13]

Certainly, once one abandons an epistemological commitment to individualism, then more encompassing definitions and considerations of violence become possible. For example, Bowie has sought to develop the category of 'organisational violence', which 'involves organisations knowingly placing their workers or clients in dangerous or violent situations or allowing a climate of abuse, bullying or harassment to thrive in the workplace' (Bowie, 2002: 6). If this still retains some commitment to intention, it at least moves beyond simple understandings of individual action, not least because it acknowledges how a general organizational demeanour of generating or turning a blind eye towards violence can be fostered 'in a growing economic rationalist climate of decreasing job security, massive retrenchments and expanding unemployment that pitted workers and unions against employers' (ibid.: 9). Of particular interest, Bowie also notes that such violence is much harder to recognize due to the tendency to 'blame' (ibid.: 6) individuals, and to develop strategies for responding to violence which are 'based on a pathology model of "mad, bad or sad" employees or clients and patients who are seen as individually responsible for the violence occurring at work' (Bowie, 2000: 8).

Similarly, Hills, in introducing a collection of case histories of 'corporate violence', defines this phenomenon as:

> Actual harm and risk of harm inflicted on consumers, workers, and the general public as a result of decisions by corporate executives or managers, from corporate negligence, the quest for profits at any cost, and wilful violations of health, safety and environmental laws. (Hills, 1987b: vii)

Through the cases presented in this collection, and in his final considerations regarding these, Hills concludes that such violence is understood 'not in the pathology of evil individuals but in the culture and structure of large-scale bureaucratic organisations within a particular political economy' (Hills, 1987c: 190). Hills's understanding of violence seems to shift beyond *both* intention and individuals. These shifts beyond intention can also be discerned in some other, recent criminological work which, if not explicitly couched in the language of violence could be re-framed as such – notably a variety of work within the rubric of 'green' criminology (Lynch and Stretesky, 2003; White, 2003), within which we would include the systematic (state-corporate) exploitation of whole classes of people (Walters, 2006).

## Conclusion: beyond criminology?

These brief appraisals of, first, mainstream criminological theory, and then understandings of violence, highlight that understanding corporate crimes against health and safety requires us to look far beyond the individual on the scene – the ship's assistant bosun who did not check whether the ferry's bow doors were closed before leaving port, the chemical plant worker who attached the hose to the methylisocyanate tank at Bhopal, or the shipping manager who sent a young man, Simon Jones, to unload cargo. This is not to deny human agency, nor that individuals at times act (or fail to act) in ways that act as decisive triggers for such crimes. But it is to argue that understandings of the production of these crimes is rarely found at this level. For to examine incidents and offences in terms of individuals is to fail to ask the question, what kind of organization or process is it that allows the actions or inactions of one or several low-level employees unintentionally to cause significant physical harm, as is often the case?

The actions, inactions, decisions, and so on of individuals must therefore be placed in the structures within which they operate – and this means taking cognizance of their immediate workgroup, their workplace, their organization/company as well as, beyond these, a far wider complex of factors. The urgency of developing such a wide-ranging explanatory framework has been raised by some commentators on corporate crime in general, who have emphasized the need to incorporate explanatory variables which range from the **micro** (individual) through to the **macro** (socio-structural) levels (Coleman, 1987; Punch, 2000; Vaughan, 1992, 1996). In truth, however, as with theory-building in corporate crime research in general (Cressey, 1989), theoretical development here remains at an early stage, although there are now a number of book-length studies which attempt to use some of this range of factors. These include studies of safety crimes in the offshore oil industry (Whyte, 1999; Woolfson et al., 1996), corporate crime in the asbestos (Tweedale, 2000), chemicals (Pearce and Tombs, 1998) and pharmaceutical (Braithwaite, 1984) industries, corporate manslaughter (Slapper, 2000), and possible corporate and state illegalities associated with the fateful launch of the *Challenger* Space Shuttle (Vaughan, 1996). All these latter studies integrate analyses of features in the production of corporate crimes that identify a range of micro and macro social processes.

First, at the micro level of the individual and of inter-personal relations, we need to take account of individual personality and characteristics, not least in terms of the kinds of personalities who are recruited or 'get on' within the organization, as well as 'individual' factors that are socially constructed as relevant such as rank/position within hierarchy, age, gender, and ethnicity. Shifting to the level of the immediate work-group or sub-unit within the organization, we must take account of inter-personal dynamics (and particularly the possibility of '**group think**'), the culture of the work-group (and the extent to which this coheres or clashes with the culture of the wider organization), and its location within the overall organization, both structurally and geographically – that is, is it relatively autonomous or highly supervised? Is it part of one large organizational complex, or is it geographically isolated?

Second, at what might be called the 'meso' level, there are also key sets of issues to be raised in relation to the organization itself. At this level, we need to understand something of its organizational structure, its internal lines of decision-making and accountability, its geographical scope of operations, and the nature, volume and complexity of internal transactions. Issues of organizational culture must also be addressed: is the organization risk-taking or risk-averse?; is it gendered?; is it authoritarian?; and is it one where a blame culture predominates? Crucially, we must also enquire into what kind of management is either valorized or deemed acceptable by the organization; and related to this point are issues related to workforce organization, notably the existence, and strength, both of a trade union, as well as of safety reps and safety committees. Of further relevance are the very products or services that are the focus of the organization: are these opaque or transparent?; are they sold to consumers or other organizations?; is their production labour-intensive or capital-intensive? Perhaps most obviously, we need to know something of the economic 'health' of the company, and of specific organizational units, as well as the ways in which and the time-scales across which profitability is calculated.

Finally, there are key sets of questions to be broached regarding the macro economic, political and social environments within which the organization operates. Among these extra-organizational features are: the nature of the market structure; the size and scope of the market; the predominant form of inter-organizational relationships within any given market; the material and ideological state of regulation; the more general nature of state–business relationships; the dominant form of political economy, and concomitant societal values, including the nature and degree of pro- or anti-business sentiment. Thus, an understanding of changing levels of corporate risk to workers' and citizens' health and safety requires attention to factors which include the following: the abilities of capital to relocate within and beyond national boundaries, and thereby to export hazard and risk; trends in labour markets and employment patterns, not least attempts to imitate models of flexibility claimed to exist in the US and Japan; the nature of, and changes in, contractual arrangements and methods of payment; and the introduction of new technologies and new forms of work organization, particularly in terms of the impact of these upon workers' skills and functions. As cases such as those at Piper Alpha, Bhopal, Morecambe Bay and the *Herald of Free Enterprise* illustrate most clearly, we also need to gain an understanding of the national and international economic conditions that shape organizational strategies.

Whether examined in isolation, or in their combination through attempts to conceptualize the range and relative importance of such factors in terms of an overarching framework, the production of corporate crimes against health and safety therefore needs to be conceptualized at a range of micro, meso and macro levels. And this requirement, for an integrated understanding of these complex levels of analysis, takes us beyond criminology. Indeed, even in our brief discussion of classicisms, and individual and sociological positivisms, it is clear that we needed to move towards disciplinary areas such as organization theory and organization studies, economics, and political science in order to fully understand how corporate crimes are produced in any given society. Only a shift away from criminology can facilitate understanding the production of corporate crimes against health and safety through prevailing systems of economic, social and political organization, dominant value systems and beliefs, and the differential distribution of power. Further, we require an integrated historical and international focus – for we cannot understand such crimes in the UK, without some understanding of how these, first, have emerged, and, second, how they fit within broader market processes that are increasingly played out internationally, if not globally.

Such an approach, alongside a recognition of the embedded biases of states and criminal justice systems, forces us to think about a much more profound question in relation to regulation: whether, under capitalist social orders, corporate crimes against health and safety can ever be sufficiently harnessed given that states see as their primary aim the encouragement of private profit maximization and capital growth? Given that under-regulation and an absence of corporate crime controls appear to be as much an embedded feature of capitalist social orders as corporate *crime* itself is, our greatest challenge is perhaps not simply to reform or tinker with the means we have to control individual corporations. Therefore, a much greater and more pressing challenge is to seek an alternative means of organizing production regimes that will neither encourage nor sustain the routine killings, injuries and impoverishment of lives wreaked by corporations.

## Notes

1 http://www.food.gov.uk/news/pressreleases/2002/feb/campaignlaunch.
2 http://www.food.gov.uk/multimedia/pdfs/ocd200506uk.pdf.
3 See http://www.simonjones.org.uk.
4 Corporate Environmental Crime covers 'a varied range of actions. This can include offences as wide-ranging as, for example, fly-tipping (the illegal dumping of waste), fly-posting (plastering public spaces with advertising posters which blight the area), and pollution incidents, whether that be as a result of chemicals, farm slurry or general sewage waste, being discharged into the watercourse' (House of Commons Environmental Audit Committee, 2005: 9).
5 http://www.hse.gov.uk/statistics/causdis/asbestos.htm
6 Merseyside Asbestos Victims Support Group, *The Scale of the Problem in Liverpool*, at http://www.asbestosdiseases.org.uk/problem.html
7 Merseyside Asbestos Victims Support Group, http://www.asbestosdiseases.org.uk/services.html, accessed 2 February 2007.
8 A network of resource centres and campaigners on health and safety at work. See http://www.hazardscampaign.org.uk/.
9 'A Little Compensation', *Hazards*, 90, May 2005, http://www.hazards.org/compensation/briefing.htm
10 One has only to watch *Wall Street* to see that the personality traits that helped to make Gekko a success were the same characteristics that allowed him, though a combination of intention and negligence, to break the law.
11 This is also one example of 'techniques of neutralization', which are crucial to understanding motivation in the context of corporate crime: see Box, 1983; Slapper and Tombs, 1999.
12 A point which we know holds for contemporary Britain, despite moral panics about 'stranger danger'. Thus BCS figures for 2002/03 show that 'In over half of violent incidents the offender/s were known to the victim in some way; in one-third of incidents they were known well' (Smith and Allen, 2004: 11).
13 And, of course, bodies of criminal law which are constructed on the basis of the individual (Norrie, 2001).

## Websites

There are numerous www sites providing useful information on many of the themes and concerns addressed in this chapter. In particular, the following (UK-based) sites are worth consulting:

http://www.corporateaccountability.org/

The Centre for Corporate Accountability, a charity concerned with the promotion of worker and public safety, provides free advice to victims of safety crimes, campaigns on law and enforcement, and undertakes related research, much of which is available at the site.

http://www.hazardscampaign.org.uk/

The Hazards Campaign, a network of resource centres and campaigners on health and safety at work, and the best source of safety contacts and campaigning groups information in the UK.

http://www.tuc.org.uk/h_and_s/index.cfm

The health and safety section of the Trades Union Congress Website.

Sites with useful material on corporate crime in general, and with some useful coverage of health and safety issues in particular, include the following:

www.corporatepredators.org

Here you will find 'Focus on the Corporation', a weekly column on illegal and unethical corporate activity, posted by two North American journalists/activists.

www.corporatewatch.org

Corporate Watch (UK) tracks similar forms of corporate activity as the US journal of the same name (below), but is independent of and unrelated to the US publication.

www.corpwatch.org

Corporate Watch (US) tracks illegal and unethical corporate activity, and business–industry relations. Its parent organization is the Transnational Resource and Action Center (TRAC), based in San Francisco.

www.essential.org

Multinational Monitor, published by Essential Information, Inc., tracks corporate activity, especially in the Third World, focusing on the export of hazardous substances, worker health and safety, labour union issues and the environment.

www.motherjones.com

Mother Jones is an independent not-for-profit US-based campaigning site and magazine whose roots lie in a commitment to social justice implemented through first-rate investigative reporting.

www.nader.org

The Nader Page. The site of Ralph Nader, long-time US anti-corporate campaigner, this site seeks to further the ability of consumers to be heard and to have a real voice and a significant role in the legislative and regulatory decision-making process on financial issues.

http://paulsjusticepage.com/elite-deviance.htm

An excellent source of corporate crime material, and many links, maintained by Paul Leighton, co-author of Reiman's *The Rich get Richer and the Poor Get Prison*.

# References

Alvesalo, A., Tombs, S., Virta, E. and Whyte, D., (2006) 'Re-imagining crime prevention: controlling corporate crime?', *Crime, Law and Social Change*, 45: 1–25.

Bablak, P. and Hare, R.D. (2000) *Snakes in Suits. When Psychopaths Go to Work.* New York: HarperCollins.

Bowie, V. (2002) *Workplace Violence*. New South Wales: Workcover.

Box, S. (1983) *Power, Crime and Mystification*. London: Tavistock.

Braithwaite, J (1984) *Corporate Crime in the Pharmaceutical Industry*. London: Routledge and Kegan Paul.

Brown, P. (2001) 'Incinerator breaches go unpunished: poisonous chemicals pumped into atmosphere, report reveals', *Guardian*, 22 May.

Catley, B. (2003) 'Philosophy – the luxurious supplement of violence', paper presented at Critical Management Studies conference, 2003, Lancaster, July. Available at www.mngt.waikato.ac.nz/ejrot/cmsconference/2003/proceedings/philosophy/catley.pdf.

Chibnall, S. (1977) *Law-and-order News: An Analysis of Crime Reporting in the British Press*. London: Tavistock Publications.

Coleman, J. (1987) 'Towards an integrated theory of white-collar crime', *American Journal of Sociology*, 93: 406–39.

Cressey, D. (1989) 'The poverty of theory in corporate crime research', in F. Adler and W.S. Laufer (eds), *Advances in Criminological Theory*. New Brunswick, NJ: Transaction Books, pp. 31–55.

Croall, H. (1995) 'Target women: women's victimisation and white-collar crime', in R. Dobash, et al. (eds), *Gender and Crime*. Lampeter: University of Wales Press, pp. 228–45.

Croall, H. (1998) 'Business, crime and the community', *International Journal of Risk, Security and Crime Prevention*, 3: 281–92.

Croall, H. (1999) 'Crime, business and community safety', *Scottish Journal of Criminal Justice Studies*, 5: 65–79.

Croall, H. (2001) 'The victims of white-collar crime', in S-Å. Lindgren (ed.), *White-Collar Crime Research: Old Views and Future Potentials*. Stockholm: Brottsförebyg ganderådet/fritzes. pp. 35–54.

Grant Stitt, B. and Giacopassi, D.J. (1993) 'Assessing victimization from corporate harms', in M.B. Blankenship (ed.), *Understanding Corporate Criminality*. New York: Garland, pp. 57–83.

Hills, S. (ed.) (1987a) *Corporate Violence: Injury and Death for Profit*. Totowa, NJ: Rowman and Littlefield.

Hills, S. (1987b) 'Preface', in S. Hills (ed.), *Corporate Violence: Injury and Death for Profit*. Totowa, NJ: Rowman and Littlefield, pp. vii–viii.

Hills, S. (1987c) 'Epilogue: corporate violence and the banality of evil', in S. Hills (ed.), *Corporate Violence: Injury and Death for Profit*. Totowa, NJ: Rowman and Littlefield, pp. 187–206.

Hilpern, K. (2004) 'Beware: danger at work', *Guardian*, 27 September.

House of Commons Environmental Audit Committee (2005) *Corporate Environmental Crime. Second Report of Session 2004/05. HC 136*. London: The Stationery Office Limited. Available at: http://www.parliament.the-stationery-office.co.uk/pa/cm200405/cmselect/cmenvaud/136/136.pdf

Lacey, N. (1995) 'Contingency and criminalisation', in I. Loveland (ed.), *Frontiers of Criminality*. London: Sweet and Maxwell, pp. 1–28.

Lynch, M. and Stretesky, P. (2003) 'The meaning of green: contrasting criminological perspectives', *Theoretical Criminology*, 7(2): 217–38.

Meier, R.F. and Short, J.F. Jnr. (1995) 'The consequences of white-collar crime', in G. Geis, R.F. Meier and L. Salinger (eds), *White-Collar Crime: Classic and Contemporary Views*, 3rd edn. New York: The Free Press, pp. 80–104.

Norrie, A. (2001) *Crime, Reason and History: A Critical Introduction to Criminal Law*, 2nd edn. London: Butterworths.

Passas, N. (1990) 'Anomie and corporate deviance', *Contemporary Crises*, 14: 157–78.

Pearce, F. (1976) *Crimes of the Powerful: Marxism, Crime and Deviance*. London: Pluto Press.

Pearce, F. and Tombs, S. (1998) *Toxic Capitalism: Corporate Crime in the Chemical Industry*. Aldershot: Ashgate.

Pemberton, S. (2004) 'A theory of moral indifference: understanding the production of harm by capitalist society', in P. Hillyard, C. Pantazis, S. Tombs and D. Gordon (eds), *Beyond Criminology: Taking Harm Seriously*. London: Pluto Press, pp. 67–83.

Punch, M. (2000) 'Suite violence: why managers murder and corporations kill', *Crime, Law and Social Change*, 33: 243–80.

Reiman, J. (1998) *The Rich Get Richer and the Poor Get Prison*, 5th edn. Boston: Allyn & Bacon.

Salmi, J. (1993) *Violence and Democratic Society: New Approaches to Human Rights*. London: Zed Books.

Schrager, L.S. and Short, J.F. (1977) 'Towards a Sociology of Organisational Crime', *Social Problems*, 25: 407–19.

Slapper, G. (2000) *Blood in the Bank: Social and Legal Aspects of Death at Work*. Aldershot: Ashgate.

Slapper, G. and Tombs, S. (1999) *Corporate Crime*. London: Longman.

Smith, C. and Allen, J. (2004) *Violent Crime in England and Wales. Home Office Online Report 18/04*. Available at www.homeoffice.gov.uk/rds/pdfs04/rdsolr1804.pdf.

Snider, L. (1993) *Bad Business: Corporate Crime in Canada*. Toronto: Nelson.

Sutherland, E. (1983) *White Collar Crime: The Uncut Version*. New Haven, CT: Yale University Press.

Szockyi, E. and Fox, J.G. (eds) (1996) *Corporate Victimisation of Women*. Boston: Northeastern University Press.

Taylor, I., Walton, P. and Young, J. (1973) *The New Criminology*. London: Routledge and Kegan Paul.

TNS (2004) *Consumer Attitudes to Food Standards Wave 4. UK Report. Prepared for Food Standards Agency and COI Communications*, London: TNS. Available at: http://www.foodstandards.gov.uk/multimedia/pdfs/cas2003.pdf.

Tombs, S. (2001) 'Thinking about "white-collar" crime', in S-Å Lindgren (ed.), *White-Collar Crime Research: Old Views and Future Potentials. Lectures and Papers from a Scandinavian Seminar, (With articles by James W. Coleman, Hazel Croall, Michael Levi and Steve Tombs)*, (BRÅ-Rapport 2001: 1). Stockholm: Brottsförebyggande rådet/Fritzes, pp. 13–34.

Tombs, S. (2006) 'Violence, safety crimes and criminology', *British Journal of Criminology*, 47(4): 531–50.

Tombs, S. and Whyte, D. (2001) 'Media reporting of crime: defining corporate crime out of existence?', *Criminal Justice Matters*, 43: 22–3.

Tombs, S. and Whyte, D. (2007) *Safety Crimes*. Cullompton: Willan.

Tweedale, G. (2000) *Magic Mineral to Killer Dust: Turner and Newall and the Asbestos Hazard*. Oxford: Oxford University Press.

Vaughan, D. (1992) 'The macro-micro connection in white-collar crime theory', in K. Schlegel and D. Weisburd (eds), *White-Collar Crime Reconsidered*. Baston, MA: Northeastern University Press. 124–45.

Vaughan, D. (1996) *The Challenger Launch Decision: Risky Technology, Culture, and Deviance at NASA*. Chicago: The University of Chicago Press.

Virta, E. (1999) 'A thief is a criminal who has not had enough time to start a company', in A. Laitinen and V. Olgiati (eds), *Crime-Risk-Security*. Turku: University of Turku, pp. 91–128.

Walters, R. (2006) 'Crime, bio-agriculture and the exploitation of hunger', *British Journal of Criminology*, 46(1): 26–45.

Weisburd, D. and Waring, E. (2001) *White-Collar Crime and Criminal Careers*. Cambridge: Cambridge University Press.

White, R. (2003) 'Environmental issues and the criminological imagination', *Theoretical Criminology*, 7(4): 483–506.

Whyte, D. (1999) 'Power, ideology and the regulation of safety in the Post-*Piper Alpha* offshore oil industry', unpublished PhD thesis, Liverpool John Moores University.

Whyte, D. (2004) 'Regulation and corporate crime', in J. Muncie and D. Wilson (eds), *Student Handbook of Criminal Justice and Criminology*. London: Cavendish.

Woolfson, C., Foster, J. and Beck, M. (1996) *Paying for the Piper: Capital and Labour in Britain's Offshore Oil Industry*. London: Mansell.

Wolmar, C. (2001) *Broken Rails*. London: Aurum Press.

## Suggestions for further reading

Bakan, J. (2004) *The Corporation: The Pathological Pursuit of Profit and Power*. New York: The Free Press.

Box, S. (1983) *Power, Crime and Mystification*. London: Tavistock.

Davis, C. (2004) *Making Companies Safe: What Works?* London: Centre for Corporate Accountability.

Hills, S. (ed.) (1987) *Corporate Violence: Injury and Death for Profit*. Totowa, NJ: Rowman and Littlefield.

Michalowski, R. and Kramer, R. (eds) (2006) *State-Corporate Crime*. New Brunswick, NJ: Rutgers University Press.

Pearce, F. and Snider, L. (eds) (1995) *Corporate Crime: Contemporary Debates*. Toronto: University of Toronto Press.

Reiman, J. (1998) *The Rich Get Richer and the Poor Get Prison*, 5th edn. Boston: Allyn & Bacon.

Szockyi, E. and Frank, N. (eds) (1996) *Corporate Victimisation of Women*. Boston: Northeastern University Press.

Tombs, S. and Whyte, D. (2007) *Safety Crimes*. Cullompton: Willan.

Tucker, E. (ed.) (2006) *Working Disasters: The Politics of Recognition and Response*. New York: Baywood Press.

# TWO

## Corporate Economic Crimes

*Laureen Snider*

## Introduction

The economic crimes of corporations are once again topical. Since the collapse of the technology 'bubble' in 2000, the subsequent wave of bankruptcies and the allied exposure of systemic fraud in what were formerly deemed reputable corporations, the world's electronic and print media have been buzzing with talk. Articles, documentaries, video clips and blogs debate the causes and remedies of corporate fraud and criticize either the paucity of enforcement or the over-reaction of government. Pundits lament the decline of business ethics while those accredited in law, criminology, accounting and business management establish think tanks, run ethics workshops and offer executive courses to businesses seeking to promote particular versions of 'corporate social responsibility'. Profiles on fallen corporate moguls such as Kenneth Lay and Jeff Fastow (Enron), Bernie Ebbers (Worldcom), Conrad Black and David Radler (Hollinger Incorporated) abound. Legal experts and politicians, government and non-governmental standard-setting bodies and professions (particularly investment brokers, lawyers and accountants' associations) have sprung into action – or at least into rhetoric and print. In 2001/2 the United States, still the world's dominant economic player (despite growing competition from China and India), passed a number of laws to prevent, deter and punish stock market fraud. The most notable was Sarbanes–Oxley (SOX to friends and foes alike), an ambitious bi-partisan statute covering a wide range of corporate fraud. And when the United States takes action to protect its stock exchanges, all the countries and companies wishing to trade or sell products in its markets are compelled to listen and/or copy.

However, such efforts by nation-states to 'crack down' on powerful corporate offenders have historically been cyclical. Backlash to new regulations is already well established and growing. In the United States, highly placed critics are calling Sarbanes–Oxley 'excessive and ill-conceived', alleging that the 'burden' of regulation is killing Wall Street (*Globe & Mail*, 2 January 2007: B5). The reform-minded William Donaldson, appointed Chair of the SEC in 2002, has been replaced by Christopher Cox, a Wall Street insider deemed more sympathetic to industry concerns. Industry lawyers are busy preparing a lawsuit to declare SOX unconstitutional; auditing rules requiring public companies to certify their internal financial controls, the provisions that forced 8 per cent of all listed companies in 2005 to 'restate' their earnings, have been targeted for revision 'to limit the auditing burden'. And the US Justice Department is presently passing guidelines to limit the powers of prosecutors to lay charges (*Globe & Mail*, 2 January 2007: B5; *International Herald Tribune*, 2006, accessed online 15 November 2006; *New York Times*, 8 April 2007). In Canada too, the Ontario Securities Commission is 'rethinking' its enforcement strategies after a high profile insider trading case was overturned on appeal (*Globe & Mail*, 9 April 2007: B2). Typically, highly public disasters such as the collapse of Enron, or the now-forgotten collapse of the Savings & Loans industry in Ronald Reagan's newly deregulated America of the 1980s (Calavita et al., 1997), generate 'get tough' rhetoric followed by new and/or resuscitated regulatory statutes. The problems that generated the particular crisis are then hailed as solved. When the media spotlight shifts and/or boom times return, the regulatory status quo reverts to status quo ante. Anti-regulatory lobbies step up the pressure and business-friendly legislators fall over themselves to deregulate, decriminalize and downsize regulatory agencies (Snider, 2000). With aggressive, proactive enforcement out of fashion, politicians are free to appoint an agency's most ardent foes to senior regulatory jobs (Calavita, 1983). Then a new round of disasters occurs and the cycle continues.

This overall sketch does not capture the nuances and exceptions to this pattern. Levels of compliance, we now know, are related to the history and internal organization of business, its sector, size, profitability and geographic location; the characteristics of the labour force (organized or not, skilled or casual); the type, size, history and resources of the regulatory agency(ies) and of the government(s) it serves; the impact of expert and technical knowledge; and the strength of third parties such as NGOs, trade and professional associations, pressure and protest groups (Braithwaite and Drahos, 2000; Gunningham et al., 2003; Gunningham and Johnstone, 1999; Haines, 2003; Hall and Johnstone, 2005; Hutter and Jones, 2006; Noble, 1985, 1986; Parker, 2002; Post, 1998; Purcell et al., 2000; Sanchez, 1998; Shover et al., 1986; Simpson, 2002; Vaughan, 1998). However, despite this variability, the overall pattern of historical cycles of boom and bust, crackdown and reversion to status quo ante, has been documented by decades of researchers in a number of different sectors (Calavita et al., 1997; Carson, 1970, 1980; Grabosky and Braithwaite, 1986; Noble, 1985, 1986; Rosoff et al., 2004; Simpson, 2002; Snider, 1993, 2004). As a result, every Anglo-American democratic state now has a complex mass of statutes covering every aspect of corporate activity. Many of these are impenetrable and ambiguous, inaccessible to lawyer and non-lawyer alike. Many contain obsolete and contradictory provisions setting up what Haines has termed 'the engineer's dilemma' – where to obey some regulations necessarily means disobeying others (Haines, 2003). The consequence is iatrogenic regulation.

Can these cycles be interrupted? Why has corporate economic crime been so resilient, so resistant to formal and informal control? Is the problem too much or too little regulation? Does it reside in inadequate laws, insufficient ethics education, too little transparency in corporate hierarchies or too much temptation? All of these factors, and many more, have been examined since Sutherland's famous researcher 'call to arms' (Sutherland, 1945). This chapter will argue that, while all of the above are important, researchers should devote much more attention to the criminogenic effects of corporate structure itself. As Harry Glasbeek memorably put it: we need to pay less attention to the rotten apples in the barrel, and more to the 'rottening effects of the barrel' (Glasbeek, 2002).

To accomplish this task the chapter is organized as follows: the first section begins with five case studies of 'typical' economic corporate crimes. Since acts of corporate fraud are not restricted to one type of business or nation-state and vary by size, impact and nature of victim, case studies were chosen to illustrate this. In the second section, the causes and patterns depicted in the first section are examined, from structure to *habitus* (Bourdieu, 1987, 1993, 1996). Finally, we look at new forces, resistance and change, reforms introduced by the latest regulatory crackdown on economic crime and their impact on 'common sense', corporate culture and *habitus* thus far.

## Case studies

### Barings

February of 1995 saw the collapse of Barings, the oldest merchant bank in Britain. At the centre of the scandal was Nicholas Leeson: a 28-year-old trader with Barings who set staggeringly large trading obligations on the Singapore and Japanese futures exchanges, which the Bank, in the end, simply could not meet. Leeson's fraud involved posting large profits for his employers by falsifying bank statements and confirmation letters while at the same time concealing continued losses in a secret account. For more than three years, Barings' management rewarded their phenomenally successful employee with huge bonuses, never investigating the details of his transactions. Nor did Barings question Leeson's large funding requests for loans to secure client positions. In fact, no such clients existed, the money was used to enrich Leeson's secret accounts as he attempted, with increasing desperation, to make up losses that had snowballed since the failure of the Japanese market to recover after the Kobe earthquake.

Barings' corporate structure facilitated poor supervision of trading activities: management was internationally fragmented, reporting structures weak, transparency non-existent. Thus Barings allowed Leeson's Singapore-based trading activities to continue long past the point where investigation and intervention might have prevented total collapse. Leeson occupied a privileged position, responsible for both the dealing desk and the back office. This made it difficult for third-party checks into his dealings to be routinized. This was compounded by the absence of risk-management protocols for monitoring Barings' Singapore branch, its poor 'matrix' management supervision and inadequate control procedures. With Leeson's continued losses and Barings' lack of supervision – no one asked how such huge profits were generated – bankruptcy was inevitable. On 26 February 1995, Barings folded, with debts of $1.4 *billion*.

Leeson stood trial in Singapore in 1995; of the original 11 charges against him, 9 were dropped. However, he was convicted on one count each of fraud and forgery and sentenced (by a judge notorious for 'heavy-handed' sentencing) to 6½ years in a Singapore jail. Leeson was the only employee of Barings to serve time in this scandal. He was released in July 1999 for 'good behaviour', serving less than four years of the total sentence.

## BCCI

The Bank of Credit and Commerce International (BCCI) scandal has been called a '$20-billion-plus heist' (Beaty and Gwynne, 1993), and is recognized as one of the worst financial scandals in history (so far!). Established in Pakistan in 1972 and eventually operating over 400 branches in 78 countries, BCCI was ultimately shut down in July 1991 after Bank of England audits revealed that fraud, improper loans and deceptive accounting practices were rampant within the company. Resulting investigations in both the USA and the UK revealed that BCCI was involved in money-laundering, tax evasion, bribery, smuggling, arms trafficking (including nuclear technologies), and the illegal purchases of banks and real estate. It was accused of catering to drug dealers, arms merchants and third-world dictators.

The sophisticated deceptions of senior BCCI officials required a highly compartmentalized organizational structure, one designed to foster deception and avoid centralized regulatory review (Kerry and Brown, 1992). BCCI's annual auditing system was also designed to be non-transparent, with complexity built in to avoid the detection of illegal accounting practices. PriceWaterhouse were the in-house, contract accountants for BCCI Overseas, while Ernst & Young audited BCCI and BCCI Holdings in Britain. Neither company, apparently, oversaw or audited BCCI's numerous satellite companies. BCCI also made extensive efforts to operate as much as possible in nation-states offering total bank secrecy.

However, it became increasingly difficult for management and auditors to account for unexplained losses of hundreds of millions of dollars. A

PriceWaterhouse audit in 1990 resulted in one of BCCI's founders, Sheik Zayed bin Sultan al Nahayan (emir of Abu Dhabi in the United Arab Emirates), making good on one loss, of hundreds of millions of dollars, in exchange for an increase in his (corporate) shareholdings to 77 per cent. This transaction resulted in the transfer of much of BCCI's record-keeping operation to Abu Dhabi. However, international suspicion continued to grow. In March 1991, the Bank of England commissioned PriceWaterhouse to carry out an inquiry, which ultimately resulted in the Sandstorm report showing that BCCI had engaged in 'widespread fraud and manipulation'. In addition to a plethora of lawsuits filed by BCCI creditors, criminal charges were filed in UK and US courts.

In 1993, Syed Ziauddin Ali Akbar, the head of BCCI's treasury division in London until 1986, was the first to face BCCI-related charges in Britain. Akbar pleaded guilty to false accounting practices involving $765 million. Authorities estimated that Akbar had personally gained or misused $61 million. Akbar was sentenced to six years in prison, a 'light' sentence resulting from a plea bargain for his guilty plea (*New York Times*, 29 Sept. 1993). Another high profile trial involved Abbas Gokal, the head of Gulf Group who secretly received hundreds of millions of dollars in unsecured loans from BCCI. Arrested in Germany and extradited to Britain in 1994, Gokal was sentenced to 14 years imprisonment in 1997. After a lengthy appeal process, the High Court upheld Gokal's sentence in 2001. Gokal was released from prison in May 2004, and he remains in violation of a confiscation order for £2.94 million issued by Britain's Serious Fraud Office, monies intended for the numerous victims of the BCCI fraud.

In the United States, investigations of BCCI began in 1988 when the bank was implicated in Panamanian dictator General Noriega's drug-trafficking and money laundering activities. US investigations eventually revealed BCCI's connections with the Central Intelligence Agency and various members of the American political elite – Henry Kissinger and associates were specifically implicated. Indictments on multiple fraud and larceny charges were drawn up in 1991 against Swaleh Naqvi, the former BCCI chief operating officer. However, it was 1994 before a complicated accord was struck between the US and Abu Dhabi allowing Naqvi's extradition to the USA. In exchange for Naqvi, the USA agreed to remove Sheikh Zayed and Abu Dhabi from a $1.5 billion civil racketeering lawsuit filed by the trustee of First American Bankshares. This was a Washington-based bank that was illegally owned by BCCI. When proceedings commenced, Naqvi admitted responsibility for $255 million in losses in the United States, and pled guilty to charges of fraud, racketeering and conspiracy. He was ordered to pay restitution and sentenced to eight years in prison. As stated in Kerry and Brown's report to Congress, 'The scope and variety of BCCI's criminality, and the issues raised by that criminality, are immense, and beyond the scope of any single investigation or report' (1992). Attempting to capture the repercussions, the victims and causes of all the BCCI frauds is equally difficult. However, it is evident that prison sentences, when and where they were handed out, although heavy in light of 'typical' sentences for corporate crime, were light in relation to the personal disasters BCCI frauds brought upon countless victims. They are even lighter when compared to sentences routinely handed out for non-violent robberies, embezzlement and theft committed by individuals lacking the corporate shield.

### Parmalat

The Parmalat scandal is another case heralded as 'the largest corporate fraud in history', earning the press title of 'Italy's Enron'. The Italian dairy and foods giant, with more than 35,000 employees in 30 nations, was forced into bankruptcy on 27 December 2003 when $4.9 billion in supposed company assets were revealed to be a complete fiction. For years, Parmalat had concealed its true financial condition from investors and financers using a combination of falsified revenue statements, offshore holding companies, and even outright forgery (done by pasting a note of asset confirmation to a Bank of America letterhead and running the form through a fax machine multiple times). The frauds were set in motion to cover up and offset losses and to allow the company to continue borrowing. Debt reports were hidden through elaborate deals with investment banks that allowed the company to claim loans as 'investments', thus allowing Annual Reports to show inaccurate borrowing figures. In addition, a system of 'double billing' to the company's retail customers ensured that Parmalat's accounts would appear to be healthier than they actually were. It is alleged that company founder and Chief Executive, Calisto Tanzi, personally siphoned $620 million from Parmalat's accounts, to mitigate losses in other businesses owned by the family-run company. All told, the secret losses over the course of a decade resulted in $17.38 *billion* in debt.

On the day Parmalat declared bankruptcy, Tanzi was arrested and charged with financial fraud and money laundering. Criminal fraud investigations were launched in Milan and Parma against Parmalat, its auditors, and the financial institutions associated with the company. These investigations have resulted in dozens of charges and multiple trials. By June 2005, 10 Parmalat employees (including Tanzi's 'right-hand man', chief financial officer Fausto Tonna) and one external advisor had been convicted on charges of market rigging, obstructing the market regulator, and falsifying audits. Though they were handed prison terms, plea bargains allowed 9 of the 11 to receive suspended sentences. Sentences ranged from 10 months to two and a half years. The proceedings of 2005 also saw Tanzi and 15 others ordered to stand trial on charges of market rigging, providing false accounting information, and misleading Italy's stock market regulator – charges carrying a maximum sentence of five years. A June 2006 preliminary hearing was held to assess fraud charges against 64 of the company's former executives, financial advisors and bankers.

Seventeen plea bargains resulted in 'light' sentences for many top executives – for example, former board member, Francesca Tanzi, was sentenced to three years, five months, marketing director, Stefano Tanzi, to four and a half years. Trials for the remaining defendants, including former CEO Tanzi, are ongoing, on charges ranging from fraudulent bankruptcy to criminal association. The most severe charges could result in prison sentences of up to 15 years.

### Bre-X

The collapse of Bre-X Minerals Ltd. amounted to the biggest stock scandal in Canadian history and the biggest mining scandal in world history. David Walsh founded the junior mining firm in 1989, and it was incorporated and listed on the Alberta Stock Exchange that same year. Until 1993, the price of Bre-X stock fluctuated between 10 and 30 cents (Cdn). This unprofitable situation led Walsh to declare personal bankruptcy in 1992. Things seemed to be turning around in 1993 when Walsh teamed up with Dutch-born Canadian geologist John Felderhof who recommended that Bre-X acquire land in Busang, Indonesia. In March 1993, Bre-X bought the rights to 475,000 acres (190,000 ha) of Busang for $80,100 (US). In 1994, Filipino geologist Michael de Guzman became the project manager at Busang; by the end of the year Bre-X reported the potential for gold reserves of more than 2 million ounces, and company stock hit $2.84 (Cdn) a share. The gold rush continued to gain momentum with estimates of Busang's worth rising to 30 million ounces in 1995, with stock jumping to $39.50 (Cdn), and again to 60 million ounces in 1996. Stock peaked then at $280 a share. Independent speculators suggested there could be as much as 200 million ounces of gold at Busang, which would have made it the largest single deposit in history.

All of this activity attracted the attention of the Indonesian government and larger mineral companies. Political connections were forged. The President of Indonesia at that time, Suharto, urged Bre-X to share the site with Barrick Gold, a large Canadian mining firm tied to Suharto's daughter Siti Rukmana. Barrick's advisors included former US President George H. W. Bush and former Canadian Prime Minister Brian Mulroney. Throughout the turmoil, Bre-X owner David Walsh confidently reassured shareholders that his small company could manage the site on its own. However, in February 1997, another Suharto family associate, Mohamad 'Bob' Hasan, coordinated an agreement where Bre-X would maintain 45 per cent ownership while American firm Freeport-McMoRan Copper & Gold ran the mine, sharing its interests with the Indonesian government. When Freeport-McMoRan began investigating the site, however, they discovered no evidence of significant gold reserves. Subsequent investigations revealed that ore samples had been systematically salted (that is, gold particles were 'planted' into the samples). On 5 May 1997, Strathcona Minerals Services concluded: 'We believe there to be virtually no possibility of an economic gold deposit,' and went on to describe the fraud as 'without precedent in the history of mining anywhere in the world' (http://archives.cbc.ca/IDC-1-73-1211-6713/politics_economy/bre-X/clip5). Within a month the Bre-X boom went bust and Bre-X stock plummeted.

As a result of the Bre X fraud, the Canadian mining industry, the Alberta Stock Exchange and securities commissions throughout Canada were humbled, some would say humiliated, on the world stage. Thousands of individuals and organizations lost their savings and pensions. The Ontario Municipal Employees Retirement Board lost $45 million; the Quebec Public Sector Pension fund lost $70 million, and the Ontario Teachers Pension Plan lost $100 million. In the aftermath of the scandal, David Walsh, still protesting his innocence, fled to the Bahamas where he died of a stroke in 1998. John Felderhof, who by 1997 was Vice-President of Bre-X, fled to his home in the Cayman Islands. Ten days before the Freeport-McMoRan Copper & Gold report was released, in February 1997, Busang project manager, the geologist Michael De Guzman fell to his death from a helicopter in an apparent suicide. Much speculation surrounded Guzman's death; his family alleged murder, others claim Guzman faked suicide and is now living a rich man's life somewhere in South America.

Despite a multitude of civil class lawsuits by investor groups and investigations by several Securities Commissions, the Royal Canadian Mounted Police (RCMP), Canada's federal police force, ended its investigations in 1999 without making any criminal charges. In various interviews and media reports, RCMP officials made clear their belief that significant fraud had occurred, but the absence of evidence that would stand up in court, given securities laws in 1999, made it impossible to lay charges. The difficulties faced by the RCMP were aggravated by the fact that their investigation of evidence and witnesses spanned four jurisdictions: the Philippines, Indonesia, the Cayman Islands and the Bahamas (http://archives.cbc.ca/IDC-1-73-1211-6717/politics_economy/bre-X/clip9). In May 1999, the Ontario Securities Commission (OSC), the largest and most powerful of Canada's 13 regulatory commissions, charged Felderhof with illegally selling $84 million worth of shares and with issuing false press releases (*Globe & Mail*, 20 May 1999: B17). Felderhof's trial was suspended in April 2001 when the OSC tried to have presiding judge Justice Peter Hryn removed, alleging bias against the prosecution. The appeal was denied and the trial resumed in 2005. On 31 July 2007, after 160 trial days, 750,000 scanned images and seven years, Felderhof was acquitted on all counts. The two remaining class action lawsuits are now on hold (*Globe & Mail*, 1 August 2007, accessed online 27 October 2007 at globeandmail.com).

### Enron

The rise and fall of Enron is a quintessential American story. It began in the 1980s as a Houston-based pipeline company specializing in the transport of natural gas. CEO Kenneth Lay quickly realized there was more money to be made in controlling distribution networks than in actually distributing energy, and Enron was transformed into a company that traded in energy assets. It grew quickly throughout the booming 1990s, aided by its Texas roots, its close ties with the Bush family (both the senior and junior George Bush), and its political contributions to Republican causes and presidential campaigns. In 1996, the Federal Energy Commission deregulated energy markets in both natural gas and electricity and the sector took off. In 2000, Enron claimed it had tripled its revenues between 1998 and 2000, by 2001 it was the seventh largest corporation in America (Rhodes and Paton, 2002: 13; Rosoff et al., 2004).

The end, when it came, happened fast. In October 2001, Enron admitted to massive losses and 'restated' its earnings to include debits of $525 million and debts of $1.2 billion. Two days later, earnings reports for the previous five years were officially 'restated'. The company filed for bankruptcy on 2 December. Four thousand employees lost their jobs and pensions, thousands of investors lost their life savings, and $70 billion in wealth vanished literally overnight (Rhodes and Paton, 2002: 10). Middle and low-level employees were doubly hard hit because, unlike senior executives, their shares were 'locked in' (McBarnet, 2005).[1] Subsequent investigations revealed that Enron had used a number of techniques to hide debts and losses and keep stock prices high, including 'Special Purpose Entities' (SPEs), 'Special Purpose Vehicles' (SPVs) – 4,300 of them – and 'Off Balance Sheet Transactions' (McBarnet, 2005).

On 25 May 2006, Enron CEOs Kenneth Lay and Jeff Skilling were convicted by a jury in Houston, Texas, of multiple counts of fraud. In July, Lay died of a heart attack in his home in Aspen, Colorado, at the age of 64 and his conviction was 'vacated'. On 26 September, Skilling was sentenced to 24 years imprisonment. Jeff Fastow, Enron's Chief Financial Officer, plea bargained for six years in return for his guilty plea and testimony against Lay and Skilling.

## Evaluation and analysis

These five cases are all different, but they share certain characteristics. They all have thousands of victims, many of whom lost their savings, pensions, houses, future prospects and, for employees and suppliers, their livelihood. All involved calculated, premeditated acts that the perpetrators knew were illegal. All were aided and abetted by high-ranking professionals – lawyers and accountants and investment bankers. And in all cases the corporation was an enabling factor, a shield protected by statute and precedent, by corporate complexity, lack of transparency and the political, economic and cultural capital routinely granted to rich white men – and, to a lesser extent, to all with truly colossal riches, like the oil sheiks in BCCI. All the crimes lasted over a series of years, but regulators and law enforcement officials were unable to move in until after disasters occurred. None, with the possible exception of Nick Leeson at Barings, can be blamed on one 'bad apple'; they were quintessentially organizational offences, requiring collective cooperation and mutual reinforcement – what might be called cultures of non-compliance.

Crimes of this nature are not unusual. While the collapse of Enron has attracted the most attention, particularly in North American media, economic corporate crimes are very common.[2] The North American Securities Administrators Association has estimated that 'Americans lose about $1 million an hour, six billion per year, to securities fraud' (Fishman, 1998: 41). The most common frauds are profit overstatements where revenues are inflated or costs and debts hidden through special reserves accounts or similar devices, and insider trading – still not a criminal offence in many countries. Now that regulators have what will inevitably be a short window during which they have cultural permission to launch proactive investigations, the long-standing ubiquity of corporate fraud has become apparent. Many reputable, blue-chip companies have been over-valuing their assets and/or hiding their debts for years, if not decades; insider trading is routine. This has allowed hundreds of senior executives, typically remunerated with a combination of salary, bonuses and stock options, to reap millions of dollars. As far as we can tell, neither the 'suspects' nor the practices were shamed within or outside the corporation. Indeed, they were more typically rewarded, with prestige, promotions and of course multi-million dollar bonuses. From 1997–2001, for example, Xerox overstated its revenues by $6.4 *billion* (Patsuris, 2002–7). Dynergy, Reliant Resources, El Paso, CMS Energy and Duke Energy all inflated revenues by recording mutual, round-trip trades as sales. Adelphia executives fraudulently excluded over $2 billion in bank loans. Sun Microsystems 'wrote down' $1.05 billion of tax reserves (ibid.). On 30 August 2005, eight accounting executives at KPMG admitted helping corporations evade 'billions of dollars in capital gains and income taxes by developing and marketing tax shelters and concealing them from the IRS' (McClam, *Globe & Mail*, 30 August 2005: B9). The firm avoided criminal charges by agreeing to pay the Internal Revenue Service $456 million (US) in penalties. KPMG's main rival in the accounting/audit business, the Arthur Andersen firm, faced criminal charges as Enron's main auditor and was forced into bankruptcy in 2002. Virtually all major corporations employ questionable SPEs and SPVs and so-called 'aggressive tax planning' (Braithwaite, 2005: 16) to avoid tax, mislead investors and maximize revenue.

To understand the ubiquity of such offences, we must look at the failure of formal social controls to transform or even penetrate individual and corporate belief systems. This is where the 'common sense' of business, the uninterrogated 'truths' of corporate conduct are forged. We must look, therefore, at how the structural realities of the for-profit corporation and the relations of power they generate, shape individual and collective *habitus* (Bourdieu, 1987, 1993, 1996). Regulatory *habitus* refers to the mentalities and sensibilities, practices and techniques that characterize regulation. It is produced by 'the dialectical interplay between incorporating … objective features of the organization of social fields' and 'externalizing ... this through ... the subject's reproductive labour' (Bourdieu, 1987: 54). Both regulators and regulated populations constitute and reproduce 'the structural conditions of social fields', and the resulting 'interiorization' generates the behaviours that characterize actors in particular settings (Bourdieu, 1991; Frauley, 2005: 181–5). While the details of regulatory interactions are ever-changing, always negotiated and constantly fine-tuned in response to market players and global events, the boundaries, assumptions and overall shape of the regulatory field reflect and reveal enduring, structurally-based relations of power.

This is where the definitions and parameters of 'social responsibility', 'ethical behaviour' and 'best practices' actually are negotiated. Compliance-related factors such as the certainty and celerity of punishment only become critical in the absence of informal controls (Coleman, 1987). If acts proscribed by law (civil, administrative and criminal) do not get translated into 'naming, blaming and shaming' at coffee breaks and in day-to-day business interaction, then formal social control is the only route left – and, as we know from dozens of studies, it is inevitably reactive and hugely problematic (for example, Braithwaite and Drahos, 2000; Kagan et al., 2003; Shapiro, 1984; Simpson, 2002).

Although hundreds of ethics consultants, compliance specialists and social responsibility institutes spring up after every financial disaster, much corporate crime is not seen as criminal, immoral or shameful by the system's dominant actors, those who live, work and shape corporate culture on a day-by-day basis through their interactions. As noted above, all major corporations employ armies of professional enablers and facilitators whose job is to maximize corporate profits through creative 'law avoidance' (Braithwaite, 2005: 16; McBarnet, 2005, 2006). Their job is to stretch the boundaries of law and of corporate culture. Studies of Enron provide empirical evidence of the vibrant 'culture of defiance' that flourished for decades in the world's seventh largest corporation. Devising new ways to 'beat the rules' and 'screw the state' was seen as smart business practice, a necessary component for success in the company (Rhodes and Paton, 2002). Those skilled in stretching the margins of legality were rewarded with bonuses, promotions and respect from peers and superiors.

The overall success of such initiatives can be seen in the remarkable freedom the business sector has enjoyed to shape the meaning of its antisocial acts, in both law and culture, and thus to negate, minimize, delay or avoid criminal charges and sanctions (Andrews, 2006; Condon, 1998; Glasbeek, 2002; Pearce and Tombs, 1998; Tombs and Whyte, 2002). On the few occasions when regulatory agencies have tried to internalize and institutionalize compliance norms in corporate culture by publicly shaming offenders, business reacted not by questioning its own behaviour, but by challenging the legitimacy of the agency (Parker, 2006). High-level business crimes continue to be defined, in the mind, body and practices of corporate executives, and of mainstream lawyers and judges, as 'illegal but not criminal', *mala prohibita* rather than *mala in se* (Geis, 1972). In contrast, when blue-collar crime offenders attempt to rationalize their offences this way, academics delegitimize their claims by labelling them 'techniques of neutralization' (Sykes and Matza, 1957)

Outside the corporation, culture-shaping initiatives by economic elites are so omnipresent that they have become part of the 'noise' of everyday life. Conservative think-tanks sponsor research questioning global warming or warning of the disastrous effects of regulation. Supreme Court and Charter challenges are mounted to entrench and extend the legal rights of corporations (Glasbeek, 2002: 33–8). Mass market advertising blankets every public and private space, cajoling us to think of corporate rights as our rights, of restrictions on corporate free speech as tyranny, of false advertising as harmless 'puffery', and of corporate crime as accidental and non-criminal. Global spending on advertising, growing at 25 per cent per year and topping $304 billion in 1999, dwarfs public sector spending. And 75 per cent of it comes from the world's 100 largest corporations, creating 'a giant propaganda/educational machine' which influences 'our beliefs, values, customs and social relations' (Glasbeek, 2002: 96).[3]

## Resistance and change?

### Change and resistance from the outside: new external forces

Discovering, preventing and sanctioning economic corporate crime is a complex, ever-changing, always-evolving process. While cycles of crime, disaster and reform continue, the players, dynamics, balance of power and politics never stand still. In the two or three decades since neo-liberal governance came to dominate democratic capitalist states (Levi-Faur and Jordana, 2005), new forces of resistance and reform have arisen. First is the establishment and growing strength of oppositional investor rights groups. With the bursting of the technology-inspired market bubble of the 1990s, such groups have become increasingly assertive. They have sometimes defied senior management by resisting – or promoting – takeover attempts, or argued against the appointment, renewal or dismissal of CEOs or other senior executives. They have demanded ceilings on executive compensation and criticized CEO payouts as excessive. Many shareholder groups now lobby legislators, demanding more disclosure and greater protection for investors, more information on corporate profit levels, salaries and debt loads. Although less common, dissident groups sometimes appear at Annual General Meetings questioning corporate environmental practices, outsourcing and/or labour conditions in third world countries (Yaron, 2002). This puts pro-regulatory pressure on regulators and the state, pressure which helps to balance the consistent, unremitting anti-regulatory arguments supplied by corporate lobbies.

Second, with 24-hour business news and increased public interest in investment and markets, investigative financial journalism has come into its own. The *New York Times*, *The Times*, the *Guardian*, the *Globe & Mail* (Canada's major national newspaper), 24-hour news channels and various on-line journals and blogs report regularly on insider trading, or the disconnect between executive salaries (rising) and profit levels in particular sectors or companies (falling). While the vast majority of business news is anything but critical, and media such as *The Wall Street Journal* and *The Economist* are primarily lobbyists for business, corporations are increasingly scrutinized and critiqued, from a number of different perspectives, in a much wider range of venues. Publicity on the costs and ubiquity of corporate crime can direct public and political attention to the massive inequality between sanctions handed to traditional offenders (bank robbers or 'welfare cheats') *versus* those received by corporate criminals. The multinational corporation steals millions and is fined the equivalent of its profits for a day while the impoverished welfare mother or burglar is imprisoned, demonized, cut off welfare forever or turfed out of public housing (Calavita et al., 1997; Rosoff et al., 1998; Slapper, 2000). Such exposés have the potential to strengthen oppositional forces by questioning public acceptance of law as impartial and corporate power as irrelevant.

This increased scrutiny is enabled by the third factor, the proliferation of new electronic technologies offering unprecedented opportunities to monitor and discipline market players. Trades can be tracked as they happen, electronic 'markers' differentiating insider trades can be purchased. Surveillance equipment is easy to acquire and install. Email has forever changed evidence-gathering, since it is impossible to render messages permanently irretrievable to those with sufficient time, resources and computer savvy to retrieve them. Technological innovations allow regulators, in theory, to intervene as soon as 'abnormal' trading patterns are discovered. They ease evidence-gathering and make convictions easier, provided investigations proceed this far. (Most do not.) They make the democratization of control possible, though not necessary or easy. If put into effect, these technologies can increase trade visibility, make it harder for government agencies and self-regulating bodies to ignore suspicious trading patterns, and lay an evidence trail that makes conviction more likely.

All of these forces resisting corporate power are contested and are constituted by networks of interests, actors and structural forces reinforcing and/or promoting it. All technologies interact with relations of power. Decisions on the design and deployment of new technologies are made by CEOs and Boards of Directors. Decisions on surveillance equipment which will be utilized by government agencies are made by politicians who depend on corporate goodwill, ideologically, economically and politically. Thus the primary targets of technological surveillance up to now, those receiving the most intensive, intrusive monitoring, have been low-level employees – clerical staff, warehouse and call-centre workers (Ehrenreich, 2001; Snider, 2002). Despite the growing prominence of the internet as an alternate source of information and the continued presence of publicly owned media in most western democracies, mainstream media belong to corporations. They are businesses out to attract an audience for advertisers and maximize profits for owners. Lengthy think pieces on corporate fraud are unlikely to deliver instant gratification for the concentration-challenged. As for shareholder rights groups, investors are still in the minority in most countries, albeit one that has increased dramatically in size since 1990 (Phelps et al., 2003). Shareholder rights groups tend to represent private, minority interests, investor lawsuits do little to protect the public and deliver basically individual 'remedies'. Investment lawsuits that succeed deliver the largest payoffs to 'secured' creditors, generally the biggest investors, and to the law firm taking the case. They offer no symbolic redress, no 'closure', nothing to compensate citizens for indirect losses when currencies decline and taxes increase to cover corporate malfeasance and theft, nothing for the majority of unsecured creditors whose life savings, pensions and nest-eggs have disappeared. And there is no redress for employees faced with job loss, pension loss and the challenge of finding a decent new job at the age of 55. However, it is foolish to speculate on which parties are 'winning' or 'losing' this regulatory tug-of-war. The struggle continues, the regulatory dance goes on (Snider, 1991).

### Change and resistance from the inside: transforming corporate ethics

With every crackdown comes a resurgent interest in corporate ethics. The post-2001 crisis is no exception: there is a renewed emphasis on ethics education in MBA programmes and law schools, and a burgeoning ethics industry (Hyatt, 2005). For researchers the key question is this: when the economy has recovered, stock markets are booming and investors are buoyant again, when regulators relax and the most committed corporate crime busters within them have burnt out or been removed, will boardroom and barroom values have changed? Can the 'rottening effects of the [corporate] barrel' (Glasbeek, 2002) be overcome?

Unfortunately, it is extremely difficult to study corporate cultures. Access is hard (often impossible) to attain, methodological problems abound. Survey research utilizing interviews or questionnaires probing management attitudes is problematic because its validity depends on the willingness of participants to give honest answers, perhaps putting themselves in a bad light in the eyes of the interviewer or jeopardizing their careers if confidentiality is breached. Moreover, these methodologies assume that those heavily invested in corporate culture have the insight and reflexivity to disentangle themselves from it, gaze dispassionately at themselves and their organization, and report this to some researcher they do not know and cannot control. Participant-observation studies of business behaviour from the inside cut that risk to a certain extent, but overwhelming difficulties in securing access mean there are very few of them. Without this, detailed patterns of interaction, communication, and naming, shaming and blaming cannot be interrogated. Thus academics have been forced to rely heavily (too heavily) on business histories, (auto)biographies of successful executives, whistleblower and investigative journalist accounts. But all of these are written with agendas which must be disentangled before they can be used for social science research; in many cases the sources of bias are simply unknown.

That said, the pictures that emerge tell us that corporate cultures, in the main, are made up of aggressive, ambitious, driven Type A personalities, primarily men, primarily white in ethnicity, primarily privileged in background. Few have class origins below upper-middle class. Women and certain racial-ethnic minorities – Asian rather than Eastern European, Caribbean, African or Latino – are among the few 'outsider' groups making inroads into senior management, though this varies by industry, sector and nation-state (Grabosky and Braithwaite, 1986; Jackall, 1988; Vaughan, 1998). The corporate culture these executives simultaneously create and inhabit is one that promotes and rewards the personal characteristics these people display. To rise to the top of the hierarchy, managers must become skilled at compartmentalizing, dividing work norms from other areas of life. They must jockey for power, privilege and promotion in a stressful, high energy environment, working long hours and networking assiduously on and off the job. As individuals, senior corporate officers tend to display varying but generally conventional upper-middle-class ethical views and values on religion, family and citizenship. Their perspectives on blue-collar crime and on law and order issues are overwhelmingly conservative. However, *corporate* offences, in general, are judged differently. While many, even most subjects strive to 'do the right thing', it can be enormously difficult to sort out exactly what this means at the top levels of the average corporation. Which behaviours, at what period of time, amount to corporate crime (and are therefore illegal and unethical), and which acts are 'smart' business practice? In the corporate pressure cooker with an abundance of conflicting definitions, conventional ethics provide little guidance (Braithwaite, 1989, 2000, 2005; Grabosky and Braithwaite, 1986).

For example, Grey's study (2003) of the Arthur Anderson accounting firm, a once-storied family firm now remembered primarily as Enron's auditor, depicted a corporate culture that rewarded conformity and loyalty. Conformity meant constant and aggressive striving to be the best, being totally client-centred to the point of 'retaining that client no matter what' (Grey, 2003: 574). Loyalty meant doing all that you could to promote the objectives of the firm – which were to maximize profits by satisfying clients, particularly clients that accounted for a substantial percentage of your business. The professional standards and values stressed in business schools and in training as a professional accountant were generally not seen as relevant to day-to-day decision-making challenges. Whether this resulted from selective memory failure or from creative reinterpretation is not clear, but either way it is indisputable that professional norms failed to function as practical guides to ethics and behaviour. Grey concludes that 'the cultural practices of the company' were **criminogenic** (ibid.: 575).

The few post-Enron studies published thus far do not indicate a sea change in corporate culture at the top. Indeed, as noted earlier, resistance and backlash to 'regulatory overkill' are flourishing. Employer-sponsored initiatives to govern the behaviour of middle management, however, may be outwardly more successful because employees either conform or risk losing their jobs. However, Roberts (2003) found that employees distance themselves from new corporate ethics codes on both moral and social levels. While employers tell employees the codes are both 'profitable and principled' (ibid.: 257), employees are simultaneously experiencing a workplace that is anything but. Employer demands that they immerse themselves in work 'to the neglect of almost everything else' (ibid.: 260) and produce ever-higher profit levels have intensified for those who have not yet been downsized or outsourced. And despite escalating demands on middle management, rigid social distance is maintained that limits their access to top ranks. Thus many employees experience the latest round of management demands to incorporate new ethics codes at yet another way to shift responsibility from those at the top to those in middle management.

Similarly, Jennings (2005) reports that the employees she studied look for, and usually find, ways to get round new ethics codes and return to 'business as usual'. Employees resist what they see as 'oppressive regulations' (ibid.: 49) whether they originate from top management or the state, and assume that such rules are intended for 'bad apples', not for them. She argues that control must be 'self-imposed', with top management emphasizing what is ethical, not what is merely legal. Only when senior management sets the bar higher for itself, she argues, will 'the spirit of ethics at individual and lower levels' emerge (ibid.: 52, 53). She finds no evidence that ethical leadership of this sort is coming.

These studies tell an old story. Management insists that generating constant and increasing profits is consistent with respecting high-level ethical standards. Employees experience the contradictions embodied in this claim and resent the fact that they are asked to 'manage' the conflicts and ethical dilemmas this creates and will be held responsible for ethical as well as legal lapses. Under these conditions, *habitus* change is unlikely.

However, efforts are also underway to fix the problem by transforming the CEOs of tomorrow while they are still in school. Ethics courses in business schools have long been low profile, low priority and low enrolment.[4] Ethics courses were optional, typically shunted off to the Philosophy Department. Post-crackdown initiatives to improve ethics training are now seen in business schools at both undergraduate and MBA levels.

How promising are these initiatives? How deep does ethics training go? Studies published thus far tell us little except that more courses are being offered. Ridler (2004), who surveyed all 49 business schools in Canada, found that 48 had at least two Introductory Business Ethics courses, typically offered by the Philosophy Department, not integrated with the main business curriculum. Of 26 schools offering MBA/Graduate degrees, while 75 per cent offered a Business Ethics course, only 13 made it compulsory. Few offered more than one such course, only two Deans identified it as a core responsibility, and many business professors saw an ethics specialization as career-impeding.

Moreover, 'ethics' is increasingly being defined as environmental management or sustainability (Finlay et al., 2005), and such courses are isolated from the mainstream curriculum. A worldwide survey of 4,123 MBA graduates from 96 schools (53 per cent were US citizens) found over 80 per cent satisfied with the ethics education they were offered. The scandals then rocking the business world – the survey was conducted in 2002 – were only worrisome to them because they created an 'atmosphere of distrust' not conducive to business prosperity. Only 37 per cent thought Enron et al. would make businesses act more ethically, although women were significantly more ethics-conscious (Anonymous, 2006). A 2005 study by the World Resources Institute reports that 54 per cent of 91 business schools on six continents now require an ethics or an ethic-related course, up 45 per cent from 2003, 34 per cent in 2001 (World Resources, 2006). A subsequent study (Aspen Institute, 2006) measured the effects of MBA education on student attitudes on the responsibilities of business. This was a longitudinal internet survey of students in 13 business schools which followed student attitudes through the course of a two-year MBA. Some 1,116 entered the first year in September 1999, 512 of these were sampled at the end of the first year, and 551 graduates in the spring of 2001. The sample was 66 per cent male; 57 per cent American, and most were between 26 and 30 years of age. The results show that 'shareholder return' becomes more, not less, relevant as business education proceeds: 66 per cent put it first in September of the first year; 74 per cent at the end of the first year, and 82 per cent on graduation. Creating benefits for the local community was well down the list: 22 per cent put it first in year 1, 18 per cent in year 2, 24 per cent of graduates. When asked how business decisions should be prioritized, shareholder interests were privileged above customers, employees or environmental/social considerations. Socially responsible behaviour was pronounced 'good' if it led to fewer legal, public relations or regulatory problems (and bad, presumably, if it did not). Corporate social responsibility was deemed useful primarily for building a better corporate image (74 per cent).

## Conclusion

This snapshot indicates little progress towards the creation of cultures of compliance thus far. Indeed, there is evidence that structural factors, one of the elements shaping cultural 'common sense', conflict with formal social control efforts. When economic factors – increasing profit levels to maximize share-holder value – dominate the real-world environment, it only *makes sense* that business will develop cultures putting this first. This means ethics discourse, law and other forces promoting greater social responsibility become second priority. Indeed, evidence indicates one effect of the crackdown has seen top management shifting the burden of reconciling competing responsibilities downward while maintaining a highly principled 'zero tolerance' rhetoric at the top.

This chapter began with case studies showing the ubiquity, resilience and variability of economic corporate crime and proceeded to ask whether cycles of disaster, crackdown and status quo ante can be interrupted. While conclusions are necessarily premature and tenuous, little transformation in corporate *habitus* (Bourdieu, 1987, 1993, 1996) is yet evident.

## Notes

My thanks to Research Assistants Suzanne Day and Jordan Watters for their assistance with assembling and writing up these case studies.

1  Ironically, the financial scandal of the preceding decade, the most financially costly corporate crime before Enron, the U.S. Savings and Loan crisis, was also enabled by deregulation. In the early 1980s, laws restricting owners and managers of Savings and Loan companies ('thrifts') to stable, 'blue chip' stocks were repealed, as were requirements that thrift owners and managers maintain a minimum percentage of assets as capital reserves (a cushion against investment losses). 'Hot deals' (land flips, nominee loans, and reciprocal lending), 'looting' (diverting investments to executive salaries, bonuses, yachts, etc.), and falsified records proliferated. By the late 1980s, 284 thrifts had failed, overall losses exceeded $500 billion, $12,420,065 per institution, an estimated $5,000 per household. Eerily, given today's scandals, every major accounting firm in the United States but one was implicated (*New York Times*, 10 June 1990; *Observer*, 8 April 1990; Calavita et al., 1997).

2  With deregulation, decriminalization and downsizing of regulatory agencies, there are fewer offences and fewer watchers (Snider, 2002; Tombs and Whyte, 2002). This is one reason offences are detected only after major disasters, such as bankruptcies, have occurred.

3  This is not to suggest that corporations are necessarily 'amoral calculators' (Pearce and Tombs, 1998). Nor is it to downplay the deep divisions and wide range of attitudes to compliance found within business, at different organizational levels, and across business sectors.

4  Law schools are also intensifying ethics education, offering courses on corporate governance and, in one case, on corporate crime (Crosariol, 2005; Paton, 2006).

## References

Advertising Supplement of the Toronto Stock Exchange (2004) *Report on Business Magazine*. Globe & Mail, June.

Andrews, N. (2006) 'Corporatism and the Toronto Stock Exchange: a new Ontario Egg Board?' *Australian Journal of Corporate Law*, 19: 65–113.

Anonymous (2006) 'Ethics and environmentalism increasing at business schools', *BizEd*, 5, 2.

Aspen Institute (2006) 'Where will they lead? MBA student attitudes about business and society', *Initiative for Social Innovation Through Business*. Aspen Institute. Available at: www.aspeninstitute.org

Beaty, J. and Gwynne, S.C. (1993) *The Outlaw Bank: A Wild Ride into the Heart of BCCI*. New York: Random House.

Bourdieu, P. (1987) 'The force of law: toward a sociology of the juridical field', *The Hastings Law Journal*, 38: 805–53.

Bourdieu, P. (1991) *Language and Symbolic Power*. Cambridge, MA: Harvard University Press.

Bourdieu, P. (1993) *Sociology in Question*. London: Sage.

Bourdieu, P. (1996) *The State Nobility: Elite Schools in the Field of Power*. Stanford, CA: Stanford University Press.

Braithwaite, J. (1989) *Crime, Shame and Reintegration*. Cambridge: Cambridge University Press.

Braithwaite, J. (2000) 'The new regulatory state and the transformation of criminology', *British Journal of Criminology*, 40(2): 222–38.

Braithwaite, J. (2005) *Markets in Vice, Markets in Virtue*. Annadale, Australia: Federation Press.

Braithwaite, J. and Drahos, P. (2000) *Global Business Regulation*. Cambridge: Cambridge University Press.

Calavita, K. (1983) 'The demise of the occupational safety and health administration: a case study in symbolic action', *Social Problems,* 30: 437–48.

Calavita, K., Pontell, H. and Tillman, R. (1997) *Big Money Crime*. Berkeley, CA: University of California Press.

Carson, W. (1970) 'White collar crime and the enforcement of factory legislation', *British Journal of Criminology*, 10: 383–98.

Carson, W. (1980) 'The institutionalization of ambiguity: early British Factory Acts', in G. Geis and E. Stotland (eds), *White Collar Theory and Research*. Beverly Hills: Sage.

Cohen, M. (ed.) (2000a) *Risk in the Modern Age*. London: Macmillan.

Cohen, M. (2000b) 'Environmental sociology, social theory and risk: an introductory discussion', in M. Cohen (ed.), *Risk in the Modern Age*. London: Macmillan, pp. 3–34.

Coleman, J. (1987) 'Towards an integrated theory of white-collar crime', *American Journal of Sociology,* 93: 406–39.

Condon, M. (1998) *Making Disclosure: Ideas and Interests in Ontario Securities Regulation*. Toronto: University of Toronto Press.

Crosariol, B. (2005) 'Whistle-blowing 101: the latest Law School offering: post-Enron era spawns corporate ethics courses across the country', *Globe & Mail*, September 6, 2004: B10.

Ehrenreich, B. (2001) *Nickel and Dimed: On (Not) Getting By in America*. New York: Metropolitan Books.

Finlay, J., Bunch, R., Prakash-Mani, K., Samuelson, J., Gentile, M. and Scully, M. (2005) *Beyond Grey Pinstripes: Preparing MBAs for Social and Environmental Stewardship*. Denver, CO: Joint publication of World Resources Institute and the Initiative for Social Innovation.

Fishman, E. (1998) 'Up in smoke', *Harpers Magazine*, December, pp. 37–46.

Frauley, J. (2005) 'Architextures of governance: a critical enquiry into the "analytics of government" through Foucault, Bourdieu and Critical Realist Metatheory', unpublished PhD thesis, Department of Sociology, Queen's University, Canada, August.

Geis, G. (1972) 'Criminal penalties for corporate criminals', *Criminal Law Bulletin,* 8: 277–92.

Glasbeek, H. (2002) *Wealth by Stealth*. Toronto: Between the Lines Press.

Grabosky, P. and Braithwaite, J. (1986) *Of Manners Gentle: Enforcement Strategies of Australian Business Regulatory Agencies*. Melbourne: Oxford University Press.

Grey, C. (2003) 'The real world of Enron's auditors', *Organization*, 10(3): 572–6.

Gunningham, N. and Johnstone, R. (1999) *Regulating Workplace Safety: System and Sanctions*. Oxford: Oxford University Press.

Gunningham, N., Kagan, R. and Thornton, D. (2003) *Shades of Green: Business, Regulation and Environment*. Stanford, CA: Stanford University Press.

Haines, F. (2003) 'Regulatory reform in light of regulatory character: assessing industrial safety change in the aftermath of the Kader Toy Factory Fire in Bangkok, Thailand', *Social & Legal Studies,* 12(4): 461–87.

Hall, A. and Johnstone, R. (2005) 'Exploring the re-criminalizing of OHS breaches in the context of industrial death', *Flinders Journal of Law Reform*, 57(8): 57–92.

Hutter, B. and Jones, C. (2006) 'Business risk management practices: the influence of state regulatory agencies and non-state sources', paper presented at *Law & Society Annual Meetings*, Baltimore, 6–9 July.

Hyatt, J. (2005) 'Birth of the ethics industry', *Business Ethics: The Magazine of Corporate Responsibility*. Available at: www.business-ethics.com/current-issue/summer-2005-birth.html.

Jackall, R. (1988) *Moral Mazes: The World of Corporate Managers*. New York: Oxford.

Jennings, M. (2005) 'Ethics and investment management: true reform', *The Financial Analysts Journal*, 61(3): 45–58.

Kagan, R., Gunningham, N. and Thornton, D. (2003) 'Explaining corporate environmental performance: how does regulation matter?', *Law & Society Review*, 37(1): 51–90.

Kerry, J. and Brown, H. (1992) *The BCCI Affair: A Report to the Committee on Foreign Relations United States Senate*. Available at: http://fas.org/irp/congress/1992_rpt/bcci/

Levi-Faur, D. and Jordana, J. (2005) 'The rise of regulatory capitalism: global diffusion of a new order', *The Annals*, American Academy of Political Science, V598, March.

Mackay, R. and Smith, M. (2004) 'Bill C-13: an Act to amend the Criminal Code (capital markets fraud and evidence-gathering)', Ottawa: Parliamentary Research Branch, Legislative summary, LS-468E.

McBarnet, D. (2005) 'After Enron: governing the corporation, mapping the loci of power in corporate governance design', in J. O'Brien (ed.), *Governing the Corporation: Regulation and Corporate Governance in an Age of Scandal and Global Markets*. Chichester: John Wiley & Sons, Ltd, pp. 89–111.

McBarnet, D. (2006) 'The meaning of "cleaner than clean" in regulation after Enron', Paper presented at Annual Meetings of American Society of Criminology, November 1–4.

Noble, C. (1985) 'Class, state and social reform in America: the case of the Occupational Safety and Health Act of 1970', *Research in Political Economy*, 8: 145–62.

Noble, C. (1986) *Liberalism at Work: The Rise and Fall of OSHA*. Philadelphia, PA: Temple University Press.

Parker, C. (2002) *The Open Corporation: Effective Self-Regulation and Corporate Citizenship*. Cambridge: Cambridge University Press.

Parker, C. (2006) 'The "compliance trap": the moral message in responsive regulatory enforcement', *Law & Society Review*, 40(3): 591–622.

Paton, P. (2006) 'Corporate counsel as corporate conscience: ethics and integrity in the post enron era', *Canadian Bar Review*, Special Edition on Ethics, 84(3): 533–62.

Patsuris, P. (2002–07) 'The corporate scandal sheet'. Available at: www.forbes.com/corporate

Pearce, F. and Tombs, S. (1998) *Toxic Capitalism: Corporate Crime and the Chemical Industry*. Aldershot: Ashgate/Dartmouth.

Phelps, M., McKay, H., Allen, T., Brunet, P., Doboon, W., Harris, E. and Tims, M. (2003) *It's Time: Report of the Committee to Review the Structure of Securities Regulation in Canada*. Ottowa: Department of Finance.

Post, J. (ed.) (1998) *Research in Corporate Social Performance and Policy*, vol. 15. Stamford, CT: JAI Press.

Purcell, K., Clarke, L. and Renzulli, L. (2000) 'Menus of choice: the social embeddedness of decisions', in M. Cohen (ed.), *Risk in the Modern Age*. London: Macmillan, pp. 62–82.

Rhodes, D. and Paton, P. (2002) 'Lawyers, ethics and Enron', *Stanford Journal of Law, Business and Finance*, 8(1): 9–38.

Ridler, J. (2004) 'Business ethics in education: the vision and the reality: Canadian perspective', paper presented at MBA Leadership Conference of Management Admission Council, 5 Feb, Newport Beach, California.

Roberts, J. (2003) 'The manufacture of corporate social responsibility: constructing corporate sensibility', *Organization*, 10(2): 249–65.

Rosoff, S., Pontell, H. and Tillman, R. (1998, 2004) *Profit Without Honor: White-Collar Crime and the Looting of America*. Englewood Cliffs, NJ: Prentice Hall.

Sanchez, C. (1998) 'The impact of environmental regulation on the adoption of innovation: how electric utilities responded to Clean Air Act Amendments of 1990', in J. Post (ed.), *Research in Corporate Social Performance & Policy*, vol. 15. Stamford, CT: JAI Press, pp. 45–88.

Shapiro, S. (1984) *Wayward Capitalists: Target of the Securities and Exchange Commission*. New Haven, CT: Yale University Press.

Shover, N., Clelland, D. and Lynxwiler, J. (1986) *Enforcement or Negotiation: Constructing a Regulatory Bureaucracy*. Albany, NY: SUNY Press.

Simpson, S. (1989) 'Corporate America', *Social Forces*, 65: 493–563.

Simpson, S. (2002) *Corporate Crime, Law and Social Control*. Cambridge: Cambridge University Press.

Slapper, G. (2000) Blood in the Bank, Social and Legal Aspects of Death at Work. Aldershot: Ashgate.

Snider, L. (1991) 'The regulatory dance: understanding reform processes in corporate crime', *International Journal of Sociology of Law*, 19: 209–36.

Snider, L. (1993) *Bad Business: Corporate Crime in Canada*. Scarborough: ITP Nelson.

Snider, L. (2000) 'The sociology of corporate crime: an obituary', *Theoretical Criminology*, 4(2): 169–206.

Snider, L. (2002) 'Theft of time: disciplining through science and law', *Osgoode Hall Law Journal*, 40(4): 89–113.

Snider, L. (2004) 'Resisting neo-liberalism: the poisoned water disaster in Walkerton, Ontario', *Social and Legal Studies*, 5(2): 27–47.

Sutherland, E. (1945) 'Is white-collar crime crime?', *American Sociological Review*, 10: 260–71.

Sykes, G. and Matza, D. (1957) 'Techniques of neutralization: a theory of delinquency', *American Sociological Review*, 22(6): 664–70.

Tombs, S. and Whyte, D. (2002) 'Unmasking the crimes of the powerful', *Critical Criminology: An International Journal*, 11(3): 217–36.

Vaughan, D. (1998) 'Rational choice, situated action and the social control of organizations', *Law & Society Review*, 32(1): 23–61.

World Resources Institute and the Aspen Institute (2006) *Beyond Grey Pinstripes*. Biennial Report, Denver, CO.

Yaron, G. (2002) *Canadian Shareholder Activism in an Era of Global Deregulation*. Vancouver: Shareholder Association for Research and Education. Available at: www.share.ca.

## Suggestions for further reading

Braithwaite, J. (2005) *Markets in Vice, Markets in Virtue*. Annadale, Australia: Federation Press.

Carroll, W. (2004) *Corporate Power in a Globalizing World: A Study in Elite Social Organizations*. Don Mills, Ontario: Oxford University Press.

Friedrichs, D. (2007) *Trusted Criminals: White Collar Crime in Contemporary Society*, 3rd edn. Belmont, CA: Thompson Wadsworth.

Glasbeek, H. (2002) *Wealth by Stealth*. Toronto: Between the Lines Press.

Hillyard, P., Pantazis, C., Tombs, S. and Gordon, D. (eds) *Beyond Criminology: Taking Harm Seriously*. London: Pluto Press and Halifax: Fernwood.

Pearce, F. and Tombs, S. (1998) *Toxic Capitalism: Corporate Crime and the Chemical Industry*. Aldershot: Ashgate/Dartmouth.

Rosoff, S., Pontell, H. and Tillman, R. (2004) *Profit Without Honor: White-Collar Crime and the Looting of America*, 3rd edn. Englewood Cliffs, NJ: Prentice Hall.

Simpson, S. (2002) *Corporate Crime, Law and Social Control*. Cambridge: Cambridge University Press.

# THREE

## The Evolving Legal Test of Corporate Criminal Liability

*James Gobert*

### Introduction

The title of this chapter contains an implicit assumption with which the reader may or may not agree: that companies should be subject to criminal liability for offences that occur in the course of their business operation for which they bear responsibility. But does it make any sense to prosecute a company, which is, after all, an inanimate, fictional entity? The criminal law was developed with flesh-and-blood human beings in mind. Central to the criminal law are the concepts of *actus reus* (wrongful act) and *mens rea* (wrongful state of mind) and the linking maxim of *actus non facit reum nisi mens sit rea* (an act is not wrongful unless accompanied by a wrongful state of mind). How can an inanimate, fictional entity such as a company act, and where is its state of mind to be located?

Proponents of the philosophy of methodological individualism, such as Popper (1957), Hayek (1949) and Wolf (1985), argue that that 'all social and economic phenomena are attributable to human agency and human agency alone' (Sullivan 1996). If so, actions of a company are traceable to, and therefore attributable to, natural persons. When the results of a corporate policy turn out poorly, the methodological individualist would maintain that the natural persons who conceived, developed, approved or implemented the policy should be blamed. In appropriate cases, these persons might also be subjected to criminal prosecution.[1]

Competing with methodological individualism is the vision of a company as a holistic entity with an identity separate and distinct from its shareholders, directors, officers, employees and agents. This 'organic' model of a company recognizes the power of coordinated collective action. What distinguishes collective decision-making from decision-making by individuals is the synergy which takes place when members of a company combine their expertises, knowledge, experience and analytical skills in tackling a common problem. Potential stumbling blocks are less likely to be overlooked by a group. Creative solutions, which may not have occurred to any one person in particular, may be sparked by a comment of a member of the group which takes the thinking of the others into a new and previously unexplored direction. Ambitious projects, which would be impossible for any one individual to develop or implement individually, become possible when many persons pool their skills, talents and energies. The resulting product clearly reflects a group effort and it would be misleading to attribute the result to discrete individuals.

The organic model of a company also seems more attuned to the realities of the corporate world. A company's personnel – from its CEO and directors to its online workers – are constantly changing, as are its shareholders. Throughout changes in ownership, management and staff, the one constant remains the company itself. Legally, companies are entities in their own right: they can own property, trade under their own name, and sue and be sued in a civil court. Further, the organic model accords with the way that ordinary people think about companies (an arguably relevant although not determinative consideration). When a defective product manufactured by Company X causes serious harm, we tend to blame the company, rather than the unknown individuals who conceived, designed, assembled or tested the faulty merchandise, regardless of the degree of fault of each of those persons.

The argument of the methodological individualist that all corporate wrongdoing can be traced to individuals may have more merit in respect of crimes whose *actus reus* consists of an identifiable affirmative act than it has in respect of crimes where the alleged fault element is a failure to have taken preventative action. In the case of an omission, who is to be blamed for not anticipating the harmful and illegal consequences of a corporate policy – the person who conceived the policy initially, the committee which reviewed and perhaps modified the policy, the senior managers who approved the recommendation of the committee, or the board of directors which gave their blessing to the proposal? Would any of these individuals have the necessary *mens rea* for a crime requiring, for example, that the offence be committed knowingly?

Even in respect of crimes whose *actus reus* consists of an affirmative act, there are problems with methodological individualism. Often acts of many persons need to occur in combination in order for a harmful and criminal result to follow. Should all of these individuals be held criminally liable or should liability be limited to the person whose acts were most directly linked in time and space to the harmful result? That person would most likely be an employee who may have been simply carrying out misguided corporate policy relying on their superiors not to have commanded the commission of a criminal offence. Employees are also well aware that the refusal to carry out the orders of a superior can lead to a reprimand and even dismissal. To pin legal responsibility for the resulting criminal harm on an ordinary worker in this position may be nothing more than an exercise in scapegoating.

Implicit in the methodological individualist philosophy is the assumption that one must choose between prosecuting individuals and prosecuting companies. This is a false dichotomy. To argue in favour of corporate liability is not to deny individual responsibility. While in some cases prosecuting individuals may make sense, in others prosecuting the company may make more sense, and in still others there may be no sound reason not to prosecute both individuals and the company. In some instances both individuals and the company might be prosecuted *but for different crimes*. For instance, if a corporate employee were to attack a customer in his office, the employee might be prosecuted for assault and battery and the company for an offence based on its failure to carry out the necessary background checks that would have revealed that it was hiring an unstable and potentially violent individual.[2]

In modern times, a consensus has in fact emerged that companies can and should be subject to criminal prosecution in their own right, regardless of whether individuals are also prosecuted. What then needs to be determined is the proper test of a company's criminal liability. When one examines this issue more closely, however, what one finds is that the methodological individualist influence continues to haunt the law. As we shall see, most of the traditional legal tests of corporate criminal liability involve imputing or attributing the crimes of individuals to the corporate entity.

## Vicarious liability

The prevailing test of corporate criminal liability in the United States holds companies vicariously liable for crimes of their directors, officers, employees and agents. In fact, however, the doctrine of vicarious liability traces its roots to English law, where it had long been available in *civil* courts as a means of providing compensation for those who suffered injuries at the hands of negligent employees. If the company were not liable for damages, the injured party would have been left to sue the likely impecunious employee who caused the harm. By allowing a suit against the company, with its 'deep pockets' (and ability to obtain insurance), the law enabled the innocent victim to receive the compensation which he or she needed and deserved.

In the criminal law, where the emphasis is primarily on punishing the culpable and blameworthy actor rather than on providing compensation to the innocent victim, vicarious liability is more problematic. Criminal liability is generally based on fault,[3] and a company may not have been at fault when one of its employees violated the law. Indeed, the company may have specifically prohibited the actions leading to the offence. Even in this situation, however, vicarious *criminal* liability can be justified. A directive not to engage in certain conduct may not be sufficient to thwart criminal violations. Where serious harm is threatened, companies should arguably have to go further and take positive action to prevent workers from engaging in conduct that is likely to lead to damage, injury or death.

In the United States, the seminal decision on vicarious liability is that of the US Supreme Court in *New York Central & Hudson River Railroad Co. v United States*.[4] Although the Court was interpreting federal law, its test of vicarious liability has subsequently been adopted by state courts as well. Moreover, the test has been extended from acts which were ordered or authorized by a company to those which were ratified or even simply tolerated.[5] While the offending employee or agent must have been acting within the scope of his or her authority with intent to benefit the company, these restrictions also have been liberally construed,[6] and even the fact that the offender's actions were expressly forbidden will not necessarily provide the company with a defence.[7]

Under a test of vicarious liability, the link between a company's criminal liability and an individual's crime is the fact that at the time of the offence the offender was engaged in the company's business and pursuing corporate goals. In other words, the company's liability is wholly derivative. Seemingly underlying that liability is the methodological individualist premise that crimes can be committed only by natural persons. Corporate liability results from imputing to the company the crime of the individual.

There are several objections to vicarious liability as a measure of a company's criminal responsibility. One already alluded to is that vicarious liability can lead to a company being convicted of an offence even though it took reasonable, even exemplary, steps to prevent the offence. The fact that a well-conceived policy designed to thwart criminality was foiled by a malcontent employee is hardly a fair reflection of how a company has organized and carried out its business. A second objection relates to the practical problems involved in forcing a company, particularly a large multinational corporation, to supervise potentially hundreds of thousands of employees. Supervision may be even a greater problem in a small business where it would be impractical for the employer to be present at all times, and cost-prohibitive to hire a supervisor to oversee a handful of employees. Finally, while vicarious liability may fairly capture a company's *actus reus* – after all, how else except through its employees can a company act? – it is less satisfactory when it comes to assigning *mens rea* to a company. While a company's acts can be conceptualized in terms of the cumulative acts of its personnel and the results these acts produce (as where thousands of employees produce millions of cars, some of which turn out to be defective and dangerous because of sloppy workmanship coupled with poor quality control), the company's mind cannot similarly be equated with the sum of the various mental states of its employees, many of which would be hopelessly conflicting. This logical fallacy, however has not prevented American courts from vicariously attributing the *mens rea* of an errant employee to the employer, ignoring the fact that the employee's state of mind might not in any way have reflected the thinking of the employer or, in the case of a company, corporate policy.

## Identification and attribution

The perceived weaknesses of vicarious liability, and in particular the problematic issue of the basis on which to attribute a mental state to a company, led the English courts in the 1940s to develop their own distinctive approach to corporate criminal liability. In *DPP v Kent and Sussex Contractors Ltd*,[8] it was held that a company's state of mind could be found in the state of mind of those empowered to speak or act for the company. If a company's officer had an intent to deceive, as the court found in the case, then the company too had an intent to deceive.

In a second case, *R v ICR Haulage Ltd*,[9] the managing director of a company *and the company* were charged, along with nine other persons, with conspiracy to defraud. The court reiterated the position that the intention, knowledge or belief of a company's officers could be attributed to the company. Although earlier cases had for the most part involved statutory violations, the offence charged against ICR Haulage was a common law crime. The court, however, held that this distinction did not make a difference.

In *Moore v Bresler Ltd*,[10] the most intriguing of the 1940s trilogy, the secretary of a company had sold corporate products for private gain and with the clear intent to defraud his company. In order to conceal his wrongdoing, the secretary did not report the sales to the revenue. Along with the secretary and an accomplice, the company was charged with submitting false documents with intent to deceive. The company, not surprisingly, argued that it was a victim rather than an offender, and that its co-defendants had not been acting for its benefit, but for their private gain and with the aim of defrauding the company. It might be observed that this argument would have succeeded if the American test of vicarious liability had been in force for under that test, in order for a company to be convicted, the individual offender needs to have been acting to benefit the company (rather than 'on a frolic of his own'). However, the English judges were not impressed with this feature of the case. For the court, the critical issue was whether the individuals were acting within the scope of their authority as officers of the company when they filed the false documents. If they were, then their acts and mental state represented the acts and mental state of the company, and their deceit in respect of the false returns could be imputed to the company. Parenthetically, and although not the rationale of the court, the result can be defended on the ground the company had put the secretary in a position to commit the fraud and had arguably failed to review his submissions to the revenue with sufficient care to have uncovered his deceit.

The rule of law established by the 1940s cases has came to be known as the 'identification' doctrine. The leading modern decision is that of the House of Lords in *Tesco Supermarkets Ltd. v Nattrass*.[11] In this case, the supermarket chain was charged with selling goods at a higher than advertised price, the offence having occurred when one of the company's branch stores had run out of a discounted item and a stocker had placed packets of the product bearing the ordinary price on the shelves. The shop manager in charge had failed to notice the substitution. After a customer complained, Tesco was prosecuted and convicted of violating the Trade Descriptions Act 1968. On appeal to the House of Lords, the company invoked that section of the Act which allowed a defence where the violation was due to the fault of 'another person' and the defendant had taken 'all reasonable precautions' and had exercised 'all due diligence' to prevent the violation.[12] The company maintained that the store manager was 'another person' for purposes of this section and that it had taken all reasonable precautions and had exercised all due diligence by instituting a system to avoid the occurrence of the offence.

While it would not have been unreasonable for their Lordships to have interpreted the term 'another person' to refer to somebody not associated with the company, such as a vandal or mischief maker, they in fact took a different tack. Seizing upon the fact that the responsibility for exercising 'all reasonable precautions' and 'due diligence' rested with those who constituted the 'controlling mind and will' of the company, they reasoned that anybody else would be 'another person' for purposes of the statute.[13] Thus by indirection the House defined who was the company for legal purposes. Even though the store manager had considerable authority and discretion, he nonetheless was obliged to adhere to policies formulated at a higher managerial level. In reaching this conclusion, Lord Reid quoted Lord Denning's well-known distinction between the 'brains' and 'hands' of a company:

> A company may in many ways be likened to the human body. It has a brain and nerve centre which controls what it does. It also has hands which hold the tools and act in accordance with directions from the centre. Some of the people in the company are mere servants and agents who are nothing more than hands to do the work ... Others are directors and managers who represent the directing mind and will of the company and control what it does. The state of mind of those managers is the state of mind of the company.[14]

The hands–brain analogy begs the question of how to determine whether an individual is part of the company's hands or brain. While courts, following Lord Denning's lead, frequently speak of 'brain work', 'nerve centres', and 'the mind and will' of the company, few, if any, job descriptions are drafted in such terms. More helpful, perhaps, may have been Lord Diplock's suggestion in *Nattrass* that the answer to the question of who constituted a company's 'directing mind and will' could be found 'by identifying those natural persons who by the memorandum and articles of association or as a result of action taken by directors, or by the company in general meeting pursuant to the articles, are entrusted with the exercise of the powers of the company'.[15] Another possibility would be for the courts to consult corporate documents filed with the state which identified the company's officers either by name or post held. Any such formulaic approach, however, may fail to capture the *realpolitik* of the decision-making structures in a given company. While their Lordships in *Nattrass* were plainly of the view that the board of directors would be deemed part of a company's 'controlling mind and will', in many organizations directors are appointed because of their public persona and the board is little more than a 'rubber stamp'. Even a CEO or corporate president may be selected because of his/her perceived gravitas and/or political contacts. Conversely, there may exist consultants, junior executives or 'shadow directors'[16] who hold no official position in the organization but who play a decisive behind-the-scenes role in formulating corporate policy.

In practice, authority in large companies must often perforce be delegated, as directors and senior managers are not in a position to oversee what every employee in the organization is doing at all times. In *Nattrass*, their Lordships accepted that a company could be liable for a crime committed by a person to whom decision-making authority had been delegated if the delegation came from a person 'identified' with the company, which of course brings the inquiry full circle. The issue is more complicated when delegation is partial, as there then arises the question of *how much* authority needs to be delegated in order to effect a transfer of 'identification'. While the store manager in *Nattrass* possessed significant delegated authority, that authority did not include the power to make policy decisions on behalf of the company. Thus it was insufficient delegation to prevent the House of Lords from reaching the conclusion that he was 'another person' for purposes of the statute. The decision would seem to establish a blueprint for corporate officials who seek to insulate their companies from criminal liability. What they need to do is assign responsibility for overseeing potentially criminogenic aspects of the company's business operation to junior executives, who would be unlikely to be deemed part of the company's 'directing mind and will', while reserving a residual veto power to themselves.

Despite the distinctive nomenclature, the identification test at heart is basically a variant of vicarious liability. It is, to be sure, a restrictive variant in that not all persons who are employed by the company or associated with it are accorded sufficient status to lead to the company's being held vicariously liable for their criminal offences; it is only a limited class of persons whose acts and state of mind can lead to the company's criminal liability. But in such cases liability is clearly vicarious: the offence of the person who is the 'directing mind and will' of the company is imputed to the company. The company's liability is derivative, grounded in the methodological individualist premise that crimes are committed by natural persons. As a result, a company still may be convicted of an offence despite having conducted its affairs in an impeccable manner.

An attempt to re-locate the identification doctrine within a broader scheme of liability was attempted by Lord Hoffmann in *Meridian Global Funds Management Asia Ltd. v. Securities Commission*.[17] The issue in the case was whether the corporate defendant had violated the New Zealand Securities Amendment Act 1988 when its Hong Kong investment managers had failed to comply with the Act's notification requirements. Writing for the Privy Council, Lord Hoffmann interpreted the identification doctrine as representing not a distinctive test of corporate criminal liability but rather a sub-category of a broader test which turned on the *attribution* of authority. According to Lord Hoffmann, for an individual's acts or state of mind to count as that of the company, the individual in question had to have the authority to act on behalf of the company with respect to the particular transaction in question. Whether or not the individual possessed that authority was to be determined by examining: (a) the company's 'primary rules of attribution' (contained in its constitution and articles of association); (b) any primary rules of attribution implied by Company Law; and (c) general principles of attribution, including rules of agency and estoppel. The joker in Lord Hoffmann's deck was that if the foregoing rules of attribution were insufficient to prevent frustration of the purpose of the statute alleged to have been violated, they could be supplemented with 'special rules of attribution' established by the court. The court then had to ask itself whether the statute was intended to apply to companies, and, if so, whose acts, knowledge or state of mind were to count as the acts, knowledge or state of mind of the company *for purposes of that particular statute*.

While expanding the basis of a company's potential criminal liability, Lord Hoffmann's 'attribution' test retains the same basic link between corporate and individual criminality that we saw with respect to the identification and vicarious liability doctrines. The company's liability is based on the fact that an individual has committed an offence which is then imputed to the company.[18] A company can still be criminally liable despite having done everything within its power to prevent the commission of the offence.


## Aggregated fault

One of the problems with the vicarious liability, identification and attribution tests of corporate criminal liability is that they require a prosecutor to identify a particular individual whose offence can be imputed to the company. But when harm that would seem to warrant criminal liability occurs in a business context, it is often the product of acts and failures by several persons, none of whom may have committed a crime. All may have behaved with less than the desired degree of circumspection but none in so egregious a manner so as to warrant a criminal prosecution for an offence requiring proof of recklessness or gross negligence, the generally invoked criminal law standards in cases where the defendant has not acted intentionally or knowingly. Yet the cumulative effect of all the individual acts of negligence may imply a higher degree of fault on the company's part than mere negligence.

Consider the nearly 200 deaths which followed the capsize of the *Herald of Free Enterprise* after water entered through the ferry's open bow doors and caused it to become destabilized. An inquiry mandated by statute identified numerous instances of negligence and poor practice that had contributed to the disaster.[19] The assistant bosun, whose job it was to close the bow doors, had been asleep at the time. The Chief Officer, responsible for assuring himself that the bow doors were closed, interpreted his responsibility to mean only that he had to assure himself that a crew member capable of closing the bow doors was in the vicinity of the doors.[20] For his part, the Master of the *Herald* had been content not to have been told that the bow doors were open and did not insist on an affirmative report that they were closed. Further, the Master accelerated out of the harbour at an excessive speed, the effect of pressure from management to depart ahead of schedule whenever the ferry was fully loaded in order to be able to achieve a timely arrival in England.[21] The Master of the fleet was also criticized for not having devised a foolproof system to ensure that the bow doors were closed. Finally the directors were rebuked for having rejected an eminently sensible proposal from the Masters to install indicator lights on the bridge that would alert a Master when the bow doors were open. The inquiry concluded that 'all concerned in management ... were guilty of fault' and that 'from top to bottom, the body corporate was infected with the disease of sloppiness'.[22]

Despite the damning conclusions of the inquiry, when P&O Ferries was subsequently charged with manslaughter, the prosecution failed because it could not be proved that any individual 'identified' with the company had committed manslaughter.[23] The trial judge rejected a theory of aggregated fault that would have allowed the Crown to establish the requisite *mens rea* by showing that the individual errors and oversights of various crew members, Masters and directors, *taken together*, amounted to sufficient fault to warrant a conviction for manslaughter. The opinion quoted of Bingham, J. (as he then was) in the related case of *R. v. H.M. Coroner for East Kent, ex parte Spooner*:[24]

> Whether the defendant is a corporation or a personal defendant, the ingredients of manslaughter must be established by proving the necessary *mens rea* and *actus reus* of manslaughter against it or him by evidence properly to be relied on against it or him. A case against a personal defendant cannot be fortified by evidence against another defendant. The case against a corporation can only be made by evidence properly addressed to showing guilt on the part of the corporation as such.[25]

Bingham's point that the 'case against a personal defendant cannot be fortified by evidence against another defendant' is undoubtedly correct. Guilt of an individual is by definition personal, and properly so for the individual on trial will suffer whatever penalty and stigma follow from a conviction. It would be unjust to convict that defendant on the basis of the fault or even partial fault of another person (unless complicity was alleged and established). But what Bingham arguably failed to take on board was the quite different rationale for aggregating fault in the corporate context. That purpose is not to hold one individual criminally liable based on the fault of another but rather as a tool for ascertaining the *company's* fault. Even if every wrongful act of a large number of corporate employees does not rise above the level of negligent behaviour, with *gross* negligence being required for criminal liability, a company's willingness to tolerate widespread negligent behaviour by its employees may constitute gross negligence on its part.

Why should the above described negligence on the part of the company be characterized as 'gross' when it consists only of cumulative acts of ordinary negligence? There are several points that can be made. First, when an individual employee behaves in a negligent manner, harm does not automatically follow. Indeed, the inquiry into the capsize of the *Herald* identified at least six other open bow crossings which had occurred without mishap. Let us therefore posit that the probability of harm actually occurring following an individual's negligent act is, say, one in ten (a figure admittedly chosen at random as the true incidence of negligent acts unaccompanied by concomitant harm can never be known). When, however, 1000 employees act in a similarly negligent manner, the probability of harm occurring would be $1000 \times 1/10$. Now the likelihood of some harm resulting from the negligence of these 1000 employees would be a near certainty. Indeed, it can be postulated that the incidence of harm following negligent acts increases proportionately (sometimes exponentially, as it may require a combination of negligent acts to produce a harmful result) to the number of persons who act in a negligent manner. Second, if we were to assume that the amount of harm resulting from a negligent act of a particular type by a single employee is Y, then the amount of harm that would follow from 1000 employees behaving in that way would be $1000 \times Y$. It can thus be seen that both the *probability* and *quantity* of harm resulting when many employees act negligently are considerably greater than when an isolated employee acts in a negligent fashion. These figures of course do not convert the acts of the individuals in question from ordinary negligence to gross negligence, but they do suggest that when companies tolerate negligent behaviour by their employees, the exacerbated risks warrant a finding that the company's *tolerance* of pervasive negligence constitutes gross negligence. Further, while an individual's negligent act may be inadvertent (anybody can have the occasional lapse of concentration), a company's decision to tolerate widespread negligent conduct by its workforce is more likely to be advertent. It is submitted that companies have a duty to be aware of how their workforce is carrying out their assignments. For a company to fail to do so, and for it to fail to take steps to prevent negligence by its employees arguably itself constitutes gross negligence.

While aggregation would have been a useful tool for determining P&O's *actus reus* in relation to the capsize of the *Herald*, the concept can also be helpful in ascertaining a company's *mens rea*. In the American case of *United States v. Bank of New England*,[26] several individuals within the bank had come into possession of various bits of information, none of which by themselves were sufficient to alert the bank to the fact that a criminal violation was about to occur. It was only by weaving together the various strands that the full picture emerged. The federal court held that 'if employee A knows one facet of the currency reporting requirement, and B knows another facet of it, and C a third facet of it, the bank knows them all'.[27] The court explained its reasoning:

> A collective knowledge is entirely appropriate in the context of corporate criminal liability. Corporations compartmentalize knowledge, subdividing the elements of specific duties and operations into smaller components. The aggregate of those components constitutes the corporation's knowledge of a particular operation.[28]

Accordingly, although no one individual in the bank had sufficient information to render the individual personally liable, the *bank's* aggregated knowledge was sufficient to render the bank liable.

The relationship between corporate liability based on an aggregation theory of corporate fault and individual criminality is of a hybrid nature. On the one hand, liability is still linked to acts and mental states of individuals, albeit more than one individual. On the other hand, there is a significant difference between the link under a vicarious liability, identification or attribution theory of corporate criminality and the link under aggregation – unlike under the first-named theories, an aggregation test of liability would not require proof that any specific individual has committed a criminal offence. As a consequence, a company could be convicted of a crime even though no individual associated with the company had committed a crime. Viewed in the latter light, aggregation represents a first step towards an approach to corporate criminal liability where a company's liability is not derivative, but where the company is liable in its own right for its own 'fault'.

## 'Corporate fault'

To briefly recap, four tests of corporate criminal liability have so far been examined – vicarious liability, identification, attribution and aggregation. Under the first three of these tests, the liability of the company is derivative. The link between corporate and individual criminality is the fact that a person who is a director, officer, employee or agent of a company has committed an offence which is then imputed to the company. Under a test of aggregated fault, corporate criminal liability will remain derivative if the courts persevere in linking corporate fault to individual fault, with the only difference being that the search is not for *that* individual whose crime can be imputed to the company but for *those* individuals whose acts and states of mind can be imputed to the company. On the other hand, aggregation may be a harbinger of a test of corporate fault that is independent of proof of individual criminality.

What considerations argue for holding companies responsible in their own right for offences committed by those working for or associated with the company? First, the companies are responsible for hiring and training their staff, and for placing them in a position where they can commit a criminal offence (as was the case in *Moore v Bresler Ltd*, discussed previously). Second, a company may have provided the offender with the means to commit the offence. Examples would be where a company supplied a driver with a lorry having known defects without informing the driver of the danger or placed a worker in charge of conducting a controlled explosion without having provided the worker with adequate training or supervision. In the financial sector, carte blanche power to spend accorded to a corporate officer may lead to bribery, fraud and corruption. Third, corporate salary, promotion, and bonus structures may encourage illegal behaviour. Nick Leeson's unauthorized and calamitous stock market trades, which led to the collapse of Barings Bank, may have been in large part driven by the extravagant bonuses on offer if his reckless gambles had succeeded. Similarly, when insurance salespersons are paid on a commission basis, can one be shocked if they misrepresent the risks associated with the company's policies in order to enhance their sales and, concomitantly, their income and advancement within the organization? Fourth, companies can be faulted for failing to put into place supervisory systems that would have prevented offences. The capsize of the *Herald of Free Enterprise* almost certainly would have been averted if indicator lights signalling that the bow doors remained open had been installed on the bridge, as lobbied for by the fleet's Masters. With respect to fraudulent telephone sales of insurance policies, recording relevant phone conversations would not only help to resolve future disputes that might arise, but also would serve to deter improper selling practices by sales personnel. Finally, companies provide individual wrongdoers with a ready rationalization for their offences. This is particularly true in the case of white-collar criminals – the claim of the typical white-collar criminal is that he or she was not seeking individual gain but was acting to advance the interests of the company (although this may be a bit disingenuous as the white-collar criminal no doubt also expects to benefit indirectly from bonuses, salary raises and promotions within the organization). Nevertheless, the deviance is easily rationalized on the basis that the wrongdoer is adhering to corporate norms. One of the major differences between ordinary crime and white-collar crime is that ordinary crimes violate the accepted norms of society and are generally condemned by law-abiding citizens, while white-collar crimes often conform to the norms of the company and, indeed, are likely to be rewarded when they lead to greater profits (Nollkaemper, 2006).

Derivative theories of corporate criminal liability locate a company's *mens rea* in individuals. What, then, takes the place of *mens rea* under a theory of 'corporate fault' for a crime that has a mental component?[29] Peter French (1984) has argued that within companies can be found what he calls semi-autonomous internal decision-making structures. These involve defined roles, established internal rules and procedures, and organizational flow-charts. Decisions are not so much made as processed. These internal decision-making structures, French submits, represent the corporate mind at work. Indeed, in an increasingly technological age, computerized models may be capable of generating solutions to corporate problems without human involvement (Dan-Cohen, 1986).

Over time a company may develop not only internal decision-making structures but also a distinctive corporate culture. Pamela Bucy (1991) asserts that this ethos or culture often plays a critical role in the commission of corporate criminal offences. For example, a company's ethos may tolerate illegal short-cuts (especially of regulatory legislation) which contribute to increased profitability.

It may not be possible, as the methodological individualists would have one believe, to neatly tie the relevant ethos to any particular individual or individuals within the company. The ethos may have evolved over time, and it may never have been made explicit. It would be naïve to expect to find a written policy that legal constraints such as health and safety regulations were to be ignored if they inhibited profitability. Indeed, if the trail of a corporate ethos were to be pursued, its roots might be traced to the founders of the company or managers who were no longer alive. In such situations Sullivan (1996) argues that the culture should be attributed to those officials who perpetuate it. But no conscious decision to this effect may ever have been taken, and corporate officials may not be aware of dangerous practices that have grown up over an extended period of time, having been passed from one generation of workers to the next (however, as has been argued, management may have an affirmative obligation to discover such improper practices).

## Capturing corporate fault in a statute

A pioneering effort to capture in statute the concept of a criminogenic corporate culture has been undertaken in Australia. In relevant part the federal Criminal Code Act (1995) provides:

(1) If intention, knowledge or recklessness is a fault element in relation to a physical element of an offence that may be committed by a company, that fault element must be attributed to a body corporate that expressly, tacitly or impliedly authorised or permitted the commission of the offence.

(2) The means by which such an authorisation or permission may be established include –

...

(c) proving that a corporate culture existed with the body corporate that directed, encouraged, tolerated or led to non-compliance with the relevant provision; or

(d) proving that the body corporate failed to create and maintain a corporate culture that required compliance with the relevant provision

...

(4) In this section ... [a] corporate culture means an attitude, policy, rule, course of conduct or practice existing within the body corporate generally or in the part of the body corporate in which the relevant activities take place.[30]

The above statute creates no new offences but would apply to existing offences which have intention, knowledge or recklessness as a fault element and allow for the prosecution of companies. The Act accordingly provides an across-the-board test of corporate fault. While part of the Act (not reprinted here) incorporates a modified and expanded version of the 'identification' test, what is truly distinctive in the Act is its recognition that a defective corporate culture can also serve as the basis of a company's criminal liability. Subsection (2)(c) allows liability to be based on an existing culture that directs, encourages, tolerates or leads to non-compliance with the law. Subsection (2)(d) goes further, imposing on companies an affirmative duty to create and maintain a corporate culture that requires compliance with the law. If a company fails to do so, it can again find itself charged with a crime of intention, knowledge or recklessness. Under Subsection (2)(d), the fact that a defective corporate culture has long been in existence will not excuse a company from failing to create and implement a law-compliant culture. Although proving a company's culture at a particular point in time may be problematic, the law's main effect hopefully will be to force companies to look critically at their existing culture and to reform that culture where it threatens to lead to violations of the law.

## The Corporate Manslaughter and Corporate Homicide Act 2007

In the UK, an attempt to capture 'corporate fault' has also been made in the limited context of homicide[31] in the Corporate Manslaughter and Corporate Homicide Act 2007.[32] The offence is set out in section 1 of the Act:

### 1 The offence

(1) An organization to which this section applies is guilty of an offence if the way in which its activities are managed or organised –

(a) causes a person's death, and
(b) amounts to a gross breach of a relevant duty of care owed by the organization to the deceased.

…

(3) An organization is guilty of an offence under this section *only if the way in which its activities are managed or organized by its senior management* is a substantial element in the breach referred to in subsection (1). (emphasis added)

(4) For the purposes of this Act –

…

(b) a breach of a duty of care by an organization is a 'gross' breach if the conduct alleged to amount to a breach of that duty falls far below what can reasonably be expected of the organization in the circumstances;
(c) 'senior management', in relation to an organization, means the persons who play significant roles in –

(i) the making of decisions about how the whole or a substantial part of its activities are to be managed or organized, or
(ii) the actual managing or organising of the whole or a substantial part of those activities.

While the 2007 Act takes the law forwards in several welcome ways, it unfortunately is also in many ways disappointingly regressive (Gobert, 2008). The Law Commission Report (1996) and the Home Office consultation paper (2000), which preceded the Act and on which the Act was based, had proposed an offence of corporate killing whose fault element consisted of a 'management failure' which fell 'far below' what could reasonably have been expected of the company under the circumstances. The term *management* failure was not intended to refer to the failures of a company's managers, but to the flawed way in which the company managed its affairs.[33]

While the 2007 Act incorporates the Commission's concept of a 'management failure' into its definition of 'gross breach' (see section 1(4)(b) above), it further requires that the actions of 'senior management' be a 'substantial element' in the gross breach (see section 1(3) above). This reference to senior management may have been intended to signify that companies should not be responsible for deaths caused primarily by junior staff, a defensible position (although arguably erroneous for reasons already articulated), but unfortunately the Act then proceeds to define 'senior management' in terms of persons who play a significant role in the formulation and/or implementation of corporate policy. By so doing, the Act deflects the inquiry from the Law Commission's intended focus on systemic failures to one where the failings of individuals again take central stage. Granted, the use of the plural ('persons') suggests that under the Act corporate liability can be based on aggregated fault and that the need to identify a specific individual within the organization who has committed the offence, as required under the doctrines of identification and attribution, is no longer indispensable. Furthermore, defining senior managers by the functional role that they play in an organization may be an advance over the use of formal job titles and offices held as the criteria of senior rank. Nonetheless, the requirement of proof of fault on the part of individuals seems to underscore the methodological individualist position that fault is to be found in persons rather than in a defective system of management.

As a practical matter, the Act's requirement that the prosecution establish fault on the part of individuals threatens to perpetuate the same kinds of evidentiary problems that plagued prosecutions under the the 'identification' doctrine. Arguments over whether a particular individual played a significant role in the formulation and/or implementation of corporate policy are likely to prove just as contentious as the question of who constituted a 'directing mind and will' of a company under the 'identification' doctrine. The Act's further requirement that the senior management failure be a 'substantial element' in the alleged breach is also likely to prove a battleground for litigators.[34] Disputes over what is needed generally to be proved in order to establish 'substantiality' will be inevitable, as will, in a given case, arguments over whether senior management's contribution to a particular alleged 'gross breach' was substantial or something less weighty. The prosecution may experience particular difficulty in cases where there are systemic failures at multiple levels of an organization, as occurred in respect of the capsize of the *Herald of Free Enterprise*.

One final feature of the Act that bears mentioning is its recognition of the relevance of corporate culture. Among the factors that a jury '*may*' consider in determining whether a 'gross beach' has occurred is 'the extent to which the evidence shows that there were attitudes, policies, systems or accepted practices within the organization that were likely to have encouraged (the management) failure ... or to have produced tolerance of it.'[35] This echoes the Australian concept of a criminogenic corporate culture, and is to be welcomed. It would have been even more welcome if a jury's consideration of corporate culture had been made mandatory rather than being simply permissive, and if it were deemed generally relevant to guilt rather than relevant only after a health and safety violation had first been established.[36]


## Conclusion

The purpose of a doctrine of corporate fault is not to substitute corporate liability for individual liability, but rather to recognize the distinctive roles played by companies and individuals in bringing about criminal offences. Sometimes individual offences are attributable to organizational forces which encourage, promote or tolerate offences. Sometimes individuals are placed in situations where in retrospect it can be seen that the offence was virtually inevitable if the individual was to achieve the assigned corporate task (as where a delivery is required to be made by a specified time but meeting this deadline will require the driver to commit road traffic offences, which may lead to fatal 'accidents'). Sometimes lax supervision creates an irresistible temptation to commit an offence. Under the identification and attribution doctrines, considerations such as these tend to be ignored or glossed over by the courts.

The argument made here is that companies should be under a legal duty not only to establish a law-compliant culture but also to put in place systems that will prevent criminal offences by personnel. Companies, however, cannot be relied upon voluntarily to adopt the relevant policies. Too often a company benefits financially from the crimes of its employees. As a consequence it may have little incentive either to discover or put a stop to the offences.

If corporate criminal liability is a desideratum, the question becomes what the test of a company's liability should be. In a principled criminal justice system, liability should be based on fault. The derivative liability embodied in tests of vicarious liability, identification, attribution and possibly aggregation can penalize companies whose way of conducting their business has been faultless. So when, then, can it be said that a company has been at fault? It is submitted that a company should incur criminal liability in three situations:

1   When it orders, aids, abets, counsels, or in any other way facilitates a criminal offence by a person for whom the organization bears responsibility (e.g., one of its directors, officers, employees or agents)
2   When it fails to prevent a crime by a person for whom the organization bears responsibility; in circumstances where:

- it had a duty to its employees, consumers or users of its product, or members of the public to prevent harm, and;
- when it was – or with the exercise of due diligence – should have been, aware of the risks that were presented by a policy or course of action or inaction;
- when it had the capacity to prevent the violation; and
- when it was not unreasonable for it do so.

3   Permits a corporate culture that tolerates, encourages, or fails to discourage crimes; or fails to establish a corporate culture that demands compliance with the law.

Each of the above situations entails a distinct form of criminal liability. In the first situation, the company's liability would be as an accessory to the offence of the person who actually commits the offence. In the second, the company would be liable in its own right as a principle. And in the third, the company would again be liable in its own right but for an inchoate offence; that is, without regard to whether or not actual harm occured.

It is submitted that the above obligations inhere in the concept of corporate citizenship. As corporate citizens of the state, companies should have a duty to ensure that their business activities are conducted in a way that does not expose employees, customers and members of the public to the risk of crimes by persons who work for or are in a significant way connected to the company. Companies need to put in place systems that will deter and prevent criminality, that will lead to prompt discovery should violations of the law occur, and that will minimize or ameliorate any injury or damage that might follow from the commission of an offence. They also have an affirmative obligation to establish a law-compliant culture that effectively deters negligence, deviance, and criminal behaviour; that does not tolerate wrongdoing or illegal shortcuts and refuses to turn a blind eye to offences committed by staff and employees

Companies are able to satisfy these obligations of corporate citizenship because they alone have the power to select and train their employees; to put in place supervisory systems; to establish a corporate culture that does not – and does not appear to – encourage, condone or tolerate violations of the law; and to organize the way their business is conducted to prevent violations of the law. Regardless of whether or not there are natural persons who may also be at fault and deserve to be prosecuted, a company should be liable in its own right when it is to blame for not preventing a crime by one of its personnel, regardless of the individual's status within the company; or when it has created conditions likely to lead to criminal conduct.

The corollary to the above proposition is that a company should not be subject to prosecution and sanction if it has conducted its affairs in a non-culpable manner. To advocate corporate fault as the basis of a company's criminal liability is also to accept defences based on the absence of fault. A company should be permitted to prove in its defence that it has taken 'all reasonable precautions' and exercised 'due diligence' to prevent the offence. Just as a fact-finder should be able to infer corporate fault from a company's actions, inactions, policies, culture or ethos, so too should the fact-finder be able to infer the company's commitment to a lawful way of doing business from the fact that it has taken appropriate steps to eliminate the risk of criminal activity by its personnel. It might further be observed that a defence based on 'all reasonable precautions' and 'due diligence' is not a novel proposition in the law. This, it might be recalled, was the defence contained in the statute at issue in *Nattrass*, as well as in many other criminal statutes designed to apply to companies.[37]

In conclusion, the context in which crimes occur in a business setting should not be ignored in developing a legal test of corporate criminal liability. That test should reflect the fault of the company. Such fault is not captured by imputing criminal liability to the company based simply on the fact that a crime has been committed by somebody who works for, or is an officer or director of, the company. Derivative liability penalizes companies whose way of doing business has in fact been beyond reproach. In a principled criminal justice system, liability should be based on fault, and this principle applies to 'legal persons' such as companies as well as to natural persons. The fault that justifies holding companies liable is the systemic failure to correct conditions that can lead to deviant behaviour and to prevent offences where the company is aware – or through the exercises of due diligence should have been aware – of the risks of illegality, where it has the capacity to prevent the crime, and when it acts unreasonably in failing to do so.

## Notes

1 Conversely, should the policies produce extremely beneficial or favourable effects the methodological individualist would assert, with perhaps more justification, that, it is these same persons who are deserving of praise, and not the organization.
2 See Health and Safety at Work, etc. Act 1974, section 3(1).
3 This is not always the case; there is a category of offences where liability is 'strict'. In these cases one can be convicted without proof of fault.
4 212 US 481 (1909).
5 See. e.g., *Continental Baking Co. v. United States*. 281 Fed 137 (6th Cir. 1960); *Steere Tank Lines, Inc. v. United States*, 330 F2d 719 (5th Cir 1963).
6 See *United States v. Hilton Hotel Corp*, 467 F.2d 1000 (9th Cir. 1972); *United States v Basic Constr. Co.*, 711 F.2d 570 (4th Cir) cert. denied 464 US 956 (1983).
7 See *United States v Twentieth Century Fox Film Corp*, 882 F2d 656 (2d Cir 1989).
8 [1944] KB 146.

9   [1944] KB 551.
10  [1944] 2 All ER 515.
11  [1972] AC 153.
12  Trade Descriptions Act 1968, section 24(1).
13  It is worth observing that this argument would not have succeeded if vicarious lia-
    bility was the controlling test, as the branch manager was clearly an employee of
    the company, was engaged in the company's business at the time of the offence,
    and had acted with intent to benefit the company.
14  *H.L. Bolton Engineering. v. T.J.Graham and Sons Ltd.* [1957] 1 QB 159.
15  [1972] AC at 199.
16  The concept of the 'shadow director' is specifically recognized in the Company
    Directors Disqualification Act 1986, section 4(2).
17  [1995] 3 All ER 918.
18  Lord Hoffmann's revisionist view of *Nattrass* received a rather cool reception in
    *A-G's Ref (No. 2 of 1999)* [2000] 3 All ER 182 with respect to its applicability to
    common law crimes such as (corporate) manslaughter.
19  Dept of Transport (1987), The Merchant Shipping Act. MV *Herald of Free
    Enterprise*: Report of Court No. 8074 (HMSO) (Sheen Report).
20  Ibid., para 10.6.
21  Ibid., para. 11.3.
22  Ibid., para. 14.1.
23  *R. v. Stanley and others*, 19 October 1990 (Central Criminal Court) (unreported).
    Since then the crime of 'reckless manslaughter' has been replaced by the offence
    of 'gross negligence manslaughter' (see *R. v. Adomako* [1995] 1 AC 171), but it is
    unlikely that this would have affected the result.
24  [1989] 88 Cr. App. R. 10.
25  Ibid. at 16–17.
26  821 F2d 844 (1st Cir) *cert denied* 484 US 943 (1987)
27  821 F.2d at 855.
28  Ibid. at 856.
29  There are some corporate crimes, such as pollution offences, that impose strict lia-
    bility, with no proof of *mens rea* being required for a conviction. See, e.g., *Alphacell
    Ltd. v. Woodward* [1972] 2 All ER 475.
30  Criminal Code Act (1995) s. 12.3.
31  The limitation of the Act to corporate manslaughter restricts the significance of
    the statute that is enacted. On the other hand, the test of liability under the Act
    may yet prove to be a model for statutes in other areas, such as a company's caus-
    ing grievous bodily harm or corporate fraud.
32  The difference in labels may reflect deeper differences between the Scottish legal
    system, where the offence will be known as corporate homicide, and the legal sys-
    tems of England, Wales and Northern Ireland, where it will be known as corpo-
    rate manslaughter
33  Law Commission Rpt, para. 8.35 (4).
34  Ibid., section 1(3).
    Ibid., section 8(3)(a).
    Compare this permissive language with that in the immediately preceeding sub-
    section(8(2)), which identifies evidence that in jury *must* rather than *may* consider.
35  One might note that, contrary to the usual approach in the law, the burden of
    proving 'all reasonable precautions' and due diligence would be on the company
    (although only by a balance of probabilities and not by proof beyond reasonable
    doubt). The justification for this shift in the burden of proof is that it is the
    corporate defendant that will know what it has done to prevent criminality.

36   Such a defence is recognized in the American Law Institute's Model Penal Code s. 2.07 (5)(1962).
37   E.g., Weights and Measures Act 1985, section 24 (1); Food Safety Act 1990, section 21; Control of Substances Hazardous to Health Regulations 2002, section 2.1.

## References

Bucy, P. (1991) 'Corporate ethos: a standard for imposing corporate criminal liability', *Minnesota Law Review*, 75: 1095–184.

Dan-Cohen, M. (1986) *Rights, Persons and Organizations: A Legal Theory for a Bureaucratic Society*. Berkeley, CA: University of California Press.

French, P. (1984) *Collective and Corporate Responsibility*. New York: Columbia University Press.

Gobert, J. (2008) 'The Corporate Manslaughter and Corporate Homicide Act 2007 – Thirteen years in the making but was it worth the wait?' *Modern Law Review*, 73: 413–33.

Hayek, F. (1949) *Individualism and the Economic Order*. London: Routledge & Kegan Paul.

Home Office (2000) *Reforming the Law of Involuntary Manslaughter: The Government's Proposals*. London: Home Office.

Law Commission for England and Wales (1996) *Legislating the Criminal Code: Involuntary Manslaughter*. London: Home Office.

Nollkaemper, A. (2006) 'International responsibility for system criminality: foundations and objectives', paper presented at the Conference on System Criminality in International Law, University of Amsterdam, 20–21 October.

Popper, L. (1957) *The Poverty of Historicism*. London: Routledge & Kegan Paul.

Sullivan, G. (1996) 'The attribution of culpability to limited companies', *Cambridge Law Journal*, 56: 515–46.

Wolf, S. (1985) 'The legal and moral responsibility of organizations', in J. Pennock and W. Chapman (eds), *Criminal Justice*. New York: New York University Press.

### Suggestions for further reading

Fisse, B. and Braithwaite, J. (1994) *Corporations, Crime and Accountability*. Cambridge: Cambridge University Press.

Gobert, J. and Punch, M. (2003) *Rethinking Corporate Crime*. Cambridge: Cambridge University Press.

Pearce, F. and Snider, L. (1995) *Corporate Crime: Contemporary Debates*. London: University of Toronto Press.

Slapper, G. and Tombs, S. (1999) *Corporate Crime*. Harlow: Longman.

Wells, C. (2001) *Corporations and Criminal Responsibility*, 2nd edn. Oxford: Oxford University Press.

# FOUR

## The Foundations of Business Ethics

*Robert Elliott Allinson*

### Egoism and ethics

While theoretically, egoism may be considered one kind of ethics, generally speaking, egoism, defined as self-interest at the expense of others is contrary to the central principles of ethics, which are, in the main, other-directed. While Adam Smith's economics is famously argued to serve both self and other, the core thesis of this chapter is that Adam Smith's position is seriously flawed. If the argument of this chapter is correct, and business is defined as serving self-interest, business ethics is an **oxymoron**.

If a business ethic is to be constructed, a very different foundation for business must be discovered which is other than self-interest. If not, if greed is considered to be the foundation for business, it is difficult to avoid the urge to increase wealth not only by unethical but by illegal means. There is, in other words, only a thin divide between greed as a motivation for business and white-collar crime. Or, to put the matter more strikingly, if the net effect of individual greed is an inequitable society, and we define the effect of crime as doing harm to another (or, oneself, in the case of 'victimless' crimes), then the net effect of a self-interest economics is the creation of a society in which crime – if we include impoverishing others under harm-doing – is legal. Legal crime is an oxymoron, indeed.

Egoism as the basis of ethics not only runs the risk of impoverishing others, outside the firm, but also runs the risk of impoverishing, both materially and spiritually, those inside the firm. If one's sole or major motivation for business is profit, then individual employees' rights will also take second place to the pursuit of profits for the firm. If there is a perceived conflict between the rights of employees, for example, and the profit margin, then there is no built-in basis for safeguarding employees' rights if the pursuit of profit is the sole or major motivation for business practice.

In the worst cases, this can result in the sacrifice of employees and civilians as in the infamous case of the Space Shuttle *Challenger* disaster in which astronauts as employees and civilians aboard were not informed of the life and death risk they were taking with regard to the known O-ring dangers.[1] If we stand by and allow others to come to harm, is this not white-collar crime? If the harm which we allow others to suffer is death, when we were in a position to prevent such harm-doing, but did not do so, is this not murder? Certainly, the decision-makers who took the decision to launch the *Challenger* in spite of advanced red flagged warnings by their senior engineer that a life and death catastrophe was possible precisely because of the known O-ring dangers, were guilty of taking an undue risk with the lives of their astronauts and the two civilians aboard. It seems as if American courts of law are taking a different view of corporate manslaughter than their British counterparts.[2]

There has always been a close connection between ethics and law. The distinctions between first degree murder, for example, and manslaughter are made in the light of ethical differentiations. First degree murder is considered ethically worse than manslaughter because intent is involved. The effect is the same, the loss of human life. The difference is simply a matter of moral intention. First degree murderers receive a harsher punishment by law than do those who are guilty of manslaughter. They are punished for their harmful intentions. The law is written to satisfy moral demands. Such is the close connection between ethics and the law. It is our concern for ethics that brings law into being in the first place.

It is clear that the decision-makers who were responsible for the launch of the *Challenger* did not intend to murder the astronauts. Thus, they were not guilty of first degree murder. It is interesting to pose the question, however, if the decisions of a corporation result in the death of employees, and the corporate decision-makers were aware that their decisions were made against the advice of expert advice-givers that their decisions were endangering the lives of their employees, should they be able to make such decisions and suffer no consequences?

What enables corporate decision-makers to make decisions that might result in the loss of lives of those who must place their lives at risk? The answer of this chapter is that it is a lack of ethics on the part of the corporate decision-makers. Corporate decision-makers, who make decisions on the basis of profit for their corporations and consequently for themselves, are forced, at the very least (assuming that they have an ethical interest) into the dilemma of a conflict of interest. At the most, if they have no such ethical interest, they may decide to override ethics for the sake of profits. Why should the basis for a business enterprise be one which forces decision-makers into a conflict of interest or, worse yet, into a situation in which ethics must be jettisoned? The solution to this dilemma is to construct a basis for business enterprise in which ethics is paramount and profit is a hoped-for result, but not the motivation for business.

It requires only a moment's thought to draw the connection between corporate decision-making that takes the safety of its employees at its main concern and an ethical business enterprise. A concern for safety is a concern for ensuring that the human life of an employee is safe. A concern that human life is safe, indeed, that the safety of human life is the highest priority of any company, is manifestly an ethical concern. A company that places safety of its employees as its highest priority is, by definition, an ethical company.

It is egoism, or placing profits first, that is the reason that ethics is not observed as a business concern. It is by bringing ethics back into business that we will be able to save human lives and increase the quality of human life. This can only be accomplished by constructing an entirely different motivational basis for the conduct of business. This new motivational basis can only be set in place by thoroughly reviewing and overthrowing the present motivational framework. Without undertaking the review and the overthrowing of the present foundation of business enterprise, it will be difficult, if not impossible, to set the new foundation solidly into place.

## On Adam Smith

The argument of this chapter, written by an ethicist and a philosopher, is that self-interest economics is fundamentally flawed and needs to be replaced by an objective, value-based economics.[3] Its argument contains two interwoven threads. One thread is an attempt to show why the fundamental philosophical notions of Adam Smith, taken as an illustration of self-interest economics, cannot lead to an equitable society.[4] Smith's *Wealth of Nations*, according to Jacob Viner:

> became a significant factor in determining the course of national policy not only in Britain but in other countries as well. This is much more than any other economic work has ever achieved; and Smith probably has had much more influence than any other economist. (1965: 326)

One wonders if it is Smith that Keynes had in mind when he famously quipped that all of us are slaves of some defunct economist. (This despite Schumpeter's trumpeted dictum ([1954] 1960: 184) that 'the *Wealth of Nations* does not contain a single *analytic* idea, principle or method that was entirely new in 1776'.)

Whether single ideas or principles were new or not, the entirety of ideas that make up *The Wealth of Nations* was certainly new. And much turns on the meaning of the adjective 'analytic'. Was the 'invisible hand' an analytic idea? Was the notion that private interest adds up to public virtue (that self-interest on the part of the individual added up to the good of the whole) an analytic idea? If one takes Viner's (1972) definition of an analytic idea to be an idea that is rigorous, possesses internal consistency and bears a close analogy to abstract mathematical operations, then neither the invisible hand nor the private interest public virtue idea qualify as analytic ideas. Nevertheless, they are extremely influential ideas. In this respect Schumpeter's dictum would appear to be of only minor import.

In his book, *Adam Smith's Moral Philosophy*, Jerry Evensky (2005) gives an historical account of what he refers to as the 'Adam Smith problem' and categorizes Smithian interpreters into two main types. Amusingly, he refers to one as the Kirkcaldian Smith (after his birthplace) and the other as the Chicago Smith (after the Chicago economists).

The Smithian version presented herein possesses more in common with the interpretation of such figures as the Nobel laureates George Stigler and Jacob Viner. But it is not that they are Nobel laureates that makes their interpretations compelling to the present author. Rather, it is that the arguments that they co-advance, that without the emphasis on self-interest, on the one hand, and the invisible hand, on the other, of Smith's theory, that Smith's entire economic theory would collapse. For if self-interest as Stigler argues, is the granite of the *Wealth of Nations*, then the invisible hand, as Viner implies, is the mortar. One recalls Stigler's famous sentence that begins his article, 'Smith's travels of the ship of state,' 'The *Wealth of Nations* is a stupendous palace erected upon the granite of self-interest.'[5] But, for wealth to be ethically distributed, it needs the mortar provided by the invisible hand.

Evensky classifies the portrait of Smith presented herein as the Chicago Smith, a portrait which he would say is painted by Frank Knight, Theodore Schultz, George Stigler, Milton Friedman, and Gary Becker. Strangely, Evensky does not mention Viner, whose stature among economists is monumental and whose interpretation of Smith is ground-breaking. In her introduction to her richly argued *Adam Smith and His Legacy for Modern Capitalism*, Patricia Werhane (1991) refers to him as 'the well-known Smith scholar'. Robbins places him as 'probably the greatest authority of the age in the history of economic and social thought' and Blaug (1991) states that he was 'quite simply the greatest historian of economic thought that ever lived'. Jacob Viner, who disavows allegiance with the Chicago School would have to belong to this category as well if we were to accept Evensky's scheme of categories. Evensky presents his interpretation of a more multi-dimensional Smith (a term devised by the present author) in which he aligns himself with Amartya Sen and James Buchanan (Patricia Werhane would belong here, as well, according to the present author). But, the multi-dimensionality aspect of Smith is not, as we shall see below, the driving force of his economic theory. It his self-interest aspect that is its driving force.

According to Glenn R. Morrow ([1923], 1973), there is no Adam Smith problem. For Morrow, Smith's ethics and economics work hand in hand if one remembers that prudence is one of the ethical virtues. One could reply to Morrow that this merely moves the problem back into the ethics. More to the point, though, is that in order to achieve the economic success of the country, one must make sympathetic impulses subservient to the rule of egoistic ones. The full title of the volume, it is to be recalled, is *The Inquiry into the Nature and Causes of the Wealth of Nations*. The egoistic impulses must rule if economics is to be served.

The consequence of this, and therefore the real problem for Smith, as seen by the present author, is that one must treat economic relations as being between non-persons in order to submerge ethical impulses under economic ones. In so doing, not only does one *ex hypothesi* treat others unethically, it also, according to Aristotelian and Confucian notions, makes oneself unethical and helps to co-create an unethical society.

Some of the former point seems to be what Jacob Viner is addressing when he states that, 'According to Adam Smith the sentiments weaken progressively as one moves from one's immediate family to one's intimate friends, to one's neighbors in a small community, to fellow-citizens in a great city, to members in general of one's own country, to foreigners, to mankind taken in the large' (Viner, 1972: 80). It is ironic that it is the thought of an economist that can give rise to so many different and conflicting interpretations. The postmodern hermeneutic theories of the possibility, or rather the necessity, of the infinite varieties of interpretation to which any text is susceptible seem to apply more in the faraway field of economics than they do in their home-grown field of literary criticism.

The second thread is a charcoal sketch of a new theory of objective, value-based economics rather than profit-based economics. It is clear that the vision of the *Homo economicus* is not proving to be a fruitful guide. Untrammeled greed, unsurprisingly, is not proving to be beneficial in an equitable sense. What happens to Smith's argument that it is good to follow one's self-interest because it best serves the interest of the whole if it turns out that the good of the whole is not so served? Does that mean that one should not be driven by self-interest? For the post-Smithian capitalist, profit is to be maximized whether this serves the good of the whole or not.

Let us analyze the most fundamental idea of economics that according to the Nobel laureate economist George Stigler (1976) 'is still the most important substantive proposition in all of economics, that is the idea of equilibrium'.[6] The idea of equilibrium is, roughly speaking, the idea that all resources will tend to equalize over the long term. Supply and demand will reach an equilibrium with each other. There are two basic questions one can raise about this most fundamental law. First, why should it be true? Clearly, it is a metaphysical law since most of the time (witness the current oil prices) resources are in disequilibrium rather than equilibrium. If there is a fundamental law, why should it not be rather that resources seek disequilibrium'? Second, one can always ask, two further questions, even if the law were considered valid: (i) At what cost in the short term and in the long term, and cost to whom, is this equilibrium reached? (ii) Who benefits from the preceding disequilibrium in the short term and its eventual equilibrium in the long term?

Equilibrium, as a notion, is value-free. It does not signify the achievement of a better condition for some parties or for all parties. In addition, it is simply mechanical. It takes place due to the operation of market forces. It has no sympathies. It has no ethical preferences.

Equilibrium is, as one may have already begun to suspect, Adam Smith's robot hand.[7] As a robot hand, it has no leanings in any ethical direction. It is purely market-driven. It distributes according to its iron law. It cares not that some receive an overabundance and others next to nothing. In the end, all will not receive a just share. In the end, there will be an equal supply of resources. But who will own these resources and who will not is left out of the mechanical equation.

The origin of the invisible hand theory may well be the idea of a Providential Order.[8] Perhaps this is why the idea of an invisible hand did not occur to the ancient Greeks or the ancient Chinese. For the ancient Greeks and the ancient Chinese, the world was not ruled by Divine Providence. The invisible hand of Smith appears to be a secular version of Divine Providence. The problem is, whereas Divine Providence supposedly has human welfare at heart, can we ascribe such an ethical motivation to the robot hand?

## Equilibrium and an invisible hand

Let us make no mistake about it: the theory of equilibrium is part and parcel of Adam Smith's theory. According to Stigler, the idea of equilibrium is central to Adam Smith's theory. In Smith's own words (2003: Book I, p. 63):

> The market price of every particular commodity is regulated by the proportion between the quantity which is actually brought to the market, and the demand of those who are willing to pay the natural price of the commodity, or the whole value of the rent, labour and profit, which must be paid in order to bring it thither.

In Amartya Sen's more contemporary version:

> The market system works by putting a price on a commodity and the allocation between consumers is done by the intensities of the respective willingness to buy it at the prevailing price. When 'equilibrium prices' emerge they balance demand with supply for each commodity. (1996: 17)

But it is not a matter exclusively of demand in the case of Smith's version or of willingness in the case of Sen's. It is a matter of capability. Demand is not ethically driven. Demand is driven by the capability on the part of the purchaser to pay the price for the commodity. Supply is not ethically driven. The price of the supply is set by the supplier in accordance with what the market – read the financially advantaged – is capable and willing to pay and how high this price can be set by the supplier without losing sufficient volume of sales which would lower the profit margin. 'Equilibrium prices' are at an equilibrium only for the financially advantaged.[9]

For the modern view of economics, distribution plays no part. According to Amartya Sen, this is true even of utilitarian welfare economics: In referring to his (1973) book, *On Economic Inequality*, he writes:

> Utilitarianism, which had been the mainstream approach to welfare economics, is profoundly unconcerned with inequalities precisely in the variable on which it focuses (and to which it attaches overwhelming importance) to wit, individual utilities. All that matters in the utilitarian view is the sum total of these utilities representing the respective individual advantages, independently of their distribution. (1997: 110)

For Smith, the general welfare is more a matter of faith than anything else. In his famous and oft quoted phrase, the one motivated by his self-interest achieves more for the common good than the one who directly attempts to further the common good. There is no proof of this. It is an article of faith. What is interesting about this article of faith is that it endorses the idea of following one's self-interest because it brings about (or supposedly brings about) the good of all. Smith is not the champion of self-interest for self-interest's sake.[10] He is already a moral economist. His economics, and he is taken as the father of economics, is not profit for profit's sake. It is profit for the sake of the general good.

Let us quote, not the well-known passage regarding the self-interest of the butcher, the brewer and the baker from *The Wealth of Nations*, but instead, a lesser-known passage from his moral tome, *The Theory of Moral Sentiments*:

> [The rich] consume little more than the poor; and in spite of their natural selfishness and rapacity, though they mean only their own convenience, though [because] the sole end which they propose from the labours of all the thousands whom they employ be the gratification of their own vain and insatiable desires, they divide with the poor the produce of all their improvements. [the trickle-down theory of the benefits of wealth, a more recent version of equilibrium theory]. They are led by an invisible hand to make nearly the same distribution of the necessaries of life which would have been made had the earth been divided into equal portions among all the inhabitants; and thus, without intending it [because they do not intend it], without knowing it, advance the interest of the society, and afford means to the multiplication of the species. (2000: 264–5)

(This passage puts lie to the theory that there are two Smiths, one of *The Wealth of Nations* and another of *The Theory of Moral Sentiments*.)

For Smith, self-interested economic behavior is inextricably linked to ethical outcomes. In particular, it is the rich, those who employ thousands for the sake of satisfying their own insatiable desires, who advance the interest of society. It is important to note that it is the division of society into economic classes that is the engine of the economic success of society. The drivers of this engine are the rich. And the fuel of the engine of the rich is insatiable greed. Let us review one of his statements from *The Wealth of Nations* in detail:

> Every individual is continually exerting himself to find out the most advantageous employment for whatever *capital* he can command. It is his own advantage, indeed, and not that of society, which he has in view. But the study of his own advantage naturally, or rather necessarily leads him to prefer an employment which is most advantageous to society. (2003: 569–70)

Smith's core belief is that self-interest pursued for its own sake is necessarily linked to the good of society. It is this core belief that is to be questioned or at least qualified. For Smith, self-interest is linked to *material* advantage and it is this notion of self-interest that is to be challenged. For Smith, 'Every man's interest would prompt him to seek the advantageous, and to shun the disadvantageous employment' (2003: 138).

Smith's notion of advantage is not moral advantage. To make this point more clear, consider the first sentence of the previous quotation: 'Every individual is continually exerting himself to find out the most advantageous employment for whatever capital he can command.' Smith is not considering that capital should be put to use as philanthropy. For his next sentence is, 'It is his own advantage … which he has in view'. He is clearly referring to capital advantage and not to moral advantage. Ironically, it is the material interest of the individual that is taken to be the basis for an ethical outcome for the whole of society. The irrelevance of Smith's own ethical theory for his economics is put in a nutshell by Viner when he points out that,

> Nowhere in the *Wealth of Nations* does Smith place any reliance for the proper working of the economic order upon the operation of benevolence, the emphasis upon which was the novel feature in the account of human nature presented in the *Theory of Moral Sentiments*.[11]

Smith, did, in his earlier *The Theory of Moral Sentiments*, also famously write, 'How selfish soever man may be supposed, there are evidently some principles in his nature, which interest him in the fortune of others, and render their happiness necessary to him, though he derives nothing from it, except the pleasure of seeing it' (2000: 3). The problem, is, what happens when one's own advantage is in conflict with one's interest in the fortune of others? In this case, his latter book would seem to trump his former because it is, as he says, 'his own advantage [and by that he means material advantage] which is most advantageous to society'. But there is no need to pit one book against the other as is commonly done in the Smith literature. For as can be recalled, it is stated in the former book that it is the rich, the greed of the rich and the division into classes that define the economic success of society. And the doctrine of the invisible hand appears in the former book as well. It is important to emphasize that the present author is not chiefly concerned with Smith and his inconsistencies. There is already a literature devoted to this. Most of the literature consists of Smithian apologetics.[12] So much so that one thinks that 'The gentlemen do protest too much.' Why the present author refers to Smith at all is because he is known as the father of economics and because the fact that there is a tension between ethical impulses and materialistic self-advantages is illustrative of the fact that this is inherent in the very nature of a self-interest or profit-based economics. It is not surprising that such a tension exists in Smith. It would be all the more surprising if it were absent.

## On classical thought

At the very least, one must say, Smith is in conflict with himself. In the cases of Plato, Aristotle and Confucius, no such conflict arises. In ancient Greek and ancient Chinese philosophy, ethics clearly takes precedence over profits. The idea that profit or advantage should be sought for its own sake and that by so doing society would necessarily benefit would be alien to classical Greek or classical Chinese thinking. For Confucius, when ethics and profits collide, one never chooses profit. It is as simple as that.[13]

In the *Symposium*, Plato described the human being as a lover, as a pursuer of beauty. For Plato (at least the Plato of the *Symposium*), the ultimate experience one strove for in life was the experience of beauty and creation in the beautiful. To put this another way, Plato saw the essence of the human being to lie in creation, in production, not in consumption. Plato thought that our ultimate experience, that for which life was worth living, was the aesthetic experience of the enjoyment and production of the beautiful. Plato realized that we were driven primarily by Eros. But Eros for Plato was not ultimately for material things. The highest stages of Eros were for the Beautiful and its products.[14]

Is it possible to say that great artists and thinkers, that Pericles, Michelangelo, Leonardo, Mozart, Van Gogh, Descartes, Spinoza and Marx were motivated by the urge to create in the beautiful rather than by the profit motive? Descartes died of pneumonia tutoring the Queen of Sweden at 5 a.m. in a cold Swedish winter. Spinoza, Mozart, Marx and Van Gogh died in poverty. If they had made profits, they would have been pleased. But, they did not do what they did for the profits.

Indeed, for Aristotle and Confucius, the purpose of life is moral self-growth. One's life assumes meaning by virtue of one's improvement of one's character.[15] One improves one's character by individual acts of moral choice. Morality, or the moral person, is defined by the choices that one makes. In Confucius' *Analects*, it is written, 'The gentleman understands what is moral. The small man understands what is profitable.'[16] Ultimately, all of these life choices that one makes along life's way lead to one's moral character.

The entire purpose of man's life, for Aristotle, since the life of pure contemplation is beyond most men, is in choosing moral acts to perform. Society exists for this very purpose. For the famous Athenians in the Golden Age of Greece, they differentiated themselves from the Phoenicians with their dismissal of this nation of merchants as 'loving only money'.

Consider this famous passage from Sophocles' *Antigone*:

No thing in use by man, for power of ill,

Can equal money. This lays cities low,

This drives men forth from quiet dwelling-place,

This warps and changes minds of worthiest stamp,

To turn to deeds of baseness, teaching men

All shifts of cunning …

This is a different universe than the universe that is formed by the logical consequences of the theory of Adam Smith. One obtains a moral society by the performance of moral actions. One cannot obtain a moral society by the pursuit of self-interest. It must be said that while Professor Smith was a Professor of Logic before he became a Professor of Moral Philosophy, there appears to be a better logic in the arguments of Aristotle and Confucius than in those of Adam Smith. For Smith the aggregate of self-interest leads to the good of all. For Aristotle and Confucius, the aggregate of moral actions leads to the good society.

*We cannot theorize morality on the one side and economic behavior on the other and hope to patch them together in some fashion.* The ancient Greeks and Chinese (these two peoples are chosen as examples not to prove that they were unique) put forth a view of humankind that held that planned ethical motivation was the motivation for living. Not so with Adam Smith. For Adam Smith, economic motivation is self-aggrandisement. In terms of economic action, ethics comes into view only as an extrinsic and unplanned outcome. He does, of course, provide separately for an ethics of sympathy and a famous one at that. But the problem is that it is not ultimately consistent with his description of what is best for society as a whole.

There is another point to be considered. When self-interest is served, as Plato well knew, the appetites grow. This is one of the problems with proclaiming self-interest to be the centerpiece of human motivation. For what is to draw the line between self-interest and greed? If one hundred thousand dollars is good as my annual income, why not two hundred thousand? And if two hundred thousand is good, why not three hundred thousand? And so on. Once greed enters the picture, the distinction between self-interest and greed, if there is one at all, begins to break down. What is to place the limits on greed? As we have seen in the creation of multi-billionaires in both the West and in China, there are no limits on greed.

The problem is not how to restrict greed, for that is well nigh impossible. The problem is with having made greed the essential motivator for economic action in the first place. The maximization of profit is the economic manifestation of the psychological motivation of greed. It is not likely by starting out with selfishness as the essential motivator that one is going to reach unselfishness at the end of this road. Why would anyone attempt to posit a theory of human motivation based on greed? Granted that it is nominally self-interest and not greed, the distinction between self-interest and greed is a slippery slope. The ancient Greeks and the ancient Chinese knew better than this. If one begins with unlimited self-aggrandisement for the individual, how can one end with equality for all? Has there ever been such an egregious *non-sequitur* in the history of humankind to rival this monstrous stroke of illogic?

Joan Robinson, the Cambridge economist has argued that:

> The emergence of industrial capitalism required the existence, on the one side, of a proletariat – that is many families who had no rights in land or possession of means of production, so that a great number of individuals were available to be employed for wages – and, on the other side, a few families with large accumulations of wealth which could be used to employ them in such a way to yield profits. I do not think that any academic economist could deny this obvious fact, but they have elaborated their theories in such a way to conceal it. (1980: 281)

And again, 'The nature of accumulation under private enterprise necessarily generates inequality and is therefore condemned to meeting the trivial wants of a few before the urgent needs of the many' (ibid.: 291).

But she could have found such a statement in the famous book by the father of economics, Adam Smith:

> Wherever there is great property, there is great inequality. For one very rich man, there must be at least five hundred poor, and the affluence of the few supposes the indigence of the many ... It is only under the shelter of the civil magistrate that the owner of that valuable property ... can sleep a single night in security. (2003: 902)

Adam Smith himself was not happy with the untrammeled pursuit of profits: 'Our merchants and manufacturers ... say nothing concerning the bad effects of high profits. They are silent with regard to the pernicious effects of their own gains' (2003: 137). And, 'No society can surely be flourishing and happy, of which the far greater part of the members are poor and miserable' (ibid.: 110–11).

But the problem with Smith is that it is his very own theory that is, according to the present author, the source of the rationalization of and therefore to some extent the toleration of the production of inequity in society. As unhappy as he might be with the results, he provides, along with his contemporary apologists, considerable self-justification for its continuance. In addition, because of his noteworthy incursion into ethics, he might also be said to be responsible for an additional burden, the division of the human being into two parts, the ethical man and the economic man. Adam Smith may be held accountable for the divided self.[17]

If a moral philosophy is designed as a guide to human action, we should not have a moral philosophy that is at odds with an economic philosophy. Otherwise, we create a divided self; we condemn one of these philosophies to the dustbin or we are hypocrites. If we base our economic theory on self-interest, then corporate social responsibility is something which comes afterwards. It is either something that flows naturally, as in Adam Smith, as a necessary result or intrinsic result of the functioning of the economic system, or it is an ethical add-on, an extrinsic function corporations must perform as an obligation of their economic power, a kind of economic version of *noblesse oblige*. In the sense of being an add-on, there is no logical connection between the corporation's pursuit of profit and its responsibility or accountability for the plight of society. Ethics is an obligation incurred by success. Ethics becomes a kind of penalty imposed upon the successful business venture.

Evidence indicates that rather than equitable distribution occurring as a result of the pursuit of private wealth, the opposite occurs. Thus, the first approach, the profits approach, results in inequity. This is not surprising since it would appear to be illogical if the pursuit of greed, that is, more than one needs, should result in economic justice.

But, there is an additional factor as well, what may be called the unhealthy mixture. This view bears some similarity with the analysis of Luk Bouckaert. While he does not use the term 'unhealthy mixture', he argues that genuine ethics may be crowded out by an ethics co-opted by management (Zsolnai, 2006). In the argument presented by the present author, when ethics is viewed as an extrinsic responsibility, then the original business ingredient is tainted by being viewed as unethical. This creates an unethical self-image of the business person. He or she becomes ethical only when performing extrinsic ethical acts. This, is, although better than a business that has no interest in social account-ability at all, an unhealthy mixture. In addition, by identifying the ethical com-ponent in the extrinsic feature, what is lost is the possibility of a greater ethical contribution that could be made by considering ethics to be a part or even a whole of the initial business concern.

What else is lost, and this may be even more pernicious, is that in daily life, if we think that every man and woman is out for his or her own self-interest, then every man or woman is met with an initial and well-justified mistrust. The self-interest model of economics creates distrust rather than trust as an initial starting point for human interaction. This is a serious reduction in the quality of interpersonal relations. How do we know when our dearest friend will slip a knife into our back when economic advantages dictate the necessity of such an action?

## Value-based economics

Our new theory of economics or value creation is the notion that all values, aesthetic, social and ethical are to be part and parcel of one's motivation for action in life, and profit is to be the secondary but not logically consequential effect. We reverse the entire equation. Action is for value creation, not for profit. Profit is the side-effect, not the goal. We build ethics and aesthetics into the business in the first place.

We may venture for a definition of the new economics the following definition:

> Value-based economics may be defined as the ownership or the use of capital investment, labour or land to produce a product or provide a service that fills a value based social need or creates a social value without creating a disvalue which is of greater harm than the value produced. The more that the good or service contributes to the social value of the underdeveloped world, the greater the value of the good or service that is provided. (Allinson, 2004a)

In a value-based economics, all car manufacturers would cease making cars that ran on oil product derivatives and all car manufacturers would sell only cars that ran on electricity or were hybrids. Since it would be easy to buy a car that was a hybrid, no surcharge for scarcity could be attached to a hybrid car. The buyer would be able to buy a hybrid easily. The seller's profit margin might be reduced (or it might increase given the volume of sales). But the main result would be that buyers would spend less money on gas; the environment would become cleaner; the price of oil would become reduced because of decreased demand; political stability in the world at large might increase when less power is held by select oil-producing nations.

In the above scenario, buyers would be able to purchase and use vehicles for transport on the basis of saving money and saving the environment. A value choice would be available to them. *A non-self-sacrificial value choice becomes available to buyers when the seller's motivation is the production of something that creates value rather than something that either reduces value or creates disvalue. Value creates value; disvalue creates disvalue.* When the seller creates disvalue, e.g., a car that pollutes and causes an unnecessary depletion in available assets in the buyer, the non-self-sacrificing buyer might be impelled to make up those funds by creating more disvalue in turn. When the seller creates value, e.g., a car that does not pollute and causes an increase in available assets in the buyer, the buyer can create value with the increase in available assets.

In a value-based economics, the car maker will want to make as many cars available as possible at the lowest possible cost to the consumer while not making any sacrifices in quality. The manufacturer will create value for others. One result of this, assuming everyone buys only hybrid cars, is that the price of oil would drop dramatically. This would mean that the oil-rich nations would lose some of their comparative advantage of wealth. The creation of value automatically creates a redistribution of wealth. *The creation of needed new value in one part results in the reduction of excess value in another part.* While it may appear that the reduction of value in the oil-rich countries is a loss, it is not exactly a loss; it is a reduction of excess. The creation of needed value where it did not exist balances excesses in parts where value is not needed (or is superfluous).

On the other hand, in a profit-based economics, every business attempts to make its greatest profit by keeping wages, quality and availability of the good or service it produces to the lowest possible level compatible with sales. Quality and availability of the product or service must always be sacrificed for profit. *There is an inverse relationship between quality and/or availability and profit. Profit inherently works in an inverse relationship to quality and universal distribution.* This is the law of disequilibrium.

Let us take an example. Country C sells goods at a lower price to country A because of lower wages in country C. This creates value and disvalue for country A. It creates value because country A can spend less for its goods that it needs. It creates disvalue for country A because country A no longer manufactures such goods for its own use or for export to country B. This creates value for country C. Country C can sell a monopoly of goods to country A. Eventually, however, country C must raise its salaries and it can no longer supply goods to country A. Now, country D sells goods at a lower price to country A. Country C begins to suffer. What was a value to country C eventually becomes a disvalue. *Whatever brings value to oneself at a price of disvalue to another eventually brings disvalue back to itself.*

If the nature of man is such that man's motivation for buying and selling is the making of profit, human beings will attempt to restrict production and supply of needed items to the quantity consonant with the greatest profit margin. If someone is manufacturing cars which do not rely upon oil, for example, one would restrict production of this kind of car to an amount that would enable the owner or manufacturer to sell that number of cars that will bring the highest amount of profit.

A system which is based on justice will result in justice. A system which is based on greed will result in greed. Adam Smith devised a system in which the basic motivator of greed was supposed to result in equality or at least equity. It is not possible to go from inequality to equality. If one starts from greed and envy, one can only succeed in producing greed and envy. *Like produces like.* Or, *Like can only come from like.* This is the general principle that governs value creation. Adam Smithian economics is inherently flawed. One cannot produce distributive justice from self-aggrandisement. The invisible hand is worse than an invisible Deity. With an invisible Deity, Abraham could at least negotiate.

When one acts out of greed or fear and pursues profit at the expense of loss for someone and distributive justice for many, one always wants more.[18] One is never satisfied. This is why for Plato and Aristotle, the pursuit of wealth could not result in happiness. Since happiness was the goal or at least the natural state for human beings, neither Plato nor Aristotle could have selected the rational economic man as the model for human action. It is not surprising that they did not. They could have, but they knew better.

Our life should be one whole. We should not need to make a dichotomy between our business decisions and our ethical decisions. Our life should be of one piece. Given our ethical nature, we should not have to go against it. It is true that the way human institutions have been set up, particularly with profit-based economics, it is difficult to combine ethics with business. At best one can minimize profit and attempt to make profit through industries that are socially contributive. But still, even if a business is socially contributive, the way it makes its profits may be creating losses for others. And if one minimizes one's profit, one places oneself at a disadvantage to others. And one's self is just as important as other selves. It is a sad lot to live and prosper in a profit-based economic system and one can only accomplish this by burying one's head in the sand. A noble attempt to rectify this situation is Prakash Sethi's replacement of corporate social responsibility with his well-argued notion of corporate accountability.

With Mencius, our nature is to be compassionate to other beings. It is our core compassionate nature, not our desire to look good in the eyes of others, that is the origin of our morality. That being the case, why should this nature not be our guide in all of our activities? Surely, our compassion does not stop at the door of our business. If it does, we have placed an artificial barrier between our nature and our business action. If we cannot satisfy our ethical nature in our business transactions, it follows that our business behavior is *unnatural*. Judged in this way, Adam Smith's counsel for each individual to pursue her or his self-interest (albeit while not doing anything unethical), is *an unnatural guidance system*.

The whole point is that capitalism constrains us to be unethical. Not only that, capitalism constrains us to be unnatural. Indeed, since it extols self-interest at the expense of (read, competition with) the other, it daily trains us to become unethical. This being the case, how difficult it must be to summon up ethical behavior in non-business situations so habituated as we must be to immoral behavior!

Indeed, though much has been written about how ethical trust is the basis for economic behavior, if one believes that the entire point of economic behavior is to take advantage of, that is, profit over the other, then one's attitude towards other human beings cannot be one other than arrogance, distrust, fear and contempt or indifference. Profit-based economics breeds arrogance in the profiteer, contempt or indifference towards the victim and ethical distrust and fear of the profiteer on the part of the victim. Profit-based economics cannot help but breed ethical contempt (or at least indifference), distrust and fear as social properties.[19] This is the ethical legacy of profit-based economics.

There is now more bite to Keynes' famous quip that we are all slaves of some defunct economist. By following a self-interest and profit-based economics, one inevitably shapes one's character, but in this case, one shapes an unethical character. This unethical character, molded by the daily pursuit of profit, must battle with one's ethical impulses, nourished on those rare occasions when one is not seeking profit but is engaged in 'pure' ethics. In addition, since the success of society is based on the existence of classes, one daily breeds an unethical society.

How can one cast aside one's moral blinders for special, unnamed moral occasions, and just as quickly don them when entering the business arena? We become, like the Mafia, gifted in being able to discriminate between actions for family and the murderous actions that are not personal, but only business.

Unlike the Mafia, whose hit men must only upon occasion practice the unethical act of murder, in the world of business, it is every single business decision that must perforce, to qualify as business, be unethical. When one is day by day, nay, hour by hour, nay minute by minute, performing cost-benefit analyses to determine which course of action to take, is it really possible to throw off this calculating brain and embrace humankind in a compassionate hug? Or, are even these rare and discrete acts of morality calculated as well so that they do not overly interfere with the daily progress and pressure of our business and professional life? These ethical actions are perforce relegated to the back stream of life, to be practiced perhaps in retirement or on Christmas Day, but for the rest of the year or one's career, surely to make up only a tiny minority of our actions, if any.

Now, it is true that Adam Smith does frequently say that one must be ethical when carrying out one's business; one must not practice any deceit, for example. One is not entitled to use any means, fair or foul, to increase one's profit margin. One must, for Adam Smith, observe basic ethical amenities. But, this does not affect the more fundamental point at issue. The whole point is that a system founded upon self-interest is inherently unethical as a system in its proper use, not unethical by its abuse. *It is unethical in its proper use.* It is exactly contrary to what we teach our children. We teach our children to share equally with each other because it is unethical to take more for oneself and give less to the other. The entire doctrine, much lauded, of comparative advantages, is an explicit articulation of this unethical ideal. My comparative advantage must be your comparative disadvantage. If it were not, it would not be my comparative advantage. Or, you must seek your comparative advantage in another situation to make up for this, *ad infinitum*.

There are those who would even argue that this is the price of economic efficiency. In these terms, poverty would always be present; it would even be required. It might even be glorified. It reminds one of Johnson's remark that 'Sir, the great deal of arguing which we hear to represent poverty as no evil shows it to be evidently a great one. You never knew people labouring to convince you that you might live very happily upon a plentiful fortune.'[20]

To conclude, it appears as if Adam Smith is in conflict with himself. His view of humans as ethical beings collides with his view of human beings as pursuing self-interest as presented in his *Wealth of Nations*. You cannot have it both ways.

But, most of us would like it that way. That is in fact the entire motivation for the discipline of business ethics. If business is self-interested, it must, to satisfy our ethical urges, be disciplined by ethics. This is where we are today.

Economics cannot exist for the sake of itself: it must exist for the sake of something else. Our work, our labours, our investments, all exist for the sake of something higher, of a higher end. As Joan Robinson once asked, 'Here we come upon the greatest of all economic questions, but one which is never asked, what is growth for?' (1980: 29).

## Notes

1  The overwhelming majority of informed opinion of relevant scholars and the testimony before the Presidential commission, including the testimony of fellow astronauts and the astronauts' representative before the Presidential commission, is that the astronauts did not know beforehand of the risk they were taking. The weight of evidence is that Christa McAuliffe, the teacher in space, also did not know. For a full presentation of opinions and a discussion of their merits, see Allinson (2005) Chapter 8, 'Post-*Challenger* Investigations', n. 5., pp. 184–7. As to the acute question, raised by my distinguished colleague and long-time friend, Professor Leonard Minkes, whether the *Challenger* disaster can be counted as a case of the pursuit of profit taking precedence over human rights, one is reminded of the famous saying of Oscar Wilde, that the truth is never pure and rarely simple. In the Presidential Report, in one chapter it is stated that pressures developed because of the need to meet customer commitments and the Commission concluded that Thiokol management reversed its position not to launch in order to accommodate a major customer. While the major customer is unidentified, at least one scholar states that it was NASA. The citing of customers certainly does imply the relevance of the profit motive. For more discussion of these and related issues, kindly see Allinson (2005: pp. 117–19, 145–6, 160–1).

2  For an extended discussion of this and related issues, kindly see Allinson (2005) Chapter 3, 'The Buck Stops Here and it Stops Everywhere Else as Well,' n. 1, pp. 55–7.

3  As to whether ethicists or philosophers are competent to comment on economics, the reader must indulge the present author in a lengthy quotation from John Rae's, *Life of Adam Smith* in which he recounts the question being raised by a Professor of Moral Philosophy, Sir John Pringle, who

> remarked to Boswell that Smith, having never been in trade, could not be expected to write well on that subject any more than a lawyer upon physic, and Boswell repeated the remark to Johnson, who at once, however, sent it to the winds. 'He is mistaken, sir,' said the Doctor; 'a man who has never been engaged in trade himself may undoubtedly write well upon trade, and there is nothing that requires more to be illustrated by philosophy than does trade. As to mere wealth – that is to say, money – it is clear that one nation or one individual cannot increase its store but by making another poorer; but trade procures what is more valuable, the reciprocation of the peculiar advantages of different countries. A merchant seldom thinks but of his own particular trade. To write a good book upon it a man must have extensive views; it is not necessary to have practiced to write well upon a subject. (Rae, [1895] 1965: 288)

It should be added to this that not only was Smith not in trade but his study in Glasgow was of moral philosophy and his later study at Balliol was of history, philosophy and Latin and Greek literature. see Lothian (1963: xiv).

4  For a comprehensive, fair and well-balanced view of the different interpretations of Adam Smith and her own well argued view, see the arguments of Werhane (1991).

5  In his article on Adam Smith for the *International Encyclopedia of the Social Sciences*, Viner appears to present a softer view of Smith. The position of the present author is that no matter how Smith qualifies his views, e.g., that the desire to better our conditions should be disciplined by internal or governmentally imposed justice, the point is that the logic of Smith's argument is that such discipline of the desire to materially improve ourselves must be counterproductive to the goal of the improvement of the wealth of the nation. See Viner (1965).

6  Interestingly, Viner considers the famous idea of 'equilibrium' to be a normative idea. It is not certain how he means this. He might mean that it is not an analytic idea. He states: 'If "analytical" as a eulogistic term is to be interpreted strictly in terms of degree of rigor, internal consistency, and close analogy to abstract mathematical operations ... Schumpeter's verdict [that there were no new single *analytic* ideas of principles in the *Wealth of Nations*] ... is difficult to challenge.' (Viner 1965: 327)

7  Grampp writes, 'The famous invisible hand of *The Wealth of Nations* is nothing more than the automatic equilibration of a competitive market' (Grampp, 1948: 334, cited in Evensky, 2005: 246). One may also trace this to the fundamental idea of the *Tableau économique* of Quesnay whose metaphor of the circulation of wealth in human societies was modeled after the circulation of blood in the human body, a metaphor which was to dominate the notions of the physiocrats. Smith even meant to dedicate his *Wealth of Nations* to Quesnay had Quesnay been alive at the time. (Rae [1895] 1965: 216). Here, in passing one must pay tribute to the power of the salons in France and thus to the association of ladies with ideas, which might account for the decline of intellectuality in the twenty-first century in which salons are no longer in vogue, for conversations with Turgot, Quesnay's famous disciple, took place in the salon of Mademoiselle de l'Espinasse (ibid.: pp. 201–4). Rae also recalls that Smith was a regular guest of the Duchesse d'Enville, herself a grand-daughter of the celebrated La Rochefoucauld, and who was popularly supposed to the inspiration of Turgot's ideas. In addition, Smith sat at table with Mirabeau and the young Duc de la Rochefoucauld, who was a disciple of Quesnay and friend of Turgot (ibid.: 192). Mirabeau famously declared the *Tableau* one of the three greatest inventions of the human spirit along with printing and money.

8  This seems to be the direction of Jacob Viner's argument in his *The Role of Providence in the Social Order*, (1972). An interesting primary evidentiary source that this idea is an opinion of Smith's cited by the early biographer of Smith, Dugald Stewart, was that in 1752 or 1753 Smith delivered lectures at Glasgow that contained the fundamental principles of the *Wealth of Nations* and in virtue of a paper of Smith's that Stewart had in his possession (that escaped Smith's own fire but later was to succumb to Stewart's son's fire), Stewart offered the following quotation of which this reproduction is but a portion:

> Projectors disturb nature in the course of her operations on human affairs, and it requires no more than to leave her alone and give her fair play in the pursuit of her ends that she may establish her own designs ... Little else is required to carry

a state to the highest degree of affluence from the lowest barbarism but peace, easy taxes, and a tolerable administration of justice; all the rest being brought about by the natural course of things. (Cited in Rae, [1895] 1965: 62–3)

While at first glance this quotation would not seem to support the idea of a providential order, upon reflection one may consider that nature is purported to have a natural direction towards economic affluence. Whether providential or natural is not to the point. Morrow identifies the concept of Nature with the Divinity in Smith, citing *Moral Sentiments*, Pt. II. Sec. II, Chap. iii (Morrow 1966: 171). What is to the point is that prosperity is perceived of as the result of not disturbing what will naturally occur. This differs not in substance from the doctrine of the invisible hand though in this instance the invisible hand (or no hand at all) has more to do with obtaining prosperity without regard to distribution. While self-interest is also not mentioned here, it still seems noteworthy that Smith thought that the highest degree of affluence was essentially linked to a notion of non-interference.

9    For an extended argument, see Allinson (2004a).
10   Strange though it may seem, Adam Smith did not even found his ideas of the motivation for trade on self-interest. According to Jacob Viner, 'Adam Smith has puzzled many commentators by his attribution of the origin of commerce to a sub-rational propensity to truck and barter, rather than to a rational pursuit of economic benefit' (Viner, 1972: 47).
11   Jacob Viner, 'Adam Smith and Laissez-Faire', in John Clark, et al. (eds), *Adam Smith, 1776–1926*, Augustus M. Kelley, 1966, p. 130. Cited in the charmingly written, Clay, (1976: 51). Patricia Werhane (1991: 37) refers to Marjorie Ann Clay's chapter as 'providing a good summary of these [the Adam Smith problem] problems'.
12   Even Viner at times takes up the cudgel of Smithian apologists. In his Adam Smith article for the *International Encyclopedia of the Social Sciences*, Viner (1965: 323) states that Smith 'would probably have demonstrated that the apparent inconsistencies were often not real ones, but were merely the consequences of deliberate shifts from one partial model to another'. The problem remains that if one's interest is for the prosperity of nations, there is no contest as to which model is to be chosen. That necessarily means the ignoring of the other model which is the ethical model.
13   Confucius, *Analects*, Book IV, 10, 16; Book XIV, 12; XVI, 10; Book XVII, 23.
14   For a preliminary account of what is offered here, see Allinson (2004b).
15   Confucius, *Analects*, Book II, 4.
16   Confucius, *Analects*, Book IV, 16.
17   One could well argue that the divided self is discoverable even within the limits of *The Theory of Moral Sentiments* for even there the good of society is accomplished precisely through the mechanism of self-interest. Logically speaking, some of the mechanism of moral sentiments, particularly that of altruism, would work against the good of society. If the rich did not pursue their self-interest, the poor would remain poorer.
18   For an extended discussion of greed and other derivative emotions, see Allinson, (2002: 147–63).
19   Luigino Bruni and Robert Sogden claim that Smith thinks that trust is a product of commercial society. For an interesting discussion, see Bruni and Sogden (2000).
20   This quotation from Boswell's *Journal* is to be found in Viner (1972: 105).

# References

Allinson, R.E. (2002) *Space, Time and the Ethical Foundations.* The Netherlands: Dordrecht.

Allinson, R.E. (2004a) 'Circles within a circle: the condition for the possibility of ethical business institutions within a market system,' *Journal of Business Ethics,*' 53: 17–28.

Allinson, R.E. (2004b) 'The birth of spiritual economics', in László Zsolnai (ed.), *Spirituality, Ethics and Management.* Dordrecht: Kluwer Academic Publishers, pp. 61–74.

Allinson, R.E. (2005) *Saving Human Lives: Lessons in Management Ethics.* New York: Springer.

Blaug, M. (1991) cited in Jacob Viner (ed.) *Essays on the Intellectual History of Economics.* Princeton, NJ: Princeton University Press.

Bruni, L. and Sogden, R. (2000) 'Moral canals, trust and social capital in the work of Hume, Smith and Genovesi', *Economics and Philosophy,* 16: 21–45.

Clay, M.A. (1976) 'Private vices, public benefits: Adam Smith and the concept of self-interest', in W.R. Morrow and R.E. Stebbins (eds), *Adam Smith and the Wealth of Nations, 1776–1976,* Proceedings of the Bicentennial Conference, Eastern Kentucky University.

Evensky, J. (2005) *Adam Smith's Moral Philosophy.* Cambridge: Cambridge University Press.

Lothian, J.M. (ed.) (1963) *Adam Smith's Lectures on Rhetoric and Belles Lettres.* London: Thomas Nelson and Sons, Ltd.

Morrow, G.R. ([1923] 1973) *The Ethical and Economic Theories of Adam Smith.* Clifton: Augustus M. Kelley.

Morrow, G.R. (1966) 'Adam Smith: moralist and philosopher', in John Maurice Clark et al. (eds), *Adam Smith, 1776–1926.* New York: Augustus M. Kelley.

Rae, J. ([1895] 1965) *Life of Adam Smith.* New York: August M. Kelley.

Robinson, J. (1980) *Collected Economic Papers,* Vol. V. Cambridge, MA: MIT Press.

Schumpeter, J.A. ([1954] 1960) *History of Economic Analysis,* ed. E.B. Schumpeter. New York: Oxford University Press.

Sen, A. (1996) 'Does business ethics make economic sense?' in T. Donaldson and P.H. Werhane (eds), *Ethical Issues in Business: A Philosophical Approach,* 5th edn. Upper Saddle River, NJ: Prentice Hall.

Sen, A. (1997) *On Economic Inequality,* expanded edition with a substantial annexe by James E. Foster and Amartya Sen. Oxford: Clarendon Paperbacks.

Smith, A. (2003) *The Wealth of Nations.* New York: Bantam.

Smith, A. (2000) *The Theory of Moral Sentiments.* Amherst, NY: Prometheus Books.

Stigler, G. (1971) 'Smith's travels of the ship of state', *History of Political Economy,* 3.

Stigler, G. (1976) 'The Successes and Failures of Professor Smith', *Journal of Political Economy,* 84(6): 1199–213.

Viner, J. (1965) 'Adam Smith', *International Encyclopedia of the Social Sciences.* New York: Macmillan, pp. 322–9.

Viner, J. (1960) 'Adam Smith and Laissez-Faire', in J. Clark et al. (eds), *Adam Smith, 1776–1926.* New York: Augustus M. Kelley. p. 130.

Viner, J. (1972) *The Role of Providence in the Social Order.* Philadelphia, PA: American Philosophical Society.

Werhane, P. (1991) *Adam Smith and His Legacy for Modern Capitalism.* New York: Oxford University Press.

Zsolnai, L. (ed.) (2006) *Interdisciplinary Yearbook of Business Ethics. The Debate Section,* Oxford, Bern, Berlin, Bruxelles, Frankfurt am Main, New York, Wien: Peter Lang.

## Suggestions for further reading

Allinson, R.E. (2002) *Space, Time and the Ethical Foundations*. Aldershot: Ashgate.

Allinson, R.E. (2004a) 'An object lesson in balancing business and nature in Hong Kong: saving the birds of long valley', in Lene Bomann-Larsen and Oddny Wiggen (eds), *Responsibility in World Business: Managing Harmful Side-effects of Corporate Activity*. Tokyo: United Nations University Press.

Allinson, R.E. (2004b) 'The birth of spiritual economics', in László Zsolnai (ed.), *Spirituality and Ethics in Management*. Dordrecht: Kluwer Academic Publishers, pp. 61–74.

Allinson, R.E. (2004c) 'Circles within a circle: the condition for the possibility of ethical business institutions within a market system', *Journal of Business Ethics*, 53: 17–28.

Allinson, R.E. (2005) *Saving Human Lives: Lessons in Management Ethics*. The Netherlands: Dordrecht.

# FIVE

## The Organization Did It
### Individuals, Corporations and Crime

*Maurice Punch*

### Introduction

Mannheim once said that Sutherland deserved the Nobel Prize for Criminology (had there been one) and Nelken remarked that he may have earned it, but it would not have been for the clarity of his concepts. For the concept of 'white-collar crime' in his pioneering work was catching but misleading (Braithwaite, 1985). Nevertheless, reading his seminal work – and it can still be read for its insights which are often as applicable today as when he penned them – it is clear he meant *'corporate'* crime (Sutherland, 1949). Whereas 'white-collar' conveys an individual – albeit the 'organization man' doing it ostensibly for the company – the material tends to illustrate that the real 'crook' is the organization: '*Corporations have committed crimes* ... they are deliberate and have a consistent quality ... the criminality of the corporations, like that of professional thieves, is persistent' (Sutherland, 1983: 217; emphasis added).

And here I wish to argue that in much corporate crime it is the organization that 'done it' and that, rather than focusing on the deviant executive, we should look at the organizational component in crime. Sutherland remains the essential starting-point but his focus is very much on 'clean hands' crime, committed rationally and in a calculating way on behalf of the company: also not much 'blood' flows in his work.

In contrast, I would argue that the field has developed in two main ways in recent years. One is related to the evidence of deaths and injuries in the workplace and to members of the public (Slapper and Tombs, 1999; Tombs, this volume). This emphasis on 'corporate violence' reveals that corporations can 'kill' and managers can 'murder' (Mokhiber; 1988; Punch, 2000). Executives can have blood on their hands: and the pursuit of business can lead to the deaths of their victims. The other is concerned with owners and managers who rip off their own companies, 'looting' them of their assets and victimizing the organization, its employees and those who hoped to benefit from its profits (as in the Savings and Loan scandal: Calavita and Pontell, 1990).

Here, then, the starting point is the *organizational* component in corporate crime. Ermann and Lundman state

> organizational deviance is consistent with normal organizational routines. The deviant behaviors are not produced by dramatic or aberrant actions of a few isolated individuals, but instead are an integral part of the organization. Deviance thus exists alongside legitimate organizational activities and frequently serves to advance important organizational goals. (1982: 91)

It draws on views of organizations as *criminogenic*, as not always rational and as even pathological. Two points are important here:

1  There is a tendency to view organizational life in general and business activity in particular as essentially rational and under control. But that is not always the case.
2  It is not organizations that set policies and take decisions but people. In a way that is correct: organizations do not exist outside of the collective efforts of individuals. Yet, this is based on a highly individualized view of social reality in institutions. As Gross puts it, 'Organizations, though inventions of biological persons and thus totally dependent upon the continuous activity of such actors, nevertheless *may take on lives of their own*' (1980: 59; emphasis added).

When people become members of a collective, an institution or organization this may in powerful ways demand conformity to group norms, to suppressing individuality and even to adopting a new identity (as in religious sects). Furthermore, that collective behaviour may lead to distortions in decision-making through processes such as group think and **cognitive dissonance**.

In effect, I wish to argue that corporate crime is made possible because the corporate setting provides *MOM* – Motive, Opportunity and Means (the trinity of all criminal investigations). Within the corporate environment, executives are provided with a range of motives (competition, rivalry, power, status, market share, profits, quarterly returns, speed to market innovation, etc.); encounter enhanced opportunities for deviance as they reach the boardroom level; and the organization – legally, financially, socially, politically and institutionally – forms the means through which the crime is committed. What makes corporate crime so interesting, and so different from 'common crime', is that the organizational component is essential: indeed, the organization can be the offender, or the victim – or both at the same time; it is the instrument, the weapon, the accomplice and the enabling, encouraging or coercing context within which the crime is conducted. In short, the *organizational* component is a defining characteristic of corporate crime; no organization, no crime (Tonry and Reiss, 1993). Are there, then, no individuals in organizations?

Of course, there are individuals in the sense of ostensibly morally autonomous actors but some people are prepared to surrender to the collective – 'my company right or wrong' – while others use the institution in deviant ways, but can only adopt that course because of their place in the institutional context or hierarchy. They are not individuals in a vacuum and executives are not languishing in some soft meadow of independent reflection and moral balancing. This is not the MBA seminar on 'Business Ethics' (the ultimate oxymoron?) where students, approached as moral individuals, deny vehemently that they would take the deviant option when faced with a moral dilemma in business. In reality, as in the British Airways/Virgin affair, a group of managers decided on a deviant solution to an issue and recruited a team to conduct a covert conspiracy; the team decided to hack into Virgin's computer to steal the passenger list and to distribute black propaganda on Virgin's financial situation (Punch, 1996). When I used to ask my MBA students if they would hack into the competitcor's computer, they reacted with strong denials; I used to reply, 'Oh yes, you will!'

For there are umpteen examples of controlled conspiracies conducted 'for' the organization – such as price-fixing, cartel forming and industrial espionage – and constructed by senior executives over a long period of time with considerable ingenuity and sophisticated camouflage (Braithwaite, 1984). In the Netherlands, for instance, a recent Parliamentary Inquiry revealed that virtually all the major companies in the construction industry had been fixing prices for years; had been using bribery and inducements to obtain inside information on tendering from officials and to influence regulators; and they had an elaborate scheme for compensating companies that lost out on a particular round of covert agreements (Parliamentary Inquiry Construction Industry Fraud, 2002).

This was *systemic* deviance and effectively a way of life in the industry. Large numbers of managers took part in an environment which was 'crime facilitative' in the sense that a battery of factors – the nature of the industry which encouraged covert alliances to cope with structural uncertainty, weak enforcement with co-opted regulators, a near collusive government engaged in prestigious projects and mindful of the importance of the industry for the national economy, etc. – made it almost 'rational and reasonable' to break the law (Gobert and Punch, 2003). Or, as Braithwaite (1985: 7) remarks, 'given the great rewards and low risk of detection, why do so may people adopt the "economically irrational" course of obeying the law'?

Furthermore, in his influential work on price-fixing (1978), Geis portrays managers who simply took it as a routine and taken-for-granted part of their job to fix prices in secret negotiations with competitors. They knew it was 'wrong', they said on exposure, but had lost sight of the fact that it was illegal: they certainly had no perception of doing something 'criminal'. Their rationalizations, or vocabularies of motive, included that if they did not do it then someone else would, no-one was really harmed, it preserved jobs and they had not profited personally: in fact, they had scrupulously not taken a cent for themselves.

Whether any individual had doubts or reservations about this is unclear: these executives in the Heavy Electrical Anti-Trust cases all seem to have gone along with the flow: 'every direct supervisor that I had directed me to meet with the competition … It had become so common and gone on for so long I guess we lost sight of the fact that it was illegal' (ibid.: 132). They did it primarily 'for' the corporation, but maybe a bit for themselves as well (say, in the hope of promotion: selflessness is, after all, not normally a characteristic with which managers are richly endowed).

Indeed, it was the service of Sutherland that he long ago alerted us to the fact that we should not be surprised by such conduct: and many of his findings were later replicated by Clinard and Yeager (1980). Managers in corporations break the law, in some companies repeatedly so they can be viewed as 'recidivists': they even displayed contempt for the law while their consciences 'do not ordinarily bother them' for they did not perceive themselves as criminals (Sutherland, 1983: 217). Yet privately they were typically the epitome of the law-abiding, church-going, respectable citizen with high social and cultural capital. It was if they had a split personality, one for inside and one for outside the corporation.

## Corporate environment and irrationality

In effect, people in organizations are capable of rationalizing and justifying their deviant behaviour: but they do this not as autonomous individuals but as corporate actors. People who are highly moral in their private lives 'leave their consciences at home' when they enter the portals of the firm and do what the organization asks them. Jackall (1989) provides an intriguing analysis of the social processes which turn managers into amoral chameleons doing their corporate bosses' bidding: not to do so, not to survive the continual testing in the 'moral mazes' of corporate politics, means ostracism, demotion, being sidelined, banishment to another position or to another location involving a house move, getting demeaning assignments and other frosty forms of exclusion.

Again, let me state that I shall review deviant behaviour which is done collectively on behalf of or against the organization or done 'individually' for or against the organization. Another major thread relates to cases in the literature which illustrate wide discrepancies in the level of control over the deviant behaviour and of the level of rationality involved (Punch, 1996). It is not always a rationally calculated means to achieve an illicit goal (perhaps in a variant of 'strain theory'). When Robert Maxwell plundered his firm's pension fund to the tune of some £470 million, for instance, it was part of an institutional drama in which one man dominated an organization as an extension of his ego. His pursuit of power and status led to undue risk-taking, lack of caution and even an element of self-destruction. Maxwell's use of his corporate empire was not rational but pathological (and it ended in his death at sea which was termed 'accidental' but which some believed was suicide). He 'looted' his own company and by filching from the pension fund he not only victimized the firm but also thousands of employees and pensioners (Greenslade, 1992).

Indeed, this strand raises the crucial issue of rationality and control in organizations. It can be argued that we are mesmerized by the external image of control and coherence that business, and other organizations, like to exude. This is the 'myth system', as Reisman calls it (1979), of glossy brochures, mission statements, corporate outreach and philanthropy, ethical codes, trendy adverts, role-model executives and an edifice of good corporate citizenship. But every account of the inside reality of corporate life from Dalton's *Men Who Manage* (1959) onwards, reveals rivalry, schisms, factions, fiefdoms, back-stabbing, dirty politics, the manipulation of data, façades and charades, collusion between various actors and lack of unanimity and coherence. And, crucially, an 'operational code' (Reisman, 1979) as to how rule-bending and rule-breaking are covertly constructed, justified and managed. This might relate to bribery, to creative accounting, to benefiting by rule-bending (as in 'churning' in banks where needless transactions are made in accounts simply to generate more income for the banker) or a cynical, informal 'code':

> The code is this: you milk the plants: rape the business: use other people and discard them: f --- any woman that is available, in sight, and under your control: and exercise executive prerogatives at will with subordinates and other lesser mortals. (Jackall, 1989: 97)

I would, then, argue that we have to revise our view of organizations and management. Modern management was originally seen as a science that would enable executives to run their enterprises on rational grounds (Reed, 1989). Indeed, early management education in the nineteenth century was conducted in Schools of Engineering (this was still the case in Cambridge, that fountain of educational innovation, until the late 1980s). And engineering is not exactly a profession renowned for its intellectual flexibility, so that legacy is one of a belief in rational control over coherent processes in a 'manageable' world. Even the vast contemporary industry of management education and publications is based on seeking solutions to business problems which enable executives to 'take charge' of processes. The archetypical manager, in this imagery, straddles the organization and skilfully steers it: and to help him, or her, there is a vast output of instant solutions and steps to success by academics, consultants, top executives as role models and an army of gurus (Knights and McCabe, 2003). In my years in management education, on programmes for young MBA students to senior executives, it became clear that the underlying paradigm is of the participant being groomed to take control at an executive level within that myth system of formal strategy, effective internal control and compliant or malleable personnel. There is little or no attention to crises, scandals, managerial mistakes, fraud, bribery, and so on: all the guest speakers tell corporate success stories to fawning audiences. No-one wants to listen to a 'loser' and, hence, no-one addresses failure, undue risk and pathologies.

For, in contrast to the paradigm of a controlled and controllable world there is an alternative institutional reality of irrationality, management that is not in control and even organizations that are effectively out of control. In an inquiry into misuse of public funds in a Dutch ship-building conglomerate, for example, the CEO stated:

> The shivers run down my spine again if I think back on it. We had completely lost our grip on the organization. RSV was damaged, battered and in many respects humiliated. There was total de-motivation. The organization was not capable of coping with the issues. It was a terrible time. (Punch, 1996: 208)

The best illustration of this duality was when executives – having participated in an expensive seminar on, say, strategic human resource management (HRM) – approached me in the breaks to tell me what it was 'really' like in their company and why none of the excellent ideas presented to them would fly in the 'real world'. These revelations ranged from 'my boss is a feudal psychopath' to 'my boss is an incompetent nitwit who is threatened by anyone who is competent, so he surrounds himself with boot-lickers, and he will deeply resent my getting this degree because he doesn't have one; in fact I'm paying for it myself and I told him it's only in the weekends because he just doesn't invest in his personnel' or 'HRM with us means reaching your monthly target: you may miss it once, but then you need a damn good excuse, but if you miss it twice you are out on your ear; my MBA was geared to corporate strategy, as if I was running a multinational, but here I'm just a corporate coolie.' Their world was one of constant uncertainty, company politics, unrelenting pressure, replaceable personnel, fickle and unpredictable bosses, simulated deference and fear of failure. This is fertile ground for authoritarian behaviour from above, obedience and servility from below and, of course, devious rule-bending and impression management.

Taking this into account I will argue that a significant element in corporate crime can be 'system failure': organizations simply do not function as they are meant to in corporate plans and the leading textbooks. Managers are caught between a world of fluctuating contingencies with uncertainty about success from pat formulas that are difficult to translate into their insecure and confusing world. As a consequence they may turn to rule-bending.

In practice, then, decision-making in corporations may ostensibly be cloaked within a rational, economic, 'strategic' paradigm, but it can also be distorted by a number of structural, cultural and psychological mechanisms that, in turn, can foster a range of distortions including undue risk and the promotion of a culture of negligence. I am not suggesting that all organizations are in perpetual turmoil or exist in a state of chaotic fluctuations (although some seem to be), but rather that there is, below the surface, a 'negotiated order' where diverse factions and interests negotiate a way though the formal rules and regulations to shape a working practice in the face of multiple pressures. This discrepancy between the myth system and the negotiated order of the operational code can best be illustrated by cases where the gap is so wide that the deviance it elicits leads to substantial harm and to outcomes which the offenders never intended.

For a range of socio-psychological explanations – group think, depersonalization, routinization, cognitive dissonance and wilful blindness – help explain why managers in organizations can take decisions, or avoid making decisions, that lead to significant harm. In the continually ambivalent worlds that they create but which take on an existence beyond them, they become capable of living with glaring discrepancies between the front they present to the outside world and the underlying reality – at Parmalat living with a 'hole' of some 12 billion or at BCCI living with continual bribery, corruption and manipulation of data (requiring a 'black treasury' to falsify documents on a grand scale) – and learn effortlessly to flit between two conflicting realties. I shall explore these themes by examining the often complex interaction between individuals, groups and organizations in a number of cases in industries involving financial services and transport.

## The cases

### Leeson and Barings

The context for this by now renowned case is that Barings, a major merchant bank in the City of London with a solid reputation, expanded its operations in the booming economy of Asia with a strong presence in the 'futures and derivatives' markets geared to the stock exchanges of Singapore and Japan. A young, inexperienced man of 24 years, Nick Leeson, was sent to Barings Singapore to sort out some administrative problem. Yet somehow he had soon inveigled himself into playing a leading role in the bank's dealing room and taking large 'positions' on the Japanese exchanges and on SIMEX (Singapore Stock Exchange). Furthermore, he was operating in both the 'front' and 'back' offices of the firm: this despite the fact that it is a fundamental principle in financial services that there should be distance between the two so that someone cannot be controlling himself or herself. The Singapore office was far removed from London not only geographically but also culturally. It was staffed by young, ambitious people in a booming environment, where large 'positions' were taken on markets, where hospitality for clients was extravagant, where the lifestyle was opulent and the rewards considerable (Rawnsley, 1996). Leeson grew into a leading position, displaying daring on the exchange floor, enjoying an almost unchallengeable status, and bringing in a large amount of business – which promised not only high bonuses for himself but also for his colleagues in Singapore and, indeed, London. He clearly had become a major player on the Asian markets in a remarkably short time. It was said that in the trading room dealers needed the 'killer instinct' and had to display 'a strong sense of personal and corporate greed. Ruthlessness. Single-mindedness. Intolerance': and Leeson was seen as a 'ruthlessly aggressive trader' (*Daily Mail*, 28 February 1995).

Then an earthquake hit Kobe in Japan and the Japanese markets dipped. Anticipating massive government support and investment in the rebuilding of Kobe, Leeson remained deeply committed on the Japanese and Singapore exchanges when others were more cautious. For a number of reasons the market did not pick up and Leeson was 'overexposed': in a desperate attempt to force the market up on his own – a very risky strategy – he kept taking further positions. In order to bolster these positions he requested large amounts of money from London which were sent virtually without murmur (Bank of England Report, 1995).

Later it emerged, however, that from very early on Leeson had actually been losing money and fraudulently 'hiding' it. He started to conceal losses through an 'error account' with the number 88888 (8 being a lucky number in Chinese society). The losses mounted and Leeson became desperate: rather than abandoning his mistakes he compounded them until he had committed more than the reserves of the bank. Eventually his losses amounted to some £780 million, the bank went under (a rescue effort in London failed) and was declared bankrupt, and was then sold for one pound to the Dutch ING Bank.

Leeson had walked out of the office and left Singapore a few days before his 28th birthday in the hope of reaching London where he hoped to cooperate with the Serious Fraud Office and face a hopefully lenient sentence in a British jail. During a landing at Frankfurt, however, he was arrested by German police and held until his extradition to Singapore. In that period he gave an interview to David Frost; he had not yet faced trial so he was understandably cautious. Nevertheless, he made illuminating comments about his path into crime. After an early release from a Singapore prison on health grounds (he had been sentenced to six and a half years), he was later far more critical of Barings in interviews. But he did not substantially deviate from this early account.

In that interview with Frost for the BBC he related how he had dug himself into a hole that he could not climb out of. He claimed that the first deviant step in Singapore involved £20,000, which gave him 'sleepless nights'. That first step was ostensibly to help a young inexperienced woman who had made a minor error: to hide her mistake he opened an 'error account'. The idea of an error account is that you 'park' your mistakes there until you can rectify anomalies at a later date. Leeson began to use the error account to hide his own fraudulent transactions: when the amount was £40,000 it was a little easier than with that first £20,000 he recounted. Apparently it became increasingly easy for him to accept the fraudulent amounts until they had reached nearly £800 million (!) and he faced exposure. He explained that on a bad day he might lose £30 million but on a good day make £40 million: this reinforced his conviction that he could make it and he tried to beat the market on his own; if he kept taking positions, then the market might just respond. He also added 'this was not like real money' as if commitment to the game had tied him to the means, the gambits in the dealing room, and clouded out the ends (that he was investing other people's money, *real* money, in a fiduciary relationship). This stance is rather like the gambler on a losing streak mortgaging the house for one final throw of the dice to win everything back – or losing everything. Indeed, Frost says, 'But that's a gambler speaking' and Leeson replies that futures and derivatives is effectively a form of gambling: he simply took a risky gamble and lost.

The significance of Leeson's account is twofold. First, he had committed a deliberate fraud with staggering consequences (although the offences were, in fact, relatively minor and technical) and on the surface it appears that he acted on his own as an 'individual'. His downfall perfectly exemplifies the social-psychology of the slippery slope metaphor. This assumes that once on the slope you will go on 'sliding'. For Leeson is quite explicit on the nature of the slope – the initial move is troublesome but each successive move became easier for his conscience – and the way he gradually became committed to deviance while able to rationalize it to himself. We will never know with any certainty what really went through his mind but he conveyed it as a business accident rather than deliberate criminality and, at least initially, committed in the interests of the company. Indeed, he stole nothing.

Second, and crucially, he could only commit and get away with the fraud because he was working in an organization that was seriously malfunctioning. The Bank of England Report (1995) and other sources make it perfectly clear that almost everything that could go wrong did go wrong:

> Barings' collapse was due to the unauthorised and ultimately catastrophic activities of, it appears, one individual (Leeson) that went undetected as a consequence of management failure and other internal controls of the most basic kind. Management failed at various levels and in a variety of ways ... to institute a proper system of internal controls, to enforce accountability for all profits, risks and operations, and adequately to follow up on a number of warning signals over a prolonged period. Neither the external auditors nor the regulators discovered Leeson's unauthorised activities. (Bank of England Report, 1995: 250)

And let us bear in mind that this was a highly experienced, respectable bank with an impeccable reputation. In brief, senior management did not understand this new business of derivatives: internal and external signals about his over-exposure on the markets were ignored; local supervision of him was truly abject; he was able to work in the back and front office at the same time; and when he asked for large sums of money from London, these were sent without hesitation although they even exceeded Bank of England limits. In effect, this was *system failure* which created a context that presented him with an enticing opportunity to commit fraud on a massive scale. The organization was complicit and virtually made him a victim of its gross incompetence so that he can even be seen as a scapegoat for serious management failure.

In this portrait there is a depiction of the psychology of a fraudster entering deviance and sliding down the slippery slope. But the metaphor could also be applied to the organization: Barings was on a slippery slope of its own and Leeson simply made the slide more precipitous until it ended in bankruptcy. This was not an individual failure but *a collective failure* – except only the individual did time.

In stepping back from this case it is important to state that Barings is not exceptional and its failure is symptomatic of a number of features of financial services. I have given seminars to bankers and when I first entered their world I assumed it would be culturally risk-averse and structurally highly controlled. In practice, the reality can be of undue risk-taking in a highly competitive environment: Leeson was not untypical of many young and ambitious people who are used by the industry to 'gamble' on the exchanges (and if they do not display the guts and gumption they are callously cast side). The reward system with massive bonuses encourages risk and often internal controls are there more to satisfy external regulators than to seriously address dodgy financial reporting. I shall return to some of these elements later when I discuss the rash of mega-frauds.

In a nutshell, Barings is not an isolated case and Leeson is not an exception. If you take away the headline-catching features of a respectable bank becoming bankrupt because of a massive fraud, then many of the elements can be found in many other financial institutions. Under the operational code, for instance, it is 'SOP' (Standard Operating Practice) for traders to have an error account: in the hectic world of dealing rooms people are left with discrepancies at the end of the day and they park these in an error account in order to sort them out later (and Leeson claimed everyone at Barings Singapore knew of his 'five eights' account).

Behind the orderly façade of banking there is, then, another world of risk, manipulation of accounts, avoidance of control, encouragement of the over-achiever, reluctance to monitor star performers and tolerance of informal practices (often with swift exit rather than prosecution for those caught with their hand in the till). The financial services industry routinely puts rich opportunity, feeble control and high temptation together and Leeson, like Oscar Wilde, could resist anything but temptation.

## Deadly transport

In the Barings case there may have been multiple victims among investors (and not that many people shed tears for them), but virtually everyone kept their job and no-one died. But there are instances where corporate crimes bring about deaths and serious injuries to innocent victims. In conventional crime, *intent* is crucial in establishing guilt whereas here the assumption is that no executive would consciously intend deaths to occur: indeed, they would doubtless argue that this is the worst case scenario for the company – and precisely the opposite to that which is intended. For example, blood banks have brought contaminated blood on the market which had catastrophic consequences for those receiving transfusions, effectively issuing their death warrants. It seems almost inconceivable that, in such a vital medical service, managers would ignore warnings and take undue risks. How, then, can we explain that companies 'kill'?

In transport, to which I will now turn, there have been occasions when managers have insisted that planes fly to schedule, or trains depart on time, despite persistent warnings about serious deficiencies in safety. In such situations, organizational demands, expectations and constraints push people into keeping to performance targets, to keeping up production or to sticking to timetables, hence forcing or inducing managers to risk the lives of hundreds of people. The ends are lost in a fixation on means.

The transport industry, for example, works routinely with risk – by road, air, sea and rail. Safety is an ever-present concern but daily, operational safety is related to factors such as quality of management, the allocation of resources, corporate culture, government policies and regulatory regimes. In the UK, for example, there has been a rash of train crashes in recent years with considerable loss of life and many injuries. In cases of culpable 'accidents' the issue is whether or not the crash is traceable back to policy decisions taken over an extended period of time at boardroom level and if there is evidence of gross negligence within a company. Indeed, the strategic environment of the industry as a whole is crucial and not just the conduct of individual companies, because **deregulation** split a state monopoly into some 100 companies with over twenty for operations and two for track maintenance and safety. These major economic decisions help shape the 'culture' of the industry and impact on individual companies, while this operating culture may unwittingly lead to deaths and disaster.

The Southall crash of 1998, for instance, happened after deregulation. Critics of deregulation have argued that this stimulated an emphasis on short-term profitability and a lack of investment in infrastructure and safety (Jack, 2001). The circumstances leading to the accident were that a Great Western Railway (GWR) train from London arrived at Swansea and was being prepared for its return journey. Standard on trains in Britain is AWS (Automatic Warning System) which sounds a claxon if the train proceeds through a red warning light: the driver then has to bring the train to an emergency halt. In a number of countries trains are fitted with ATP (Automatic Train Protection) which stops a train automatically without driver intervention if it should pass a red light. In fact, the Southall train had been fitted with ATP on an experimental basis but the system was not functioning. Then, when the driver went to the original rear of the train for the return journey, he discovered that the

AWS was not functioning. He asked the station management at Swansea to switch the locomotive from the rear to the front so he could return with AWS. In fact, this driver had never driven without AWS. However, local management refused to turn the locomotive train around because it would cause undue delay: and this might lead to the company incurring a penalty for late arrival in London.

On the return journey the train passed two warning lights and a red light and crashed into a freight train, causing seven deaths and numerous injuries. If the locomotive with AWS had been switched to the front, or if ATP had been mandated in Britain, or if there had been a second driver assigned to the cab, then the accident would almost certainly not have happened and lives would have been saved.

There were three main factors which combined to produce the crash. First was the decision of station management at Swansea not to switch the locomotives (this would probably have taken 10–12 minutes). This follows a pattern in transport where a fixation on keeping to schedules takes priority over safety. The government may even have contributed to this mind-set by its practice of ranking rail companies on their arrival times and by imposing penalties for delays. The second was that the driver was almost certainly negligent. In reporting the accident – he survived the crash and alerted management with a phone-call that was recorded – he admitted that he had been 'packing his bags' at the time of the crash. A third, and crucial, factor was the decision taken by senior management to allow drivers to proceed in some instances without a functioning AWS and without a back-up driver. Whereas one might think, in the interests of passenger safety, that a fully functioning AWS would be mandatory, there were some weasel words in the regulations allowing for exceptions.

It might, then, appear that the immediate cause of the crash was the driver's negligence in not paying sufficient attention (Uff, 2001). But in a wider context there was the decision not to introduce ATP. However, this was not a decision of GWR alone. The *British rail industry as a whole* had decided against the adoption of ATP on the grounds of expense. This was a strategic decision which the industry was perfectly entitled to take on economic grounds: and in a deregulated industry the government was impotently sidelined.

The crash led to a prosecution for manslaughter against both the driver and the operating company but the Crown Prosecution Service's case against GWR failed in court. The company, however, did admit to breaches of health and safety regulations and was heavily fined (Gobert and Punch, 2003).

What lessons can one learn from the Southall crash? It can be argued that the corporate culture of profit orientation and lack of investment in safety fostered an operational climate in which lower-level functionaries felt pressured not to cause delays and to place adherence to schedules above passenger safety. Managers took permissible and ostensibly legitimate decisions that had fatal consequences. The strategic decisions at boardroom level were deemed too far removed from their likely consequences to warrant the criminal conviction of the company itself. But beyond the individual factors in the case, the deregulatory climate that had swept the UK (and the United States) had led to the downgrading of safety departments and research and development aimed at improving safety. Management at GWR claimed to have lost confidence in ATP, but the rejoinder is that they probably were not prepared to invest the time, money and resources needed to make ATP operate effectively. An emphasis on maximizing profitability also had led to the recruitment of directors from other industries with little or no knowledge of the railways, no engineering background and no affinity with the operational dangers that were faced by actual train drivers on a daily basis. The main concern of these directors was a return on investment. While in their public utterances they paid lip service to the paramount importance of safety, the record of the industry in practice suggested the disingenuousness of such pronouncements (Jack, 2001). Although none of the relevant executives could have wished for a mass disaster, their collective behaviour produced just such an occurrence.

This particular case needs to be put in a broader context of accidents causing death and injury including Bhopal, the Ford Pinto, the capsizing of the *Herald of Free Enterprise* at Zeebrugge and other rail accidents in Britain (Potters Bar, Paddington and Hatfield). Analysis tends to reveal that certain structural features of the industry stimulated operational practices which combined to contribute to an accident when a specific constellation of events occurred. For example, company pressure from above for results led at Zeebrugge to an emphasis on ships leaving on time; this in turn led to departing with the bow doors open and this just happened to occur when the bosun responsible for closing the doors was not on duty but was asleep while his supervisor had gone to the bridge on the assumption that the bosun was at his post. The ships' Masters had requested warning lights on the bridge so that they could see that the bow doors were safely shut: this was rejected by management on the grounds of cost. As a result of this multiple negligence nearly 200 people died (Punch, 1996).

In brief, three factors are important in explaining why people who are responsible for the safety of the people they transport end up taking decisions that lead to fatalities and injuries.

1   Operational managers become fixated on schedules, delays and punctuality (perhaps geared to wider institutional pressure or perceived rewards and penalties) and ignore safety. The station managers at Swansea refused to turn the locomotive around even though the safety device AWS was not working in the driver's cab and he was unaccompanied.

2   Why did the driver of the GWR train not simply refuse to take the train back to London on the grounds that he had never driven without AWS before, felt responsible for the lives of his passengers and valued his own life? Surely a 'rational man' would have said 'Sorry, but the risks are too high.' One answer is 'obedience'. There are many instances in the literature where you would expect an individual to flatly refuse to carry out something

dangerous or devious but they acquiesce. Organizations can be seen as replications of Milgram's famous or infamous experiments on obedience (Milgram, 1974). Individuals in organizations tend to do what they are asked to do even if that puts others, or even themselves, at risk of death.

3   Another mechanism allied to risk taking is the ability of managers to blind themselves to the consequences of their actions. For example, in a particular trucking company in Britain, the management encouraged drivers to work to the point of exhaustion which meant sending 'time-bombs' out on the roads because the risk of a crash was high: but the drivers acquiesced in risking their own lives for extra pay and all concerned engaged in *wilful blindness*; presumably this evaporated when a driver, driving erratically from exhaustion, collided with another vehicle, causing a crash on the M25 motorway which the driver survived but which killed two other people (Gobert and Punch, 2003).

In essence, there is a belief in the autonomous individual who is capable of making dispassionate decisions in his or her best interests or those of others, but in the corporate context people may become occupationally and collectively fixated on means rather than ends. They may take risks for themselves, or for others in their company's care, because they are being put under pressure and end up effectively 'following orders'; they do not possess the ability or willingness to dissent. And, as in the blood-bank scandals, they function with a split personality whereby one personality adheres to the myth system while another engages in an operational code of systemic deviance. To cope with this discrepancy they ignore the consequences of their action through wilful blindness (which is both a legal concept and possibly a form of cognitive dissonance which not only filters out disconfirming evidence but also reinforces their belief in what they are doing).

In this trucking company, the façade was of a respectable company fulfilling safety and quality requirements but, in practice, there was systematic manipulation of the devices to record driving times and a hidden policy of bonuses for driving beyond the legal limits. Everyone involved must have known of the risks involved – this is common knowledge in the industry – yet there was a collective burying of heads in the sand.

## Road to destruction

In this third, and final, case I shall attend to the mega-frauds of recent years, particularly in relation to companies such as Enron, WorldCom, Ahold and Parmalat. In the previous section I touched on cases where managers took risks that put others, but also themselves, in danger. Here, it can be argued that the actors' conduct was so extreme that it threatened the very stability of economic markets on which the continuity of capitalism depends (Partnoy, 2003). Again this reflects the view that managers are not always in full control of their organizations and blind themselves to the consequences of their conduct.

In the US and European financial scandals and affairs of recent years, many major companies engaged in systemic rule-bending and breaking (Elliot and

Scroth, 2002). A number were seen as exemplary companies: Enron was praised for its performance, winning awards, and was seen as the paradigm of the new economy, Ahold and its senior management were revered in the Netherlands and Parmalat was held up as a model for the rest of Italy. On the surface, they appeared to be strong and well-led companies. So where did it all go wrong?

Of importance is that we are talking of respected corporations with good reputations. The financial services industry in which they were operating was, however, changing significantly:

- There was a bull market for a number of years in the second half of the 1990s and the early part of this century, there was globalization and deregulation and increasingly major companies began dealing for themselves. Enron was ostensibly in the energy business but was making much of its profits from speculation. Daimler-Benz was generating some 50 per cent of its profits from dealing on the foreign exchanges and major companies were increasingly operating as if they were investment banks.

- In the bull market and new economy there were vast sums of money involved. A new generation of dealers arose who were capable of developing increasingly sophisticated, innovative and complex financial instruments. Of crucial significance is that the bosses of the new financial 'whiz-kids' did not always fully understand the new business they were in (Gobert and Punch, 2003: 20; think of the ignorance of Barings' senior management on derivatives). However, the dealers and their team were often 'winners' with untouchable status who were generating most of the firm's income. This brought them substantial bonuses, with one dealer receiving $23 million in 1990, while their financial success was also shared by their bosses (but who might only have one-tenth of their star performer's amount). There was, then, a general reluctance to intervene. This also arose because in that mercenary and fiercely competitive world, 'star players' displayed no loyalty whatsoever to their company and, if they were not satisfied, then they would simply decamp to the competition taking their entire team with them. They could virtually hold senior management to ransom.

- This lack of understanding and the institutionalized dependency on the reward system blinded people to the fact that many of the new instruments contained a high measure of undisclosed risk. It became clear later from testimony, e-mails and recorded phone-calls that many dealers were contemptuous of their clients and did not feel obliged to inform them of the risk. A former director and senior derivatives saleswoman at Bankers Trust, for instance, spoke of an 'amoral culture': 'She said: "You saw practices you knew were not good for clients being encouraged by senior managers because they made a lot of money for the bank." One salesman noted, "Funny business, you know. Lure people into that calm and then just totally f... them"' (Partnoy, 2003: 55). This was cynical, predatory and rapacious while also many investment analysts, who were meant to be giving objective advice to clients, had effectively become a covert marketing instrument for their companies.

- The seductions of the new economy and of a 'shareholders' democracy' attracted investments from many new players including public and professional bodies: financial advisors encouraged universities, schools (including a school board in the Shetland Isles) and many individuals to take out investments, to change their mortgages and to reinvest their life savings. And, as mentioned, many industrial and internationally operating companies took to dealing on their own account.

- In this cumulative system failure one might think that the regulators and controllers would act as a restraining influence. But regulation was not only weak but also virtually co-opted by the industry: the prime regulator was the SEC (Securities and Exchange Commission) which operated a revolving door with the industry, with executives and regulators frequently swapping roles. Many of the 'discrepancies' which occurred were plea-bargained to a settlement with a slap on the wrist fine following a *nolo contendere* plea (as Geis quipped, amounting to the company saying 'I didn't do it and I won't do it again' (in Braithwaite, 1984: 15) but there was no conviction and, crucially, no grounds for further criminal or civil actions. This was no real deterrent.

- Of particular concern was that the key controlling agency, the accountant firms, were essentially colluding in covering up the 'discrepancies' (as with the shredders working overtime at Arthur Andersen to destroy incriminating evidence when Enron started to unravel). These firms had become entwined with the companies they were meant to audit because they wanted to keep their business and because their consultancy branch had placed large numbers of personnel inside the firms to steer many of their primary processes. Andersen had a close relationship with Waste Management in the 1990s, saw it as a 'crown jewel' client bringing in high revenue from auditing (but even more from consultancy), every chief financial officer and accounting officer had worked at Andersen and umpteen former Andersen staff had gone to work for Waste Management. This intimate relationship was clearly a conflict of interest. Then, in 1996, a thorough audit revealed that the company had overstated its earnings by $1.4 billion! This was the largest corporate financial restatement ever until then, and the SEC fined Andersen $7 million for approving Waste Management's inaccurate financial statement. Subsequently, following a criminal trial in the wake of Enron, Andersen disappeared as a firm and accountancy firms have also since then divested themselves of their consultancy branches.

These *systemic* characteristics (well analyzed by Partnoy, 2003), led to many victims – individual and institutional – losing large sums of money (for individuals their pension, life-savings or mortgage, and for institutions their investments of public money which affected public spending and collective pension funds). One German company, Metallgesellschaft, lost $1.4 million and Orange County in California lost $1.7 billion of public money. Indeed, the fall on the NYSE after the collapse of several major companies was greater than following the attack on the Twin Towers in Manhattan and other targets on 9/11. If we examine the conduct of senior executives at Enron and other firms, as well as in the investment banking sector, then an accumulation of factors had effectively created a criminogenic environment (Fusaro and Miller, 2002).

> Today the key issues behind the recent financial scandals are the complex instruments used to skirt legal rules; the rogue employees who managers and shareholders cannot monitor; and the incentives for managers to engage in financial malfeasance, given the deregulated markets. (Partnoy, 2003: 402)

The rapaciousness of the players, however, was such that it not only threatened the stability of markets but even the very collapse of the capitalist system. These corporate crooks almost brought the system they were feeding off crashing around down around their ears: the global consequences, with the Great Crash of 1929 in mind, would have been truly catastrophic.

## Conclusion

In this chapter I have argued that the organizational component of corporate crime is fundamental. Also that behaviour in organizations is not always rational, coherent and under control. Indeed, in a number of cases we can see that a combination of factors can stimulate crime or cause significant 'system failure' that enables crime. What features can be said to distort conduct to the extent that managers seek a deviant solution?

- **Goals and pressure**. Given the competitive nature of capitalism and the need for business organizations to achieve in various ways, it is inevitable that companies set goals and exert pressure on personnel. But, as Gross observes (1980: 72), 'Whatever the goals may be, it is the emphasis on them that creates the trouble.' Some managers rise to the occasion and achieve the targets, others retreat and step out or are moved out, but others turn to rule-bending and rule-breaking either for the organization or for self (but perhaps, like Leeson, with the rationalization that it was really for the firm).
- **The company as total institution**. In some ways a company can come to dominate a manager's life personally, professionally, socially and financially. This can produce the 'company man (sic)' who is deeply loyal to the firm. It is possible that when the BA conspirators were selecting a 'dirty tricks' team, that those they approached felt they could not refuse out of commitment to the company (which is why I said to my students 'Oh yes, you will!').
- **Motives and rationalizations**. The corporate environment can provide motives for deviance (related to competition, rivalry, power, status, market share, profits, quarterly returns, speed to market, innovation, etc.) and generate 'vocabularies of motive' which justify and rationalize law breaking (such as denial of harm and of responsibility or condemning the condemners).
- **Corporate leaders**. Some senior executives display dominance, despotism, ruthlessness and unbridled egoism: they can intimidate subordinates to break rules. In extreme cases, the thirst for power leads to abuse of that power and to pathological processes: the company can become the neurotic arena for power battles and leadership struggles which nearly destroy the company. Kets de Vries (1995: 199), for example, in his book on *Life and Death in the Executive Fast Lane: Irrational Organizations and their Leaders* writes:

> [Robert] Maxwell's strong need for control was also reflected in the highly secret world he created around his private companies. Because secrecy and security were prime concerns, Maxwell had a passion for security devices. He even had the phones of his fellow directors of the Mirror Group Newspapers bugged – without their knowledge of course. Furthermore, only Maxwell himself had any idea about all the links between his myriad companies [400 of them]. There was no management structure; everything revolved around and depended on him. Through this kind of fragmentation, which created a considerable amount of insecurity, he kept control over all decisions.

In the BCCI case, the bank was suffused with the mission to become a major Muslim bank competing with the large western banks; its founder, Agha Hason Abedi, was both devout and charismatic and when he spoke at meetings some of his personnel listened spellbound: the unquestioning loyalty that he generated was doubtless one of the elements that fostered one of the largest frauds in banking history (Punch, 1996).

- **Obedience**. In much of the literature and many of the cases there emerges an authoritarian and collective culture in companies which allows little space for individual autonomy and discretion: subordinates often find it difficult to refuse to carry out an instruction. Managers suppress individuality, do not challenge the hierarchy, blend in and, as in the military, follow orders (see Kelman, 2006, on 'crimes of obedience'). Writing of entrepreneurs, Kets de Vries (1995: 198), remarks 'Some even create a culture that prohibits any form of contrarian thinking. In such a culture, disagreement is impossible: there is no tolerance for subordinates who think for themselves: give-and-take – the process of real dialogue – is not permitted.' Those who think 'outside the box' are likely to land outside of the corporation.
- **Group think**. Another psychological mechanism which can distort decision-making, but which is difficult to avoid, is group think (Janis, 1985). When, say, a managing group board gets locked into group think, it tends to neglect critical external information, to be overly positive about its own potential, to stereotype those who do not fit in, to suppress dissent and diversity and to intimidate doubters. People who may be opposed to a proposal or who reject a solution remain silent in the face of group pressure.
- **Cognitive dissonance**. A by-product of group think can be cognitive dissonance whereby disconfirming evidence is rejected and the belief in one's position is, rather than being undermined by the negative reports, strengthened. In several cases (Thalidomide, Dalkon Shield), the growing evidence of negative side-effects arising from the products, including severe deformation in babies and serious infections in women (with several deaths) respectively, led not to caution and re-assessment but to a marked increase in marketing and production.

Finally, the aim in this chapter has been to touch on some of those social-psychological factors that lead to rule-breaking and that blind managers to the consequences of their conduct. A major factor has been to argue that, while western morality and the law are based on the individual who is held to be fully conscious of his or her decision, corporate actors are placed in a context where their choices are shaped by some of the features mentioned above. People do have a choice – they can refuse, try to dissuade others, exit or blow the whistle – but we have seen that in practice the pressures are high to fit in and to adopt the deviant option. In some cases the corporate environment is 'crime coercive' (managers feel they have no option but to break the law in order to survive) whereas in other sectors the culture is 'crime facilitative' (providing enticing opportunities). There are situations where there is high senior management involvement (price fixing at Hoffmann La Roche), where a sub-group within senior management conducts the deviancy (manipulating markets at Guinness); where almost an entire industry is routinely bending the rules (cartel forming in the Dutch construction industry); or where an individual is the main offender, as with Maxwell or Leeson (Punch, 1996).

But in a sense Maxwell and Leeson were not 'individuals' as they operated in a corporate context which facilitated their crimes. They needed the organization as a backcloth, as a resource, as a facilitator, as camouflage, as a tool and as an excuse. On their own they would have been able to achieve nothing. But the corporation provided motive, opportunity and means. This was not 'individual' but organizational crime: *the organization did it.*

# References

Bank of England Report (1995) Report of the Board of Banking Supervision Inquiry into the Circumstances of the Collapse of Barings. London: HMSO.

Braithwaite, J. (1984) *Corporate Crime in the Pharmaceutical Industry*. London: Routledge and Kegan Paul.

Braithwaite, J. (1985) 'White Collar Crime', *Annual Review of Sociology*, 11: 1–25.

Calavita, K. and Pontell, H. (1990) '"Heads I win, tails you lose": deregulation, crime and crisis in the savings and loan industry', *Crime and Delinquency*, 36(3): 309–41.

Clinard, M.B. and Yeager, P.C. (1980) *Corporate Crime*. New York: Free Press.

*Daily Mail* (1995) 'Blunders behind the Barings straits', 28 February.

Dalton, M. (1959) *Men Who Manage*. New York: Wiley.

Elliot, A.L. and Scroth, R.J. (2002) *How Companies Lie*. London: Nicholas Brealey Publishing.

Ermann, D. and Lundman, R. (eds) (1996) *Corporate and Governmental Deviance,* 3rd edn. New York: Oxford University Press.

Fusaro, P.C. and Miller, R.M. (2002) *What Went Wrong at Enron?* New York: Wiley.

Geis, G. (1978) 'White collar crime: the heavy electrical equipment antitrust cases of 1961', in M. Ermann and R. Lundman (eds), *Corporate and Governmental Deviance,* 2nd edn. New York: Oxford University Press.

Gobert, J. and Punch, M. (2003) *Rethinking Corporate Crime*. London: Butterworths.

Greenslade, R. (1992) *Maxwell's Fall*. London: Simon & Schuster.

Gross, E. (1980) 'Organization structure and organizational crime', in G. Geis and E. Stotland (eds), *White-collar Crime*. Beverly Hills, CA: Sage.

Jack, I. (2001) *The Crash that Stopped Britain*. Cambridge: Granta Books.

Jackall, R. (1989) *Moral Mazes: The World of Corporate Managers*. New York: Oxford University Press.

Janis, I.L. (1985) *Victims of Groupthink*. Boston: Houghton Mifflin.

Kelman, H.C. (2006) 'The policy context of international crimes', paper presented at conference, *System Criminality in International Law*, University of Amsterdam, Faculty of Law.

Kets de Vries, M.F.R. (1995) *Life and Death in the Executive Fast Lane: Essays on Irrational Organization and their Leaders*. San Francisco, CA: Jossey-Bass.

Knights, D. and McCabe, D. (2003) *Organization and Innovation: Guru Schemes and American Dreams.* Maidenhead: Open University Press.

Milgram, S. (1974) *Obedience to Authority*. New York: Harper and Row.

Mokhiber, R. (1988) *Corporate Crime and Violence*. San Francisco, CA: Sierra Club Books.

Parliamentary Inquiry Construction Industry Fraud (2002) *Pariementaire Enquetecommissie Bouwfraude*. Den Haag: Staatsuitgeverij.

Partnoy, F. (2003) *Infectious Greed*. New York: Holt.

Punch, M. (1996) *Dirty Business: Exploring Corporate Misconduct*. London: Sage.

Punch, M. (2000) 'Suite violence: why managers murder and corporations kill', *Crime, Law and Social Change*, 33: 243–80.

Rawnsley, J. (1996) *Going for Broke: Nick Leeson and the Collapse of Barings Bank*. London: HarperCollins.

Reed, (1989) *The Sociology of Management*. New York: Harvester/Wheatsheaf.

Reisman, M.W. (1979) *Folded Lies*. New York: Free Press.

Slapper, G. and Tombs, S. (1999) *Corporate Crime*. Harlow: Longman.

Sutherland, E.H. (1949) *White Collar Crime*. New York: Holt.

Sutherland, E.H. (1983) *White Collar Crime: The Uncut Version*. New Haven, CT: Yale University Press.

Tonry, M. and Reiss, A.J. Jr. (eds) (1993) *Beyond the Law: Crime in Complex Organizations*. Chicago: The University of Chicago Press.

Uff, J. (2001) *The Southall Rail Accident Report*. London. Department of Transport.

## Suggestions for further reading

Braithwaite, J. (1985) 'White Collar crime', *Annual Review of Sociology*, 11: 1–25.

Clinard, M.B. and Yeager, P.C. (1980) *Corporate Crime*. New York: Free Press.

Ermann, D. and Lundman, R. (eds) (1996) *Corporate and Governmental Deviance*, 3rd edn. New York: Oxford University Press.

Gobert, J. and Punch, M. (2003) *Rethinking Corporate Crime*. London: Butterworths.

Kelman, H.C. (2006) 'The policy context of international crimes', paper presented at conference, System Criminality in International Law, University of Amsterdam, Faculty of Law.

Punch, M. (1996) *Dirty Business: Exploring Corporate Misconduct*. London: Sage.

Sutherland, E.H. (1949) *White Collar Crime*. New York: Holt.

# SIX

## Organizational Decision-Making
### Economic and Managerial Considerations

*Brian J. Loasby*

## Introduction

In this chapter we shall first examine some fundamental characteristics of human beings, then explain how these characteristics not only encourage the emergence of an organizational economy but influence the forms of organization, and how organizations in turn affect individual behaviour; finally, we shall explore decision processes within organizations, with particular reference to the ways in which interactions between individuals in these processes affect outcomes.

## Cognition, motivation and human knowledge

Herbert Simon was a scholar of extensive range and sharp perception; but he is particularly associated with two themes: organizational behaviour and **bounded rationality**, which are closely associated in his work. This association is fundamental to this chapter; however, I shall avoid the term 'bounded rationality' for both presentational and substantive reasons. The presentational reason is that it has been rather easy for many economists to avoid the implications which Simon believed to be important, by arguing that what Simon calls '**satisficing**' is simply optimizing when the costs of collecting and processing information are allowed for; so there is no need for the substantial, and unwelcome, changes that Simon proposed. Organizational behaviour, it is claimed, can be predicted by the analysis of individual optimizing agents who have access to well-defined production possibilities and are equipped with standard self-interested preferences, and the economic significance of formal organizations lies solely in providing incentive structures which will guide such optimization. This practice ignores the dependence of human choices on specific frames of reference, which are dependent on circumstances and experience, and on alternatives which are either readily accessible to the particular decision-maker or evoked by particular stimuli, and then assessed in relation to their more obvious and directly relevant consequences (Simon, 2005: 93–4). Though these characteristics are quite general, they are especially relevant to choices in organizations, because organizational structures and the patterns of interactions which develop within them clearly affect their manifestations and therefore the choices which are made. Furthermore, the standard simplified assumptions about human motivation exclude all recognition of 'the radical difference between the process of decision in organizations, when decision is in its important aspects a social process, and the process of decision in individuals when it is an individual process socially conditioned', emphasized by Chester Barnard (1938: 198–9), from whom Simon drew inspiration.

However, in this chapter, the substantive reasons for avoiding 'bounded rationality' are decisive. Not only is the concept of rationality (even when freed from its strict interpretation by economists) an inadequate label for human cognitive operations, which are often non-logical because there are insufficient premises for strict reasoning (Barnard, 1938: 305); it gives no hint of the fundamental problems of human knowledge or the important human motivations which we shall need to include in our analysis. Simon (1985: 303) recognized both in emphasizing the crucial importance of 'our view of the nature of the human beings whose behavior we are studying', not least in understanding behaviour in organizations. Therefore, I propose to explore these issues of cognition and motivation, and to set this exploration in the context of uncertainty, demonstrating that this context is fundamental to the very existence of formal organizations.

The classic treatment of uncertainty in economics is by Knight (1921), who defines it by the absence of any demonstrably correct procedure for assigning probabilities to a complete set of rival possibilities. Shackle generally preferred a broader treatment, writing about situations in which there is no demonstrably correct procedure for enumerating a complete set of possibilities; this is sometimes called radical or structural uncertainty. It may be argued that difficulties in assigning probabilities can be traced back to the impossibility of specifying all the different ways in which alternative outcomes might emerge and all the ways in which each of them might be prevented; and it is this inherent insufficiency of knowledge on which Shackle chose to focus (notably in Shackle, 1972). Whether this insufficiency is a fundamental property of a universe, as conceived in non-equilibrium thermodynamics, which evolves through processes of self-organization that are inherently unpredictable (Prigogine, 2005), or a logical consequence of the limited capacity of the human brain in relation to an interconnected universe, which compels us to rely on conjectures which are drastically simplified and which, as Hume pointed out, can never attain the status of general empirical proof, need not concern us here.

The absence of a demonstrably correct method of probability assignment was sufficient for Knight's purposes. In a definitively probabilistic world, there could be no dispute in establishing all possible courses of action, evaluating the outcomes of each, and writing precise contracts. Knight points to three logical implications which are straightforward but momentous. Since all opportunities would be precisely defined there would be no possibility in an open society of outcompeting rivals and therefore no profit which was anything other than a disguised wage; for the same reason there would be no scope for entrepreneurship; and there would be no firms with employees because all economic activities could be regulated by contracts in which all parties would commit to specific actions (linked, if necessary, to a correctly defined set of contingencies) for known rewards. Indeed, Knight (1921: 268) argues, in such a world, all organisms would be automata, programmed to respond appropriately to all relevant stimuli. This would not, he suggests, be an attractive prospect for humans (ibid.: 348); but it is a world in which it seems highly unlikely that anything like present-day humans would have evolved. In particular, 'it is doubtful whether intelligence itself would exist in such a situation' (ibid.: 268).

By arguing that uncertainty is a precondition of intelligence, Knight is sharply distinguishing this human capacity from the ability to calculate optima, which requires the absence of uncertainty. It therefore offers to protect us from 'the error ... of imputing logical reason to men who could not or cannot base their actions on reason' (Barnard, 1938: 305), an error which, Barnard believes, impedes our understanding of the mental processes required to deal with many business problems. Though he does not use the terminology, Knight (1921: 206) associates intelligence with pattern-making: 'in order to live intelligently in our world, we must use the principle that things similar in some respects will behave similarly in certain other respects even when they are very different in still other respects'. In arguing that such classifications and connections must be appropriate to 'the purpose or problem in view', he is clearly allowing for multiple structures of knowledge, each with its own domain of application, while also acknowledging that the adjustment between structure and domain is problematic. As we shall see, the potential for diverse principles of order, each adapted to a particular domain, opens up the possibility of creating formal organizations with external boundaries and internal divisions which are designed to exploit particular knowledge structures, and also to develop new structures. In Marshall's (1920: 138) words, '[k]nowledge is our most powerful engine of production ... Organization aids knowledge; it has many forms', because different patterns are appropriate for different purposes or different problems – thus opening up the potential for entrepreneurship, and for entrepreneurial failure. It also provides a basis for explaining the difficulties, cited by Barnard (1938: 301–2), of adjusting to a new kind of work or achieving understanding between people from different backgrounds, both of which result from differently structured mental processes, directed to different objectives. These difficulties may create unanticipated problems following a merger, and provide everyday challenges for managers.

Knight's conception of intelligence is broadly compatible with the work of three extremely distinguished economists – though this work seems much more like psychology than most modern economics. The commonality, and some particular emphases, are worth investigating.

## Human mind and human knowledge

The most substantial account of the human mind is provided by Friedrich Hayek, who studied psychology as an experimental subject, including the dissection of brains as a means to understanding the physical processes involved. This led him to produce a theoretical manuscript, which was set aside for many years, then retrieved, reworked, and eventually published in 1952 as *The Sensory Order*. Hayek's fundamental proposition is that all human knowledge about our surroundings, and even ourselves, is not an imprint of reality but a mental – indeed neurological – construction.

> [T]he qualities which we attribute to the experienced objects are not qualities of that object at all, but a set of relationships by which our nervous system classifies them. … *all* we know about the world is of the nature of theories and all 'experience' can do is to change those theories. (Hayek, 1952: 143)

Such theories 'are generalizations about certain kinds of events, and since no number of particular instances can ever prove such a generalisation, knowledge based entirely on experience may yet be entirely false' (ibid.: 168). This is, in effect, a restatement of Hume's (1875: 33) demonstration of the insufficiency of induction: it is not possible that 'arguments from experience can prove this resemblance of the past to the future; since all these arguments are formulated on the supposition of that resemblance'.

Since all human knowledge is a created representation, more than one knowledge structure may develop to represent a particular phenomenon, or group of phenomena. Such alternative representations, Hayek argued, account for the frequent disparities between our sensory experience and the classifications developed by the physical sciences: objects which look alike may behave very differently, and objects which behave alike may appear to be very different (Hayek, 1952: 5–6). Hayek believes that the sensory and the physical orders both emerge from processes of trial and error, which lead to convergence within each order. However, they do not lead to a convergence between the two orders: each structure of knowledge is compatible with a domain of 'experience', but they are not compatible with each other. We may think of them as different paradigms which are not reducible to a common measure; but if so we must acknowledge that, in contrast to Kuhn's ([1962] 1970) theory of the succession of scientific paradigms, they continue to exist in parallel – presumably because they serve different purposes, as we shall shortly see. This is a warning that some human attributes are extremely resistant to change, as well as a reminder that such persistence does not exclude substantial potential for the creation of new knowledge through development within individual brains – though, as we shall see, there are substantial restrictions on the exploitation of this potential, and significant implications of the ways in which this is undertaken.

Hayek's theory of human knowledge as a set of representations which are created by the formation of selective neural connections offers the neurological equivalent of Adam Smith's theory of 'the science of the connecting principles of nature' (Smith, [1795] 1980: 45). Like Hayek, Smith was trying to understand the processes by which knowledge develops, recognizing that, as Hume (1978: 164) had observed, this could not be by deduction because 'no kind of reasoning can give rise to a new idea'. In offering an explicit account of the motivations which 'lead and direct' this process, including an explanation of how it shapes not only knowledge but the system of knowledge production through the progressive differentiation of sciences, Smith effectively complements Hayek's theory.

He focuses on the human reaction to the unexpected and the inexplicable and the human admiration for order; the link between them is supplied by imagination. The imagination 'anticipates … every event which falls out according to [the] ordinary course of things' and if this course is indeed followed, then '[t]here is no break, no stop, no gap, no interval. The ideas excited by so coherent a chain of things seem, as it were, to float through the mind of their own accord' (Smith, [1795] 1980: 41). But if this coherence is disturbed, and the disturbance is repeated, then there is an urgent need 'to introduce order into this chaos of jarring and discordant appearances, to allay this tumult of the imagination, and to restore it … to that tone of tranquillity and composure, which is both most agreeable in itself, and most suitable to its nature' (ibid.: 45–6). The creation of a new form of order is an imaginative act; it is neither an imprint of the phenomena nor deducible from them; and as Smith shows in tracing the succession of cosmological systems, it may subsequently be confronted with jarring and discordant appearances which stimulate efforts to create yet other forms of order. By insisting that Newton's cosmological theory is the product of Newton's imagination, Smith (ibid.: 105) admits the possibility that it might eventually meet the fate of its predecessors. In the broad sense, this is clearly an evolutionary theory of trial and error, in which success is always provisional – as in Popper's view of science (and also Kuhn's, despite their substantial differences).

### Order and imagination

It should be clear from Smith's theory of the growth of knowledge and from Hayek's theory of neurological structures that the fundamental cognitive capability of our species is not rationality but pattern-making, the crucial operation of which is the non-rational invention of new connections. This appears perfectly reasonable as soon as one recognizes that rationality is of very little use without the material on which it can work. This material is constructed within the human mind, and the construction is driven by a particular set of human motivations. As Smith notes, these motivations have a significant aesthetic dimension; he cites Copernicus's concern to replace the 'confusion, in which the old hypothesis represented the motions of the heavenly bodies' with a system in which 'these, the noblest works of nature, might no longer appear devoid of that harmony and proportion which discover themselves in her meanest productions' (Smith, [1795] 1980: 71). Smith even provides in advance an explanation for the co-existence of the sensory and physical orders for which Hayek supplied the mechanisms. Copernicus had transformed the earth from a stationary object, as our senses affirm, to a sphere in rapid and complex motion; and Smith (ibid.: 77) comments that

> [nothing can] more evidently demonstrate, how easily the learned give up the evidence of their senses to preserve the coherence of the ideas of their imagination, than the readiness with which this, the most violent paradox in all philosophy, was adopted by many ingenious philosophers.

The sensory order and the physical order can co-exist because they serve different purposes.

The appeal of imaginative constructions to deliver extensive connections through the application of simple principles receives attention in Smith's *Lectures on Rhetoric* when he considers the methods of communication that are most effective for different purposes. In giving an account of a system of science, we may take the several branches in turn and offer a specific explanation for each, or begin by defining a coherent structure which will account for them all. 'This latter which we may call the Newtonian method is undoubtedly the most philosophical, and in every science ... is vastly more ingenious and for that reason more engaging than the other' (Smith, 1983: 146). However, a more powerful appeal to the imagination is not a reliable indicator of truth; Smith immediately observes that it was not Newton but Descartes who first used this method, and was thereby able to gain with assent for 'a work which we justly esteem one of the most entertaining Romances that has ever been wrote'. The imaginative and aesthetic appeal of systems which present the appearance of comprehensive order may be observed, and experienced, in many contexts, not least within large and complex organizations; the preservation of order may become a powerful motive, overriding other considerations.

Smith's theory of the growth of knowledge included an explanation of the development of the knowledge-producing system, from the beginnings of specialization in what we now call pre-scientific activity, through an increase in the number of specialists as standards of living rose enough to support them, into a differentiation of focus among specialists, which encouraged the recognition of particular anomalies which were not apparent in a broader view and the incentive to imagine novel forms of order which would encompass them – without, as Smith notes, necessarily satisfying those who had specialized in other directions. This theory of the co-evolution of knowledge and the knowledge-creating system subsequently became the foundational principle of the *Wealth of Nations* (Smith, [1776] 1976b).

Why the division of labour should be so important is to be explained by the evolved potential of the human brain for creating new knowledge, coupled with the limitations on the range of applications which can be developed by any single person. Hayek (1952: 185) noted that 'the capacity of any explaining agent must be limited to objects with a structure possessing a degree of complexity lower than its own': even the most capacious human brain must trade off the breadth and depth of knowledge. However, by appropriate variation within a population, the total knowledge available to a community can be enormously greater than any single person, or single family, could attain. As Hayek emphasized, knowledge is dispersed and incomplete; and the only means of making it less incomplete is to allow it to become more dispersed. The limitations of individual cognition may be partly circumvented by the distribution of cognitive tasks between people. This, of course, raises new problems, not only in the allocation of these tasks, but in the destruction of self-sufficiency that it entails, requiring some arrangements to allow each person to benefit from the activities of others.

Adam Smith recognized that the growth and application of knowledge are inherently social processes; what appears to be a competitive economy with many independent agents is inherently a co-operative economy. He therefore considered the human characteristics which can support a co-operative economy and which influence its operation. Each person's first concern is his or her own welfare, which is appropriate because no outsider can be as well informed; this argument clearly supports a presumption for individual liberty and against state regulation. However, it does not lead to an argument for self-regarding individualism; on the contrary, Smith's systematic exploration of the bases of social order begins with a strong declaration of the principles which give everyone an interest 'in the fortune of others, and render their happiness necessary to him, though he derives nothing from it except the pleasure of seeing it' (Smith, [1759] 1976a: 9).

Imagination, by creating order, allows one person to understand another, and to envisage how others would view possible actions that he or she might perform. As well as benefiting from other people's knowledge, or the products of their knowledge which are embodied in artefacts, we may therefore draw on others as a guide to behaviour. By choosing to participate in groups and to conform to social norms, we greatly simplify our problems of deciding what to do, limiting the range of potential options and the factors to be taken into account in deciding between them to what is manageable, and making room for selective expressions of individuality. As the writer G.K. Chesterton remarked, 'a man must be orthodox on most things, or he will never have time to practise his own particular heresy'. This argument has also been made by Simon (2005), though without reference to Smith.

Underlying these possibilities is the capacity of the human brain to imitate apparently effective actions, which, while not unique to the human species, is certainly unparalleled in its extent, and essential to permit the rapid diffusion of new practices and new ideas which are fostered by finer divisions of labour. This ability to use others as resources tends to encourage an attitude that works against the incentive to act opportunistically, which has been emphasized by economists as a means of explaining the creation of firms as hierarchical structures. One should also note that opportunism makes cognitive demands, which may be substantial for the more complex schemes, and so it may often simply be crowded out. However, there are dangers which are more subtle and more pervasive than opportunism, as we shall see almost immediately.

These attitudes and activities provide an appropriate environment for the development of language, which would be both difficult and of very little value without a good deal of social interaction. Language allows people to indulge that delight in persuasion which Smith suggested was a major reason for the 'propensity to truck, barter and exchange'; this in turn was a necessary condition for the emergence of an extensive division of labour in economic life (Smith, [1776] 1976b: 25). The delight in persuasion, and the pleasure in doing deals for which it is a prerequisite, are characteristics to which we shall return; they are not prominent in most economic analysis or studies of organization.

This combination of an interest in others, the recognition of their value as a resource, delight in persuasion, and pleasure in doing deals, entails an important pathology. To facilitate persuasion and to protect valuable relationships, it may seem desirable to avoid, if possible, any action or any communication which might be resented by other people with whom we are interacting, and to judge what this entails by the characteristics which we attribute to these people. These attributions in turn are not tested because of the possibly unwelcome effects of explicit enquiry. Such behaviour may easily become self-reinforcing – an institutional pattern which appears to deliver good results while economizing cognitive and emotional resources – however, it prevents some potentially important kinds of learning (Argyris, 2004). These pathological consequences are likely to be particularly important in formal organizations, where the incentive to protect both one's own position and the group to which one belongs is likely to be especially powerful.

Smith's and Hayek's conceptions of the growth of knowledge as pattern-formation may be considered as inherently economic theories, because they are based on the fundamental concept of scarcity – the limitations of individual cognitive powers in relation to the potential demands and opportunities of each person's situation. The formation of patterns compresses the range of phenomena by assimilation, thus reducing demands on storage capacity, and allows repeated use of established connections in response to subsequent events, thus reducing demands on processing capacity and so leaving scope for the imagination of new schemes of order. It is in focusing on the interaction between creativity and routine that Alfred Marshall's model of the mind, developed as a young fellow of St John's College, Cambridge, offers the most valuable complementarity to Hayek's and Smith's accounts.

Arguing that the workings of the human brain could be represented by mechanism plus consciousness, Marshall (1994) devised a thought experiment to indicate how much might, in principle, be accomplished by mechanism. He took care to avoid any direct impact of the environment by postulating a machine in which a 'body' received impressions and took actions, while the 'brain' had contact only with the 'body' and was therefore required to work with 'ideas of impressions' and 'ideas of actions'. (As with Smith and Hayek, knowledge is constituted by created representations.) He then developed a simplified mechanistic version of the formation of classification systems and impression–action linkages by simple trial and error; success leads to the formation of routines, releasing resources for new sequences of trial and error for other purposes. He adds a second, more complex circuit, in which potential ideas of action are confronted with potential ideas of consequences in a kind of off-line experimentation based on imagination; this may avoid some costly errors, but requires so many resources that it must be used sparingly, requiring a full complement of routines which are already working well.

This emphasis on the preponderance of routine as a necessary condition for imagination is fully consistent with Hayek's and Smith's theories; it also facilitates both imitation and co-operation. Heiner (1983) argued that it is precisely because people do not react to the specific features of every situation, but to general and more readily observable characteristics, that much of their behaviour can be predicted and understood sufficiently to be either imitated or adjusted to. Choi (1993), who explicitly sets his analysis in the context of Knightian uncertainty, uses Heiner's work in arguing that the value of this understanding and the transferability of repeated action patterns lead to the diffusion of many conventions to guide private behaviour, and that this predisposition to adjust our actions to the apparently successful behaviour of others facilitates the emergence of those intersecting action patterns which are commonly called institutions. In turn, an extensive development of shared patterns of understanding and action, and of institutions as means of regulating interactions, often with no need for explicit agreement, greatly facilitates the establishment of formal organizations – if, indeed, they are not essential precursors.

## Organizations

Raffaelli (2003) has shown how Marshall's account of economic organization is related to two essential features of his model of the brain: the development of domain-limited cognitive structures and the dialectical relationship between automatic processes and imagination. Marshall (1920: 366) observes that it is 'necessary for man with his limited powers to go step by step; breaking up a complex question, studying one bit at a time, and at last combining his partial solutions into a more or less complete solution of the whole riddle'. Though this is his prescription for economic investigation, it is also his account of how the economic system works, by decomposition both between and within organizations. It is Simon's account too; but Simon (1969) also explains that it can work this way only because our complex universe has a hierarchical structure: the overall system is composed of major subsystems, each of which is composed of smaller subsystems, and so on for many levels; and at every level the behaviour of the system depends on its immediate components while it is this overall behaviour which contributes to performance at the next level above. Thus each level has a substantial degree of independent stability, which he argues is a major, and perhaps decisive, advantage in the evolution and preservation of a complex system.

'The boundedness of uncertainty is essential to the possibility of decision' (Shackle, 1969: 224); and firms set boundaries by the creation of pools of resources and defining areas of responsibility. We have already seen how and why every individual also needs both an internal cognitive structure and external linkages which supplement that structure and help to develop it; and the structure of every economic system provides many boundaries for many classes of decision. Marshall observed that every firm requires both an internal and an external organization; and this is also true of every industry and geographical area, including the special cases of industrial districts where the two overlap but never precisely coincide. If new ideas arise from making connections, it is the avoidance of many possible connections by what seems to be an appropriate decomposition which allows a focus on a particular system and gives protection against disturbance. The protection may, of course, be illusory, and its failure may prompt recrimination, cover up, and various actions of doubtful legality or morality.

Every formal organization is a **framing device**, based on a conjecture about the appropriate decomposition of an overall process into subdivisions which will focus attention on locally appropriate activities, thus stimulating the identification and resolution of problems and the imagination of opportunities. In defining the firm as 'a pool of resources the utilization of which is organized in an administrative framework' Penrose ([1959] 1995: 149) recognized that this framework provides a distinctive environment in which particular combinations of resources are developed, used to provide particular services, and directed towards particular opportunities, in what she noted is a smaller-scale version of **Schumpeterian** entrepreneurship (ibid.: 36n). Simon noted that complex human social and economic systems are not completely decomposable, but it may be thought that he did not give enough attention either to the problems that might result from unanticipated interactions or to the arrangements, formal and informal, that might emerge to avoid such problems. It is not surprising that people are often reluctant to change a familiar structure even when it no longer seems to deliver adequate results; as Smith noted, the appeal of attractive schemes of order can be very resistant to evidence.

The value of shared patterns of knowledge and behaviour and the automatic regulation of many activities explain why people are so often ready to accept '*a social prescription of some, but not all, of the premises that enter into an individual's choice of behaviors*' (Simon, 1982, 2: 345; italics in original); joining an organization may be attractive for this reason. Barnard (1938: 163) suggests that we should primarily think in terms of acceptance rather than enforcement: 'the decision as to whether an order has authority or not lies with the persons to whom it is addressed, and does not reside in "persons of authority" or those who issue those orders'. A prime function of every manager is to ensure, both by his general conduct and in specific instances, that the recipients of his communications will accept them as authoritative. However, we should not forget that even a CEO must decide whether to treat as authoritative all kinds of messages received from all kinds of people; and of course none of us could function if we were not willing to accept the word of many other people in appropriate contexts. By an apparent paradox, authority is a matter of trust – not only in intentions (on which economists have concentrated) but also in competence (Casson, 1997: 94). In simple terms, one can decide to trust, or not to trust, a particular person in a particular situation; a decision to trust is a refutable conjecture, and therefore an opportunity of learning, whereas a decision not to trust offers no opportunity of learning – as does a decision (often implicit) not to test any other characteristic which has been attributed to another person. The potential for learning, and the potential costs may of course vary enormously across people and situations; and so therefore should reasonable decisions.

### Formal and informal organization

As Barnard emphasizes, every formal organization requires the support of an informal organization – but compatibility between the two is not guaranteed. Organizations incubate their own institutions within their own contexts, notably by providing opportunities not only to undertake experiments in trust but also to observe experiments made by others. Partly by prescription, partly by the internal structure, and partly through their own interpretations of the behaviour and the outcomes which they observe, every member of an organization internalizes notions of what to think about and who should be asked or told about what, thus shaping the allocation of what Simon called 'the scarce resource of attention'. The practices which result from these notions, of course, may be at variance with the organizational design, and may require the protection of nominal conformity and selective omission. Such interlinking practices constitute the routines which Nelson and Winter (1982) defined as the skills of an organization. These skills produce efficient performance of standardized activities (even if this is not exactly the efficiency that the senior management are, at least nominally, aiming to achieve); they also provide the elements for new combinations, and release the cognitive resources which may conceive the possibility of such combinations and shape these new combinations to deliver successful outcomes. All this is set out by Penrose ([1959] 1995), though since there are no demonstrably correct ways either of choosing between ideas or of turning ideas into effective products and services, releasing cognitive resources is not sufficient to guarantee their successful deployment.

In his early model of cognition, Marshall recognized that machines of identical design might easily develop different routines, either because they were operating in different environments or because they happened to try out different ideas which were good enough to establish connections that were sufficiently effective to end the sequence of trials. In his subsequent account of the working of economic systems, this potential for emergent variety supported the proposition that knowledge is likely to grow faster if the division of labour is supplemented by variation within each specialism. Marshall assumed that this variation would more often occur between firms than within them, because he associated it with differences between individuals and their situation, but he included among the faculties required in a successful businessman

> a power of first choosing his assistants rightly and then trusting them fully; of interesting them in the business and of getting them to trust him, so as to bring out whatever enterprise and power of origination there is in them. (Marshall, 1920: 297–8)

To bring out the enterprise and power of origination that is latent in members of an organization seems to be what is intended by a policy of 'empowerment'. This is therefore not a new idea; moreover it was reinvented between forty and fifty years ago as an emphasis, notably by McGregor (1960) and Drucker (1964), on the role of personal achievement as a motivator, leading to suggestions for organizations to change their ways to produce both greater internal satisfaction and improved performance; and for a time the concept of 'management by objectives', in which managers would be encouraged to agree on a set of objectives towards which they would work according to their own ideas, became fashionable in Britain. However, there was a fundamental ambiguity in this scheme; one enthusiastic advocate explained to me that it was a perfect means of obtaining precise commitments which would allow no excuse for failure and so make dismissal easy. Argyris (2004: 21) cites statements by three CEOs who appear to be sincere believers in empowerment but nevertheless emphasize its value in ensuring that processes are 'reliable, repeatable and in control'.

Marshall was clearly aware of the tendency in large firms for the suppression of variety, either in the interests of co-ordination or simply because so much of the activity was inwardly focused that only a few members would make the external contacts that tend to set the imagination speculating on possible new forms of order. More recent ideas about the power of forecasting, the potential for deductive reasoning, systems of targets and performance measurement, and recipes for business success (some of which appear to be highly profitable, at least for their authors) may also suggest that variety is wasteful. However, although routines may reduce the demands on cognitive resources, they do not ensure that these resources are then directed to imaginative conjectures; and of course routines may themselves expand (with encouragement from those who devise and monitor them) to fill the time available. Moreover, no method of setting bounds to uncertainty can guarantee that the uncertainty which is excluded is irrelevant to the decision-making which occurs within those bounds.

## Decision cycles

In standard economics, decision-making has a simple structure. There is a set of possible actions, each of which is associated with a set of possible consequences; and the decision-maker chooses the action with the most attractive set of consequences, as judged by the decision-maker's preference set. However, we need to enquire, not only how any decision-maker acquires the relevant knowledge about possible actions and their consequences, but how a particular issue comes to be identified as an occasion for decision.

As we have seen, the contrast between the potential of the human mind and its limited processing and storage capacity implies a continuing problem of deciding what to think about – and even the word 'deciding' in that phrase is open to question. Nor can we assume that the recognition of an occasion for decision carries with it a set of possible responses, or that such a set can be deduced from the situation. Simon has suggested that the process of decision-making should be divided into three phases: 'finding occasions for making a decision; finding possible courses of action; and choosing among courses of action' (Simon, 1965: 54), which he summarizes as intelligence, design and choice. He also recognizes that carrying out a decision requires a further decision, or series of decisions, which requires specific attention by decision-makers and by those who wish to analyse either individual or business behaviour. However, he is prepared to treat making and implementing decisions as separate, if related, units of analysis (ibid.: 56), whereas there are significant advantages in treating the sequence as a single unit, and indeed extending it to include a subsequent review of outcomes. This extended sequence was proposed by a former colleague, David Clarke, who chose to call the last phase 'control', in the accountant's sense.

Including implementation as a phase of the decision process allows us to consider whether implementation is actually included in the original specifi cation of the problem, and also to enquire which of the people involved in the process takes an interest in implementation. An experienced consultant, reflecting on his experiences, found it fairly easy to divide his colleagues into two groups: those who defined the success of a consultancy project as the successful implementation of the consultants' report, and those who defined it by the client's acceptance of that report, taking no interest in what happened afterwards. These two motivations are likely to lead to different definitions of the consultancy assignment, different decision processes, and different outcomes. The same, of course, may be true within a large organization: success in a research department may be judged by delivery to manufacturing, success in manufacturing may be judged by handover to marketing, and success in marketing may be judged by success in devising a specification for a new product which may nevertheless be impossible to produce at an adequate level of quality and at a reasonable cost.

As with implementation, arrangements for review may also be included in the problem specification, and here too whether it is or not may influence the choice of action; it is even possible that some of those involved will wish to avoid the possibility of a clear retrospective assessment in order to escape responsibility in case of failure. Whether or not a provision for such assessment is included in the course of action that is chosen, any subsequent review, in Clarke's (unpublished) words, 'will provide a stimulus to the appreciation of new events or to a new and better understanding of old facts and this will ultimately lead to the revising of old decisions and the taking of new ones', thus (in Simon's phrase) 'finding occasions for making a decision'. If the decision-making process is not very effective, then the management of a complex project may provide the spectacle of an organization 'lurching around the decision cycle, cannoning off the constraints', as a former colleague summarized the history of an attempt at innovation in a major company.

Clarke also pointed out that each phase of a decision cycle might exhibit its own complete sub-cycle. The process of deciding whether a particular situation does indeed justify the time and effort that would be needed to formulate and implement a new course of action may include an initial perception, the design of possible ways of testing this perception, the choice of one or more of these possibilities, carrying out these tests, and a review of the results – which might raise the question whether further work might be desirable. Deciding how to construct an appropriate set of possible actions, how to choose between them, how to carry out the selected action, and how to judge the outcome may similarly entail mini-cycles. There may be recourse to short-cuts, for example, drawing on a standard repertoire of actions or a simple rule for choice; in the limit there may be a direct link between perception and action which reduces the process to a simple routine. Because of the limits of human cognition, supplemented by the need for low-cost co-ordination between people, most decision cycles must be greatly compressed, and even when a problem is receiving careful attention, many sub-problems and sub-sub-problems will receive cursory treatment; a very important part of learning how to act effectively, in a profession or an organization, is developing a sense – which is at least semi-automatic – of what short-cuts are appropriate when.

It is characteristic of complex problems that the phases of each major decision cycle are likely to be decomposed to groups who are thought to have the appropriate technical skills or organizational experience and responsibilities. These groups may include people who are not members of the organization; indeed, some groups may consist wholly of outsiders. Consultants provide the obvious example (and, as previously observed, they introduce new motivations as well as new skills); but it may be instructive to think of outsourcing as a way of distributing the overall problem of running a successful business into organizationally differentiated decision cycles. The potential gain from outsourcing lies in the advantages of the division of labour: because of its distinctive focus, an organizationally distinct supplier may be able to develop better practices and generate novel ideas which would not occur to people in the customer organization. The potential danger is that some of these practices and ideas will not match those requirements of the customer which are not specified because they are assumed to be obvious. This danger may apparently be avoided if outsourcing is achieved by spinning-off a well-established department; but over time the members of that department will change, and the practices and working assumptions of the separated businesses will be modified in ways which are not communicated between them. Whatever the scheme of decomposition, there is always the possibility that it will elicit solutions in search of problems, which may be promoted for intellectual or emotional satisfaction as well as to enhance salary or status.

To explain what is identified as a problem we may turn to Cyert and March's (1963) theory of business behaviour. Here managers are motivated by a shortfall of achievement compared with aspiration, whereas achievement in excess of aspiration creates managerial slack; this frees managerial resources for other purposes, which may range from self-indulgence or schemes of self-advancement to the imagination of new products, as explained by Penrose ([1959] 1995). Pounds (1969), who had worked with Simon, Cyert and March, generalized this idea with the proposition that problems are defined by differences, and suggested three categories of reference standards which could generate such differences within firms: (1) historical – some record or recollection of a past situation deemed relevant; (2) external – the apparent situation in some other supposedly relevant context; and (3) planning – the situation that had been intended. It is convenient to add a fourth category, suggested by a manager of innovation, of imaginative standards – some imagined possibility which will require fresh action to create. Both Schumpeterian 'new combinations' and the more modest redirection of resources towards productive opportunities which shape the growth of Penrosian firms are driven by the need to make and implement decisions which will turn imagined futures into reality; indeed, the imagination of possible futures that require present action to achieve (or, if unwelcome, to avoid) is an important function of long-range planning (Loasby, 1967).

Now it is immediately obvious that the appropriateness of each of these reference standards is always debatable – not only whether the category is relevant but whether the particular instance is: what particular historical episode (and whose interpretation of it), which other organization (or even which other part of our own organization), which plan or target, which idea for change should be allowed to absorb our time, thought and effort. Different individuals may disagree, and these disagreements will often be associated with the implications of the choice of reference standard for personal or departmental responsibilities. Especially when the problem appears complex, an elaborate decision process, perhaps involving several turns around the decision cycle, may be required, and its incidence may fall very unevenly within the organization; members of one department may feel that they are being expected to do most of the work on someone else's problem, when they have much better things to do.

On the other hand, being designated as crucial to success may be used as a source of power, especially if those in other parts of the organization and its senior management are unable to judge the reasonableness of demands for additional resources. The thesis that power within an organization tends to accrue to those who are in a position to manage critical dependencies was developed by Pfeffer and Salancik (1978) with particular reference to transactions across the firm's boundaries: for example, whether customers, skilled labour, government contracts or finance are seen (or can be plausibly portrayed) as the most crucial determinant of success. Promotion to the board and the prospect of succession as CEO may be at stake. There may be important pathologies in such situations. It does not seem to be a coincidence that the major US financial scandals of recent years occurred in companies which had become stock market favourites and had therefore become dependent on reporting profits which matched earlier high expectations in order to ensure a continuing flow of funds. It seems likely that the incentives to preserve status and finance were also supported by the powerful motivation to preserve visions of a new order, based on such notions as the revolutionary impact of internet-based trading or the revelation of methods of pricing options which abolished uncertainty.

## Conclusion

'Much of the error of historians, economists, and all of us in daily affairs arises from imputing logical reason to men who could not or cannot base their actions on reason' (Barnard, 1938: 305). There is scope for reason, but this scope is defined by the patterns which serve as representations of the phenomena or situations about which we try to reason; and as has been shown by various writers, some of whom have been cited here, there is no demonstrably correct way to form patterns – and, indeed, pattern formation is by no means entirely under conscious control. Where rationality cannot suffice, the best available alternative is trial and error, and the normal result in any particular case is failure. Moreover, as financial advisers ritually acknowledge, past performance is no guarantee of future success. Indeed, over a long run, continued success tends to lead either to slow decline or rapid collapse, because it becomes very difficult for individuals to abandon a complex interpretative structure which has worked very well, and even more difficult for an organized collection of individuals simultaneously to abandon an interlocking network of such structures.

George Kelly (1963) explained how individuals suffered personal breakdowns through being locked into an interpretative framework which could neither cope with the situations being currently encountered nor be amended without disrupting critical interpretations which were still serviceable – and often apparently indispensable. Like Smith, Marshall and Hayek, Kelly recognizes that any such framework must be a representation, which is at best appropriate within a limited range, of a system which is only partly decomposable; he also notes that '*time is the ultimate bond*' (Kelly, 1963: 6; italics in original). Such breakdowns can certainly happen to individuals within organizations; moreover, because the functioning of organizations depends on highly imperfect representations of the relationships between individual (and departmental) responsibilities and activities whole organizations may find no acceptable way of responding to threatening situations. As Argyris has long argued, in organizations (as in many interpersonal relationships), there are often important issues which are undiscussable; and this undiscussability may itself be undiscussable, even – or perhaps especially – when the whole structure of assumptions is in question. We should not therefore be surprised that 'successful co-operation in or by formal organization is the abnormal, not the normal condition. What are observed … are the successful survivors among innumerable failures.' It was this observation that prompted Barnard's (1938: 5) analysis of the functioning of organizations.

## References

Argyris, Chris (2004) *Reasons and Rationalizations: The Limits to Organizational Knowledge*. Oxford: Oxford University Press.

Barnard, Chester I. (1938) *The Functions of the Executive*. Cambridge, MA: Harvard University Press.

Casson, Mark (1997) *Information and Organization*, Oxford: Clarendon Press.

Choi, Young B. (1993) *Paradigms and Conventions: Uncertainty, Decision Making and Entrepreneurship*. Ann Arbor, MI: University of Michigan Press.

Cyert, Richard M. and March, James G. (1963) *A Behavioral Theory of the Firm*. Englewood Cliffs, NJ: Prentice-Hall.

Drucker, Peter F. (1964) *Managing for Results*. London: Heinemann.

Hayek, Friedrich A. (1952) *The Sensory Order*. Chicago: The University of Chicago Press.

Heiner, Ronald A. (1983) 'The origin of predictable behavior', *American Economic Review*, 73: 560–95.

Hume, David (1875) *Essays Moral, Political and Literary*, vol. 2, ed. T. H. Green, and T.H. Grose, London: Longmans, Green and Co.

Hume, David (1978) *A Treatise on Human Nature*, ed. L.A. Selby-Bigge, 2nd edn, revised by P.H. Nidditch. Oxford: Oxford University Press.

Kelly, George A. (1963) *A Theory of Personality*. New York: W.W. Norton.

Knight, Frank H. (1921) *Risk, Uncertainty and Profit*. Boston: Houghton Mifflin.

Kuhn, Thomas S. ([1962] 1970) *The Structure of Scientific Revolutions*. Chicago: The University of Chicago Press.

Loasby, Brian J. (1967) 'Long-range formal planning in perspective', *Journal of Management Studies*, 4(3): 300–8.

McGregor, Douglas H. (1960) *The Human Side of Enterprise*. New York: McGraw-Hill.

Marshall, Alfred (1920) *Principles of Economics*, 8th edn. London: Macmillan.

Marshall, Alfred (1994) 'Ye machine', in *Research in the History of Economic Thought and Methodology, Archival Supplement 4*. Greenwich, CT: JAI Press, pp. 116–32.

Nelson, Richard R. and Winter, Sidney G. (1982) *An Evolutionary Theory of Economic Change*. Cambridge, MA: Belknap Press.

Penrose, Edith T. ([1959] 1995) *The Theory of the Growth of the Firm*. Oxford: Oxford University Press.

Pfeffer, Jeffrey and Salancik, Gerald R. (1978) *The External Control of Organizations: A Resource Dependence Perspective*. New York: Harper and Row (reprinted, 2003, Stanford, CA: Stanford University Press).

Pounds, William F. (1969) 'The process of problem finding', *Industrial Management Review*, 11: 1–19.

Prigogine, Ilya (2005) 'The rediscovery of value and the opening of economics', in Kurt Dopfer, (ed.), *The Evolutionary Foundations of Economics*. Cambridge: Cambridge University Press.

Raffaelli, Tiziano (2003) *Marshall's Evolutionary Economics*. London: Routledge.

Shackle, George L.S. (1969) *Decision, Order and Time in Human Affairs*, 2nd edn. Cambridge: Cambridge University Press.

Shackle, George L.S. (1972) *Epistemics and Economics*. Cambridge: Cambridge University Press.

Simon, Herbert A. (1965) *The Shape of Automation for Men and Management*. New York: Harper and Row.

Simon, Herbert A. (1969) *The Sciences of the Artificial*. Cambridge, MA: MIT Press.

Simon, Herbert A. (1982) *Models of Bounded Rationality*. 2 vols. Cambridge, MA: MIT Press.

Simon, Herbert A. (1985) 'Human nature in politics', *American Political Science Review*, 79: 293–304.

Simon, Herbert A. (2005) 'Darwinism, altruism and economics', in Kurt Dopfer, (ed.), *The Evolutionary Foundations of Economics*. Cambridge: Cambridge University Press.

Smith, Adam ([1759] 1976a) *The Theory of Moral Sentiments*, ed. A.L. Macfie and D.D. Raphael. Oxford: Oxford University Press.

Smith, Adam ([1776] 1976b) *An Inquiry into the Nature and Causes of the Wealth of Nations*, ed. R.H. Campbell, A.S. Skinner and W.B. Todd. Oxford: Oxford University Press.

Smith, Adam ([1795] 1980) 'The principles which lead and direct philosophical enquiries: illustrated by the history of astronomy', *Essays on Philosophical Subjects*, ed. W.P.D. Wightman and J.C. Bryce. Oxford: Oxford University Press.

Smith, Adam (1983) *Essays on Rhetoric and Belles Lettres*, ed. J.C. Bryce. Oxford: Oxford University Press.

## Suggestions for further reading

Argyris, Chris (2004) 'Introduction', in *Reasons and Rationalizations: The Limits to Organizational Knowledge*. Oxford: Oxford University Press.

Barnard, Chester I. (1938) Chapter 11 'The economy of incentives' and Chapter 13 'The environment of decision', in *The Functions of the Executive*. Cambridge, MA: Harvard University Press.

Loasby, Brian J. (2000) 'Decision premises, decision cycles and decomposition', *Industrial and Corporate Change*, 9(4): 709–31.

Pfeffer, Jeffrey and Salancik, Gerald R. ([1978] 2003) 'Organization and social context defined', in *The External Control of Organizations: A Resource Dependence Perspective*. Stanford, CA: Stanford University Press.

Simon, Herbert A. (1969) 'The architecture of complexity' (esp. pp. 84–102), in *The Sciences of the Artificial*. Cambridge, MA: MIT Press.

# SEVEN

## Crime and Culture
### Corporate Crime and Criminal Justice in a Different Cultural Environment

*Omi Hatashin*

## Introduction

This chapter aims to discuss and illustrate the ways in which the law deals with corporate crime in Japan in its cultural environment, which is different from that of the West. (In this chapter, the West primarily refers to Western Europe, North America, Australia, New Zealand, etc.)

This chapter gives a specific focus on the question of corporate '*mens rea*' (the *moral* element of a crime, as the French put it).[1] A criminal offence consists of a 'moral' or 'mental' element, e.g., malice aforethought, negligence, etc., and a 'physical' element (*actus reus*), e.g. the killing of a man. It is the 'mental' element which distinguishes between murder and manslaughter. The question here is whether or not a corporation has a 'mind' (*mens*), as distinct from an individual's mind, which can be the subject matter (*res*) of criminal proceedings; or how to define the *moral* element of corporate crime.

Different countries approach this question differently. The United States (federal common law), for example, punishes a corporate employer 'vicariously' for an offence committed by an employee within the scope of employment and on behalf of the corporation, even where no individual employee is convicted.[2] A corporation may be deemed to have a guilty knowledge (*mens rea*) even where different employees come by different parts of the knowledge but do not share the whole between them.[3] The Netherlands Penal Code (as amended in 1976) recognises that a juristic person (corporation) can commit a crime in its own right under Article 51. The corporation's *mens rea* is supposed to be gathered or collected from the criminal mental elements of those individuals whose conduct is seen to be the corporation's conduct in some *social* context, as distinct from the individuals' legal relationship with the corporation (de Doelder, 1996: 304). The French Penal Code (as amended in 2004) punishes juristic persons where an offence is committed on their account by their organs or representatives (Article 121–2). The law in England and Wales punishes 'bodies corporate' both under the common law and statutes unless the contrary intention appears in statutes.[4] The common law deems the *mens rea* of an individual officer, who is identified as the controlling mind of a body corporate in question, to be the *mens rea* of the body corporate.[5] In Germany, a juristic person cannot commit any crime[6] under any law, whether Code, statute, regulation whatsoever, although a juristic person (and unincorporated association) may be ordered to pay 'mending money' (*Geldbuße*), which is not a punishment, for a 'regulation breach' (*Ordnungswidrigkeit*), which is not a crime, done by its organ (and representative, respectively)[7] (Tiedemann, 1989: 157).

The law of Germany is not extreme, as a Lord Chancellor of England is reported to have said (Coffee, 1981: 386; French, 1984: 187), 'Did you ever expect a corporation to have a conscience, when it has no soul to be damned and no body to be kicked?'

Even so, some countries do punish corporations, and Japan, as examined below, is no exception in this respect. There are a variety of reasons why these countries do. It is necessary, for example, to deprive an illicit business of money which has been procured and pooled in a company, in order to teach a lesson that the illicit business does not pay. The target may be an illicit business or illicit business conduct. A penalty is also necessary to reinforce the administrative supervision and control of corporate business activities. There is potentially another reason: that is a collective 'guilty mind' (*mens rea*) on the part of a business organization whether incorporated or not,[8] which is not reducible to the mind of any individual member of that organization.

As a matter of social reality, company directors, managers and employees tend to be reduced to 'anonymous functionaries', less personal and less autonomous in decision-making, than a self-employed person or than themselves when they are outside the corporate context e.g. Mr Smith, Mrs Cox, John or Mary. In other words, individuals are technically reduced to 'cells' making up a number of 'organs' comprising an organization. It is actually wrong to say that a business organization is an 'abstract', because people make it up. In reality activities of an organization are collective activities. Its mental or managerial or directory function is discharged *between* functionaries, often at divergent levels, and is often not reducible to any particular individual. A brain itself actually consists of a great number of cells. Its proper function rests on the extremely rapid and extremely well co-ordinated transmission of an immense volume of information *between* the cells. It may be actually wrong to reduce the invisible concept of 'mind' to the function of the brain. The human mind exists across the cells comprising the whole body. Similarly, it is probably wrong to assume that the guilty mind (*mens rea*) can only exist in a single individual. Where individuals are reduced to functionaries of an organization, and have thereby lost their full 'individual' capacities, in other words, they are no longer 'indivisible' units of self-determination; the guilty mind of the organization exists *between* functionaries, and often not merely between the members of the board of directors. It is hoped that the exploration of some Japanese examples in this chapter will shed some light on this rather difficult question of the *moral* element of corporate crime.

A cultural issue, which may be pertinent to this question, is that the degree to which an individual is reduced to a functionary in business organizations seems to be generally greater in Japan than in the West. Of course, different companies have different 'cultures' in this respect. For example, Mitsubishi Motors and Honda Motors seem to share little in common except that they are car manufacturers. The question here is a somewhat broader comparison.

There are some stereotypical background reasons why Japan is different from the West. First, trade unions in Japan tend to be organized company by company, not *across* companies. Second, the system of employment for life, which some observe to have been eroding in recent years but without the development of a free labour market, has enforced the loyalty of individual employees to their company. The erosion at the system's peripheries apparently tends to strengthen the loyalty and obedience on the part of individual employees, who are seen to be 'dispensable at any time'. Third, the now eroding practice of 'cross-share holding', in which those companies belonging to the same group or family of companies hold their shares among themselves, has long defied the very idea of 'public' companies, even among those 'companies by shares', which are listed on the first division of the Tokyo Stock Exchange. The concept of corporate accountability (to shareholders) and that of corporate governance (of the high managerial 'agents' supposedly acting on behalf of the shareholders who own the market value of a company) have had little real foundation in Japan, at least until very recently. There is *still* quite a long way to go to make these concepts have some bearing on the Japanese realities.

Against such a backdrop, a company, especially in the Japanese context, tends to become a moral whole and its individual members its derivatives. Put in another way, a company tends to become a closed moral community in which individual members are ethically so inward-looking that they are often unable to see any higher moral value outside their company. A quasi-religious education which still tends to be practised in Japanese companies, such as early morning exercises and gatherings to sing a company's anthem, to recite its mottoes, to salute its flag or logo or an image of its establisher, etc., actually reminds the pre-war generation of the school education directed by the army in which they were taught to sacrifice everything down to their own lives for the Emperor. To the extent that the Emperor at that time was an anonymous embodiment of absolute authority for ordinary children, a company seems to have replaced the Emperor easily after 1945. As Japan before 1945 represented self-aggrandisement at the expense of others' lives and a 'culture of non-compliance' with the norms of the society of nations, the widespread copying of the imperial education at the company level may appear alarming for the promotion of corporate social responsibility. It follows that it may be more necessary in Japan than in the West to punish corporate crime.

How correct are these observations and what bearing might these observed realities have on Japanese law? These clearly represent the kinds of issues which this chapter has to address: the questions of corporate crime and organizational business ethics. It is also hoped that the Japanese examples will give the audience some insight into the situations in the societies of the Koreans and the Chinese, who, traditionally, shared relatively similar cultural and social patterns of behaviour with the Japanese, even if primarily in the eyes of the West.

## Japanese law

Somewhat unfortunately, the current law of Japan derives almost entirely from modern (pre-war) Franco-German law with some US influence and only a few elements seem to have survived the modernization/Westernization. It is known that the pre-modern Japanese had no vocabulary for 'individual' and they did not hesitate to punish individuals comprising a group 'jointly and severally'. In other words, vicarious punishment was not rare. They also punished a group as such by banning its business operations in the City of Yedo (Tokyo), and imposing that which the English used to call 'community service', although there was admittedly no distinction between the administrative measure and the judicial measure at that time. After the modernization, the Japanese tended to consider their past practice as bad and barbarous.

Currently, the six Codes, namely, the Constitutional Code, the Civil Code, the Commercial Code, the Civil Procedure Code, the Penal Code and the Penal Procedure Code, set the general principles and basic rules in the respective areas of law. These are contrasted with statutes, which are supposed to be 'special' and 'particular'. For example, the Ministry of Justice's yearly Crimes White Paper differentiates between the 'Offences under the Penal Code' and 'Offences under Special Legislation'. The nuance is that statutes are improvised by some exceptional necessity.

### The Penal Code

Japan's Penal Code, which was promulgated in 1907, has no explicit general provision making a juristic person criminally liable, even after a series of subsequent amendments to this day. However, the principle under Article 38 that no act is punishable without *dolus* (intent),[9] which is personal and subjective, has long been interpreted to deny that a juristic person (corporation) which is deemed to have no personal and subjective intent of its own, is able to commit a crime: *societas delinquere non potest* (Dando, 1978: 63 and 113).

The Penal Code actually has the offence of 'homicide by occupational negligence'.[10] The word 'occupation' or 'profession or business' is, in practice, construed widely and does not need to be connected with commercial activities. For example, driving a car is an 'occupation' for this purpose. This offence carries the same consequences as 'homicide by gross negligence (*culpa lata*)'.[11] In other words, a higher standard of care is expected of those who practise something, just as English law differentiates between the standards of care of a reasonable man, 'driver', 'engineer', 'medical practitioner', etc., case by case, without inventing a generic word for those in inverted commas.

In theory, negligence is different from *dolus* (intent) so that the personal and subjective intent principle, *supra*, does not necessarily apply here. Moreover, the very idea of 'occupational negligence', i.e. punishing a person on account of his 'occupational and objective' duty of care, as opposed to 'personal and subjective' fault (*culpa*), seems more than sufficient to exclude the application of the principle.[12] In addition, this offence is punishable by a fine. Nevertheless, so far, no juristic person has ever been prosecuted for this offence in practice.

Japan's Penal Procedure Code, which was completely revised in 1948, does have a provision defining procedural arrangements in cases where a juristic person is a suspect or a defendant (Art. 27). However, such a procedural or 'adjectival' provision is regarded as incapable of influencing the interpretation of the substantive law. So far, the Grand Court of Judicature ruling in 1935 that a juristic person is not punishable without some statutory basis to that effect,[13] remains intact.

Among academics, there have been proponents of the theory of corporate *mens rea*, of whom the late Professor Hideo Fujiki (1972: 136–8), and Professor Hiroshi Itakura (1973: 21) were pioneers. As shall be discussed later, *infra*, their theory, has influenced the application of the occupational negligence manslaughter, *supra*, in some cases. However, their argument tends to be 'ought to be' rather than 'is'. On balance, few academics seem to interpret that a juristic person is criminally liable under the current Penal Code (Maeda, 2006, pp. 100, Suda, 1998: 977 ff.).

Japan seems so far very unlikely to follow the French development from 1992 to 2004 in which the Penal Code made a juristic person punishable (Art. 121–2), let alone the Netherlands' 1976 amendment to the Penal Code (Art. 51). This is partly because virtually no useful statistical data has been compiled in the Crimes White Paper since 2000, with respect to the commission of offences by juristic persons (Hideo Takasaki, a prosecutor of the Tokyo Superior Prosecution Service, letter addressed to the present author, 2006). This has been the case despite the substantial changes in the law of juristic persons, which were completed in 2006.

## Statutes

Unlike German law, however, Japanese statutes do punish juristic persons. The relevant statutory provisions have been explained to be 'exceptions' under the proviso of Article 8 of the Penal Code, which otherwise makes its General Part provisions applicable to the statutory and regulatory offences.

*Legislative history*   The first statute, which made a juristic person punishable was an 'Act concerning cases where juristic persons have committed offences related to taxes and the monopoly of leaf tobaccos' (Statute of the 33rd Year of Meiji, i.e. 1900, No. 52). About a hundred pieces of legislation in the fields of taxation and the regulation of a variety of industrial activities, followed or applied the relevant provisions of this Act (Utsuro, 1984: 183): 'Where the representative or an employee or other similar operative of a juristic person has breached on account of the juristic person's business, the punishments of relevant provisions shall apply to the juristic person' (Art. 1).

The rationale behind the provisions is obviously to punish the 'principal', in financial terms, of some illicit business conduct (i.e. the pool of the proceeds of an offence), which was committed by its 'agent' (broadly construed). Japanese law first imposed a criminal 'vicarious liability' upon a juristic person. It is not clear whether the agent had to be prosecuted and convicted as well. Nor is the nature of the moral element of the corporate criminal liability clear under this 1900 formula of provisions (Utsuro, 1984: 183). In the late 1920s, however, Parliament desisted from enacting such 'corporate' criminal vicarious liability provisions, but instead, made provisions punishing the individual representative of a juristic person 'vicariously' for breaches by employees.

In 1932, an 'Act for Preventing the Flight of Capital' (Statute of the 7th Year of Showa, No. 17), which became the Foreign Exchange Control Act (8th Showa, 28), the following year, had introduced a new formula to punish a juristic person:

> Where either the representative of a juristic person, or an agent or servant or other similar operative of a juristic or natural person, has committed the breach of on account of the business of the juristic or natural person, the person who committed the breach as well as the said juristic or natural person shall be punished by the said Article's fine.

This 1932 formula restored the 1900 formula in order to punish the business 'principal', this time, not only a juristic person but also a natural person, for the conduct of its business 'agent' (broadly construed). Because the 1932 formula made it explicit (unlike the 1900 one) to punish *both* the direct culprit and his business principal, the formula is called *Ryoubatsu Kitei* 'provisions to punish *both*'.[14]

There are two judicial authorities on the nature of the corporate liability under the 1932 formula of statutory provisions. In 1957, the Supreme Court (Grand Chamber) rejected the strict liability theory, i.e. liability without the guilty mind (*mens rea*), and ruled that some negligence, e.g., some breach of such a duty of care as was necessary to prevent the relevant breach, should be presumed on the part of the business principal who was statutorily made punishable along with the direct culprit.[15] The business principal in this case happened to be a natural person. In 1965, the Supreme Court (Petit Chamber) further ruled that negligence should be presumed on the part of a business principal who happened to be a juristic person.[16] But the Court did not give any explanation as to the exact nature of such 'corporate negligence' and its relationship with the *mens rea* of the individual defendant.

Did the Supreme Court recognize in 1965 the idea of 'corporate *mens rea*'? Apparently, yes. However, technically, the fact that the 1965 ruling was that of a Petit Chamber suggests that the authority is tainted. To recognise corporate *mens rea*, as distinct from individual *mens rea* is a radical departure from the case law, which can only be decided properly by a Grand Chamber.

So far, the 1965 ruling has not been overruled. At the same time, it has never been applied to any Code offence. Nor has there been any ruling, which elaborates on the nature of the corporate *mens rea* under the 1965 ruling.

In 1981, an amendment to the Act Against Monopolies (22nd Showa, 54) introduced a further innovation to the 1932 formula, making the representative of a business organization (whether incorporated or not) punishable along with the organization and direct culprits (Art. 95–2). This provision, which seems to be unique to this Act, was never used as of 1992 (Shibahara, 1992: 42). The nature of these apparent vicarious liabilities is not explained. So far, there are no statutory provisions making a middle manager punishable. The criminal liability of an unincorporated association has some examples in the Act Against Monopolies (Art. 95 (2)), the Securities and Exchange Act (23rd Showa, 25, Art. 207), etc.

In terms of the number of statutes making a juristic person punishable, it is voluminous and overwhelming in percentage. In the early 1980s, there were no less than 470 pieces of legislation which contained provisions whereby to punish juristic persons by fines, of some 700 pieces of legislation then in force (Itoya, 1984: 188). It is difficult to have up to date statistics here because of the subsequent changes in the way in which statistics have been compiled, but the number of such statutes has no doubt increased substantially by now (2007). The Crimes White Paper 2005 has a list of a number of cases which have been brought to the Public Prosecution Service with respect to offences under 42 statutes (on pp. 148–9). The criteria for the selection of these statutes are not clear, but they supposedly include those statutory offences most frequently being brought to the attention of the prosecutors. Out of the 42 statutes, 34, comprising more than 80 per cent, have provisions making a juristic person punishable under the 1932 formula.

*Is corporate crime truly criminal?*　Most statutory offences, which may be committed by a juristic person (or an unincorporated association, as the case may be) under the 1932 formula, seem to be those which the English Court of Appeal would call 'regulatory offences' as opposed to 'true crimes'.[17]

In Japan, by contrast, the 1932 formula is provided even for a true 'crime',[18] with all its moral implications, under an 'Industrial Crimes Against Human Health Act 1970' (45th Showa, 142). The Act was enacted in response to a number of environmental disasters caused by heavy industrial activities at the height of Japan's post-war economic growth, harming seriously large sections of members of the public, such as the mass mercury poisonings in and around Minamata and Niigata, the mass cadmium poisonings along the River Jintsuu and the massive air pollutions in Yokkaichi. The Act's sister statutes are the Air Pollution Prevention Act (43rd Showa, 97); the Pollutions and Disasters at Sea Act (45th Showa, 136); the Waste Disposal and Cleaning Act (45th Showa, 137); the Water Contamination Act (45th Showa, 138), etc.

The significance of the Industrial Crimes Act, as distinct from its sister statutes, is in its purpose (Art. 1) and the mode of trial (Art. 7). In essence, the Act says that it constitutes a 'crime' to create a risk to the health and safety of members of the public by the emission or disposal of substances harmful to human health, and that the purpose of the Act is to punish such a crime. The trial is to be held in a full trial court,[19] consisting of three professional judges.[20] By contrast, 'breaches of provisions' under the sister statutes are to be tried by a single judge in a summary court.[21]

The Industrial Crimes Act is somewhat anomalous in that it presumes causation between the emission/disposal of the substance and a risk, even where there is the same substance from other sources, as long as the amount of emission/disposal by the defendant is sufficient to create the risk (Art. 5). This places the legal burden of proof on the defence to rebut the presumption. However, the Act's title precludes an explanation that the reverse burden of proof is justified for 'regulatory offences which are not truly criminal'.[22]

The idea of 'industrial crime', i.e. 'crime committed by way of industrial activities', is quite explicit in the Act's purpose clause (Art. 1) as well as the definitions of a crime with 'intent and recklessness' (*dolus*) (Art. 2) and a crime by occupational or business negligence (*culpa*) (Art. 3). These mental elements are questioned as regards the creation of risk. However, the Act has no definition of the *mens rea* of a juristic person defendant (Art. 4). There is only the 1932 formula, *supra*, as in the Act's sister statutes. So far, the Act has rarely been used in practice, and the first conviction of a juristic person for a breach of the occupational duty of care under the Act, Art. 3, did not discuss the corporate *mens rea*.[23] The Court said that it punished the company because its employees committed the crime on account of the business of the company[24] – mere recital of the Act.

*Punishment*    The only means of punishment of a juristic person currently available is a fine. The Japanese legislation does have a distinction between 'punishment money' (*bakkin*) and 'breach fees' (*karyou*). However, this is different from the German distinction between two different kinds of 'fine', namely 'money punishment' (*Geldstrafe*) for a 'true crime' (*Justizstrafe*) and 'money mending' (*Geldbuße*) for a 'regulation breach' (*Ordungswidrigkeit*). In German law, there shall be 'no punishment without a crime' (von Feuerbach, 1799: 148)[25] so that a juristic person who cannot commit a crime cannot be punished. In Japan, a very substantial 'punishment money' applies to a juristic person, whereas small 'breach fees' only apply to a natural person.[26]

In 1992, amendments to the Securities and Exchange Act, Art. 207, to the Act Against Monopolies, Art. 95, etc. initiated a new development in this respect: the provision of a separate and substantial maximum amount of fine exclusively applicable to a juristic person or a group, which is no less than a thousand-fold the maximum amount applicable to a natural person. The number of statutes with this modified 1932 formula has increased rapidly since then, with the maximum amount of fine ranging from one to five thousand million Yen (from £4.5 to 22.5 million) in recent years. This trend is particularly observable in the following areas of legislation: environmental safety,[27] food safety[28] (after the BSE crisis and the mass food poisonings by Snow Brand Dairy Ltd in 2002), road safety[29] (after the 2000 uncovering of Mitsubishi Motors Ltd's failure to recall), building safety (after the 2005 uncovering of the massive sale of unsafe buildings),[30] intellectual property and competition law, banking, debts, taxation, etc. In the general field of 'health and safety', the maximum is normally one thousand million Yen, whereas it has been raised to three to five thousand million Yen in the securities and exchange, competition, banking and taxation laws. So far, the maximum fine under the Industrial Crimes Against Human Health Act 1970 remains three million Yen (£13,500), despite inflation. All these can be contrasted with the UK Health and Safety at Work etc. Act 1974, under which an unlimited amount of fine is chargeable on indictment against a corporation.

In Japan, a fine is chargeable against a juristic person, often in order to provide a longstop lest any 'loose ball' escape the hands of the administrative regulators. Their administrative measures actually include some of the means of 'punishment of a juristic person' under the French Penal Code, Art. 131 39, e.g. the suspension of the whole or part of a business.[31] The legality of such an administrative order may be reviewed by the judiciary in Japan, which has abolished the system of the administrative court (*Verwaltungsgericht, Couseil d'État*) within the executive branch.

## Killing by occupational negligence

Although only natural persons have been prosecuted for the Code offence of occupational negligence manslaughter, two such cases are often cited as examples where the theory of corporate *mens rea* had some bearing on the reasoning of the decision: the case of Morinaga Dairy Ltd and the case of Japan Nitrogen Ltd.

### The case of Morinaga Dairy Ltd[32]

According to the announcement of the Health Ministry in 1956, Morinaga Dairy Ltd caused the arsenic poisoning of babies who consumed the cheapest of the Dairy's powdered milk products. The poison killed 130 babies and injured 12,214 more. Arsenic was found in some disodium (hydrogen) phosphate compounds, which the Dairy's factory in Tokushima had mixed with their powdered milk. They reduced cost by processing a range of milks supplied at different times from different farms. Different particles of the milk powder of such mixed origins melt in water at different speeds. The sodium phosphate compounds 'stabilized' the milk powder's dissolving speed. The particular sodium phosphate chemicals were manufactured by Japan Light Metal Ltd, a manufacturer of aluminium. They 'recycled' their industrial wastes. Matsuno Pharmaceutical Ltd marketed the 'recycled' chemicals. The National Rail purchased the chemicals in order to wash their locomotives. They tested the chemicals before use for the health and safety of their employees, discovered arsenic in the chemicals, and returned them. The chemicals were therefore cheap in the marketplace. The Dairy had not specified in their order which sodium phosphate products they wanted from Matsuno Pharmaceutical. Nor did the Dairy test the chemicals before use. The factory manager and the manufacturing manager of the Tokushima factory of the Dairy were indicted on 49 counts of negligent manslaughter. The Defence argued that the defendants were right to trust Matsuno Pharmaceutical because the latter's products had caused no accident for many years.

The Court (consisting of Noma, Ōyama and Shigeyoshi JJJ) ruled,

> In terms of the constituting elements (*mens rea* and *actus reus*) of the offence in question, we shall firstly look objectively at the conduct of the factory as a business organization, by abstracting from the conduct of each of the individual defendants; secondly, to examine the duty of care which ought objectively to have been owed by the factory manager and the manufacturing technician under the particular circumstances of this case in order to determine whether or not each of them breached the duty of care.[33]

The Court found the manufacturing technician guilty, and acquitted the factory manager. The crux of the matter is the structure of its reasoning. The Court examined, first of all, the conduct of the business organization as a whole, whether or not such a corporate conduct satisfied the constituting elements of the offence. This structure suggests the application of the aggregation theory, which questions whether or not the aggregate sum of the conduct of each of the individuals comprising a company fell far below the standard of care, as distinct from whether or not the conduct of each individual did so.

This approach is somewhat remarkable because a 'corporate' disaster tends to be caused by the combination of a number of small faults, indeed, a chain of small failures, which taken individually, hardly constitutes any criminal offence. Had the Court examined the conduct of individual defendants first, then, it would have been extremely difficult to convict anyone.

The Court said in relation to sentencing:

> This accident occurred against the following backdrop: the lack of rigour on the part of the State in their exercise of administrative supervision [a Ministry was asked by the manufacturer of the chemicals whether they could sell the recycled chemicals, and failed to answer], *the failure by the Morinaga Dairy Ltd as a whole with respect to their system of managing [the safety of] additives*, and the particularly immoral conduct of Matsuno Pharmaceutical Ltd.[34]

Here, as a mitigating factor for the sentencing of the manufacturing technician, the company's 'management failure' is blamed.

Apparently, the ruling represented a compromise between the corporate *mens rea* theory and the prosecution practice of not prosecuting the company (in accordance with the prevailing 'individualism' in criminal responsibility). For reasons, which do not necessarily concern this chapter, there was no appeal on this ruling. However, the Court's doctrine of 'a reasonable man's fear' of damage, as distinct from the foreseeability of damage, has been criticized as being too remote to punish anyone (Maeda, 2006: 283; 287–8).[35] This doctrine was seen to provide leeway by which to attribute the blame arising from the abstracted corporate *mens rea* back to some individual defendant.

## The case of Japan Nitrogen Ltd

Japan Nitrogen Ltd's[36] factory in the fishing village of Minamata became known worldwide at the height of Japan's post-war industrial development for having caused the organic chloro-methyl mercury poisoning of a great number of people over many decades by way of their industrial waste disposal into the sea. Mercury was a catalyst in making acetaldehyde from acetylene. According to the 'unified Government opinion' of 26 September 1968, the relevant chemical reactions produced a by-product, chloro-methyl mercury, which, through the food chain and bioaccumulation in the sea, became toxic enough to damage, often fatally, the nervous system of those who ate contaminated fish.[37] On 22 March 1979, the relevant Chief Executive Officer and the relevant factory manager were jointly convicted of, *inter alia*, one count of manslaughter.[38]

The ruling of the Court (Ishida, Matsuo, Katoya JJJ) did not make such an explicit structural reasoning as in the Morinaga Dairy ruling. Only as a matter of 'mitigation', the Court declared that the case was 'a crime caused by the corporate business activities'.[39] However, the same structure emerges on analysis, especially when their reasoning is contrasted with the classical approach. The classical approach would have been to examine the criminal liability of a technician directly responsible for the manufacturing of acetaldehyde, who is most likely to have contemplated a risk associated with the disposal of its by-product. In fact, the person convicted in the Morinaga Dairy case was the manufacturing technician of the factory in question. However, in this Japan Nitrogen case, the Court examined directly the conduct of the company's Chief Executive Officer in Tokyo, many hundreds of miles away from the factory in question, and that of the manager of the relevant factory, indeed without examining at all the conduct of the technicians at the site. Some academics therefore interpret that the Court established the corporate *mens rea* first, and then imputed it to some senior managers of the company (e.g. Numano, 1979: 48–9). Clearly, in terms of 'white-collar' crime, the Japan Nitrogen ruling is more remarkable than the Morinaga Dairy ruling.

Japan Nitrogen's case was far more complicated than Morinaga Dairy's in that the former was the consequences of the industrial activities which lasted for many decades from 1934 to 1973. Nobody at first imagined that such serious damage would be caused. A great number of CEOs and of the factory managers came and went while the problem gradually grew bigger and bigger. The case thus required a series of robust and acrobatic prosecution decisions, for example, the selection of individual defendants from among a wide range of successive office holders; the latest point in time by which their duty to stop the disposal had 'crystallized', etc. The prosecutors' usual meticulous care in detail disappeared in this prosecution. Against such a backdrop, it appears that the prosecution's genuine target was the company itself,[40] and the individual defendants its substitutes. The Court found that the defendants, despite their full awareness of the gravity of the epidemic after 1956, trusted their own and their technicians' expertise in chemistry so unreasonably and blindly, that they failed to take heed of a series of authoritative views attributing the cause of the epidemic to some chemical in the industrial wastes of their company, and thus failed to stop the disposal (until 1973) and so caused the deaths.[41] This blame equally applied to the defendants' predecessors.

The Fukuoka Appeal Court and the Supreme Court dismissed the appeal by the convicted defendants. It is technically difficult to say that these binding judicial authorities approved the corporate *mens rea* theory, because the original judgment was filled with explicit word usage contradicting the adoption of the theory, even if it had adopted the theory implicitly.

## The case of Osaka City Council

The legality of the corporate *mens rea* theory was challenged in the Osaka Appeal Court on a gas explosion case and was implicitly rejected by its ruling of 22 March 1991.[42] The appellants argued that the Osaka Trial Court erred in law by establishing the duty of care of the City Council (who contracted out the construction of an underground railway), that of Steel Builder Ltd and that of Osaka Gas Ltd first, and then examined whether or not each of the individual defendants belonging to the three entities had breached the respective duty of care. The Appeal Court dismissed the appeal by holding that the trial court did not adopt the corporate *mens rea* theory, but examined the three 'categories' of duty of care, which merely coincided with the three organizational affiliations of the defendants, because the foreseeability of damage was clearly examined at the individual level, as opposed to the corporate level (Maeda, 1993: 148). This is slightly different from saying that the corporate *mens rea* theory is illegal, but the ruling tends to be accepted as such. It is noteworthy, however, that the trial court, in mitigation, condemned the City Council and the gas supplier for their sloppiness in managing the risk of a gas leak from an exposed turning joint.[43]

### The case of Mitsubishi Motors Ltd

On 5 July 2000, Mitsubishi's concealment of no less than 64,000 customer complaints dating back as far as 1977 was uncovered. This followed an unidentified informer's suggestion that the Transport Ministry inspect private lockers on the eighth floor of the company's Tokyo office on which its recall department was located.[44] In the meantime, the rupture of a hub fixing wheels to an axle, killed a pedestrian on 10 January 2002, and a clutch failure killed a lorry driver on 19 October 2002. Wilfried Porth, whom Daimler Chrysler had sent to direct a new lorry manufacturer it had acquired from Mitsubishi Motors in January 2003, could only blame Mitsubishi's 'culture of concealment'.[45] The pedestrian killing caused not only the prosecution of the company's two recall officers for the Code offence of manslaughter, but also that of the company itself and its three top officials for the statutory offence of knowingly making false reports to the government recall authority, i.e. a particularly notable instance of the company's 'culture of concealment'. The Yokohama Summary Court (Kojima J) acquitted the company on 13 December 2006 on a technical ground that it was not ordered by the Cabinet Minister himself (but by his recall deputy) to report so that there was no element of the offence charged, while finding that the reported figures were fabricated and that there was no evidence to support Mitsubishi's allegation of overload and poor maintenance.[46]

### Amagasaki Rail Crash

At 09.18 hours and 54 seconds on 25 April 2005, near Amagasaki Station in Western Japan, a commuter train belonging to one of the privatized and partitioned entities of the former National Rail crashed, killing 106 passengers and the driver himself. It transpired that two of the rail company's employees who happened to be on the train and survived the crash, went straight on to operate their respective trains, as scheduled, without any attempt whatsoever to rescue injured passengers.[47] They said that they were so thoroughly disturbed by the accident that they were unable to help. Their explanation was hardly persuasive because many injured passengers helped each other. Why did not the company employees feel a strong ethical obligation to help? The two employees, in fact, feared a penalty which the company imposed on those train drivers who delayed. The penalty was internally known as 're-education'. It meant not only the suspension of pay, but also humiliation and abuse. The sessions at a 're-education camp' were not about driving skills but consisting of grass picking in the camp yard under verbal abuse by overbearing superiors, the submission of self-incriminating essays to them, repeated copying by hand of the company's code of values, etc.[48] In the years 2003 and 2004, the rail company conducted 1,182 instances of such 're-education' and the longest one lasted for 52 days.[49]

The Transport Ministry's Commission of Inquiry into Air and Rail Accidents suggested in its interim report of December 2006 that the fear of 're-education' caused the crash itself.[50] The requisite punctuality by the 'Japanese' standard meant that a train timetable was measured by seconds. The Commission found that the rail company had shortened the 'standard operation time' between Itami Station and Amagasaki Station from 350 seconds, as of March 1997, to 320 seconds in October 2004. The driver of the train, Mr. Takami, aged 23 at the time of the crash, was particularly apprehensive about the 're-education'. This was because he had undergone a one-day session for having fallen asleep while driving in August 2003 and a 13-day session for having overrun by one hundred metres in June 2004. After the privatization, the train drivers' working hours were extended as the train timetable became busier while far fewer new recruits joined the company. Their average sleeping hours, according to a survey of the relevant trade union, were four hours and 50 minutes. On the fateful morning, Mr. Takami was again behind the schedule by 30 seconds when he reached Itami Station. There, he overran by 72 metres. This made his delay 80 seconds. To add to his predicament, the next station, Amagasaki, was impressed upon him as the 'absolute punctuality station',[51] where most of his passengers were going to change their train in the space of 100 seconds to another train at the other side of the same platform. He entered a curve, the semi-diameter of whose arc was 304 metres, at the speed of 116 kilometres (72 miles) per hour, while the speed limit was 70 kilometres (43 miles) per hour, and derailed. The Commission found that the driver, his steward and the command centre were engaged in wireless communication about the delay for the last 50 seconds prior to the crash. The driver had asked his steward to report a shorter overrun to the command centre, and apparently felt stress when the command centre asked the steward for clarification of the alleged figures and began to talk to the driver directly. The train crashed while the command centre kept calling the silent driver to answer. The Commission found that more than a third of the company's drivers had made mistakes while talking to stewards and the command centre over wireless phones about delays.

It was alleged that the company decided not to fit an automatic train stop (ATS) speed monitor near the curve in question.[52] There had been criticisms of the company's delay in introducing a better system of automatic train control (ATC), but the existing system of ATS, had its speed monitor been fitted at the relevant point, was seen to have been capable of averting the accident.[53] The managers decided not to fit it there in order apparently to enable and overlook occasional over-speed operations at the curve for the sake of punctuality.[54] If the managers had, as professional train operators, knowingly accepted the risk of over-speed operation, i.e. the risk of the kinds of accident which actually happened, it would be possible to prosecute the managers for Japan's capital offence: murder with the wilful acceptance of a foreseen risk. A relevant branch manager of the rail company helped the police with their enquiries concerning the company's management of the safety system, train timetables and train drivers.[55] The police investigation was thereafter suspended until the publication of a final report of the Commission of Inquiry. The final report, which was published on 28 June 2007, however, failed to address the question of the managerial decision concerning the ATS monitor.

## Conclusion

In English law, 'bodies corporate' are punishable unless the contrary intention appears in statutes. Therefore, there is some remote possibility of convicting a small company of common law manslaughter by regarding the *mens rea* of some individual, who is identified as the 'controlling mind' of the company, as that of the company itself. By contrast, in Japanese law, no juristic person is punishable without some statutory provision to that effect. No juristic person has ever been prosecuted or convicted of any offence under the Penal Code, which, unlike the Dutch and more recent French Codes, has no explicit provision making a juristic person criminally liable.

Unlike in Germany, however, Japan has a large and ever-increasing number of statutes, which make a juristic person criminally liable and punishable. The criminal liability of a juristic person tends to be provided as a last resort in order to enforce the administrative control and supervision of corporate activities.

In practice, a juristic person is prosecuted and convicted, where and only where, some natural person is also prosecuted and convicted with respect to the same statutory offence. There is a somewhat tainted binding judicial authority to the effect that the juristic person's own *mens rea* (negligence) is presumed in such a case. But in practice, such corporate *mens rea* is hardly examined. It is simply presumed to exist after the guilt of an individual defendant is established. Therefore, it is very far from the 'aggregation theory', which some US authorities and the Dutch practice suggest.

There were at least two 'persuasive' judicial authorities in Japan, which did not involve the prosecution of a juristic person at all, but which nevertheless *de facto* followed the logic of the 'aggregation theory' in arriving at the convictions of some natural persons of the Code offence of (occupational) negligent manslaughter, i.e. to establish 'corporate negligence' first by abstracting from the conduct of individuals comprising a juristic person, and then attributing the resulting blame to some individual defendants. There is no explicit binding judicial authority on the question. Rather, the absence of cases which unequivocally follow the Morinaga Dairy and Japan Nitrogen cases, as well as the appellate ruling in the Osaka City Council case, militate against such an approach.

Looking at these cases from some distance, however, the negligence of the convicted individual defendants in these cases tends to be so slight that it appears that they would have never been convicted without some 'corporate' context. The judges' remarks in these cases in mitigation, blaming some organization for its failure in the management of some risk, are very much indicative of the real presence of 'corporate *mens rea*', i.e. the moral element of corporate crime, independent of that of a natural person.

The combination of the manslaughter prosecution of the recall managers and the statutory offence prosecution of the company and its top officials in the Mitsubishi case, for example, seems to confirm the practical awareness, on the part of the prosecution, of the desirability to punish the company's corporate 'culture of concealment'.

The rail crash case illustrates graphically a very 'Japanese' style of personnel management in an organization, which tends to seek humiliation and self-incrimination of employees for their mistakes, over and above the pragmatic training of their skills and the management of their safety operations, thereby generating the 'culture of concealment',[56] e.g. a false report to the command centre, which constituted the backdrop against which the fatal accident occurred. The law seems to have failed to devise a Japanese solution to this problem so far.

## Notes

1  *L'élément constitutif moral du crime.*
2  For example, US v General Motors Corporation, 121 F.2d 376 (7th Cir.), cert. denied, 314 US 618 (1941).
3  US v Bank of New England NA, 821 F.2d 844 (1st Cir.), cert. denied, 484 US 943 (1987); US v T.I.M.E.-DC Inc. 381 F Supp. 730 (W.D.Va. 1974).
4  An 'Act for further improving the Administration of Justice in Criminal Cases in England' of 1827 (7th & 8th Geo. IV, c. 28), s. 14; followed by the Interpretation Act 1889, s. 2 (1); and currently the Interpretation Act 1978, s. 5 and Sch. 1.
5  Tesco Supermarkets Ltd v Nattrass [1972] AC 153.
6  *Societas deliquere non potest.*
7  *Gesetz über Ordnungswidrigkeiten* (OwiG) 1968, art. 30 (1) for more details.

8   Cf. the UK's Corporate Manslaughter and Corporate Homicide Act, 2007 (cf. Gobert in this volume).

9   It covers contingent intent (*dolus eventualis*), which is the wilful acceptance of a foreseen consequence of one's conduct, similar to 'recklessness'.

10  *Gyoumujou Kashitsu Chishi*, Penal Code, article 211, from *Amts-, Berufs-, Gewerbs-fahrlässige Tötung*, Article 222 (2) of the German Penal Code before 1940.

11  *Juu Kashitsu Chishi* (*homicidium culposum latum*, in Latin) Penal Code, Art. 211.

12  Indeed, Germany removed this offence from the Penal Code in 1940 and never brought it back after 1945 in order to remove this anomaly from the Code.

13  Grand Court, Judgment, 25 November, 10th Year of Showa (Emperor Hirohito's reign), Criminal Reporter, vol. 14, p. 1217. The Grand Court of Judicature was the final court of appeal in civil and criminal cases in Japan before 1947. A breach of the Savings Bank Act was alleged.

14  Some writers use a term 'double punishment', but this is misleading.

15  Supreme Court, Grand Chamber, Judgment, 27 Nov., 32nd Showa, Crim. Rep. vol. 11, no. 12, p. 3113. The Supreme Court is the final court of appeal in all cases, including constitutional and administrative cases, under the Constitution of 1947. A breach of the Tax on Entry into Controlled Premises Act (22nd Showa, 142) was alleged.

16  Supreme Court, Judgment, 26 Mar. 40th Showa, Crim. Rep. vol.19, no. 2, p. 83. A breach of the Foreign Exchange and Trade Control Act, Art. 73 was alleged.

17  David Janway Davies v Health and Safety Executive [2002] EWCA Crim. 2949.

18  *Hanzai*.

19  *Chihou Saibansho*, lit., 'Local Court', located in each of the 47 prefectures. This has full sentencing powers.

20  From 2009, six lay judges are going to join the bench of three professional judges.

21  *Kan-i Saibansho*, lit., 'Easy Access Court'. The sentencing power is limited to a fine only.

22  Cf. David Janway Davies v HSE [2002] EWCA Crim 2949, on the reverse burden of proof under the Health and Safety at Work etc. Act 1974, s. 40. cf. criticisms in Cooper (2003: 352).

23  The Act was applied to Japan Aerogel Ltd in relation to an accident in its Yokkaichi factory. Tsu Local Court, Judgment, 7 Mar., 54th Showa, *Hanrei Times*, no. 382, p. 75.

24  Hanrei Times, no. 382, p. 75, at p. 85.

25  In fact, von Feuerbach wrote, *nullum crimen sine poena legali* (no crime without legal punishment) and *nulla poena legalis sine crimine* (no legal punishment without a crime), a bit of tautology.

26  Amphetamine Control Act (26th Showa, 252), Art. 43; Banking Act (56th Showa, 59) Art. 65, etc.

27  Waste Disposal and Cleaning Act (45th Showa, 137)

28  Food Sanitation Act (22nd Showa, 233), etc.

29  Road Transport Vehicle Act (26th Showa, 185): two thousand million Yen.

30  Building Standards Act (25th Showa, 201), Architects Act (25th Showa, 202) etc. as amended by an Act (18th Heisei, 92); Fire Defence Act (23rd Showa, 186), Art. 45.

31  In May 2006, Aiful, a consumer loan company based in Kyoto, was ordered to suspend the whole of its businesses nationwide for up to 25 days by a Cabinet Minister under the Money Lenders Act (58th Showa, 32), Art. 36.

32  Tokushima Chi-Han, Showa 48.11.28, Keiji Geppou vol. 5, no. 11, p. 1473; *Hanrei Jihou* no. 721, p. 7. The 48th year of Showa was 1973 (Chi-Han is the acronym of a Judgment of a Trial Court).

33  *Hanrei Jihou*, vol.721, p. 10. The words in brackets are those of the present author.

34 *Hanrei Jihou*, vol. 721, p. 16. The words in brackets are those of the present author who also added the emphasis.

35 Arguably, the responsibilities of the pharmaceutical company, rather than the Dairy, should have been questioned.

36 *Nihon Chisso Hiryou Kabushiki Kaisha* (Japan Nitrogen Fertilizers Ltd) was established in 1908 by the merger of Japan Carbide Ltd and Sogi Electricity Ltd, both belonging to Shitagau Noguchi. The company was liquidated after the loss of their properties in Japan's former colonies, and the 'new' company (with the word, 'new' at the beginning of the name of its predecessor) was established in 1950 in their only surviving factory in Minamata. The 'new' company changed its name into *Chisso* (Nitrogen) in 1966, apparently in its attempt to evade civil liabilities.

37 It was on 1 May 1956 when the Minamata Factory Hospital of Japan Nitrogen Ltd reported to the local health authority an unknown very severe brain disease, which later became known as 'Minamata Epidemic'.

38 Kumamoto-Chi-Han, Showa 54.3.22, *Hanrei Jihou*, vol. 931, p. 6.

39 *Hanrei Jihou*, vol. 931, p. 33.

40 Indeed, the Prosecution had to calm down the national public outrage against the prosecution of the leader of the Minamata Epidemic sufferers for a minor assault occasioned when the sufferers approached Japan Nitrogen's headquarters in Tokyo. Those who physically pushed the sufferers back were never prosecuted.

41 *Hanrei Jihou*, vol. 931, p. 24.

42 Osaka-Kou-Han, Heisei 3.3.22, *Hanrei Times*, No. 824 (1993.11.1), 83 at 116 ('Kou-Han' is the acronym of a judgment of an Appeal Court, a court of second instance located in each of the eight judicial regions of Japan).

43 Osaka-Chi-Han, Showa 60.4.17, *Hanrei Times*, No. 567 (1985.12.15), 86 at 138.

44 BBC News, 8 September 2000.

45 BBC News, 20 May 2004.

46 Asahi Shimbun, 14 December 2006, p. 36.

47 Kobe Shimbun, 4 May 2005.

48 asahi.com, 24 April, 2006.

49 Ibid.

50 Asahi Shimbun, 20 December 2006, p. 1 and p. 37 reporting on the Interim Report of the Ministry of Land and Transport, Commission of Enquiry into Air and Rail Accidents.

51 Kobe Shimbun, 15 May, 2005.

52 asahi.com, 6 September 2005.

53 Ibid.

54 Ibid.

55 Ibid.

56 An eighteenth century Japanese scholar, Nakamoto Tominaga (1715–1746), characterized the linguistic and cultural propensity or dispositions of the religious teachings in India (through the medium of Buddhism) in China (through that of Confucianism) and in Japan (through the medium of Shintoism) as those towards magic, those towards linguistic hyperbole and those towards concealment, respectively (Pye, 1990: 68–70). It is noteworthy that Nakamoto had argued in 1745 that the religious teachings in India and China were conditioned by the particular linguistic and cultural dispositions of the respective audience of the respective countries of the time, suggesting that the Indians at the time when Buddhism was influential there were magic-oriented, while the Chinese at the time when Confucianism was influential there were linguistic-hyperbole-oriented (Pye, 1990: 123 and 164). The arguement follows that the Japanese at the time when Shintoism was influential there, were concealment-oriented.

# References

Coffee, John C. (1981) 'No soul to damn, no body to kick', *Michigan Law Review*, 79: 386.

Cooper, John (2003) 'Criminal regulatory offences: two tier justice?' *New Law Journal*, 153: 352.

Dando, Shigemitsu (1978) *Keihou Kouyou* [Die Grundsätze des Strafrechts], *Souron* (Algemeiner Teil), revised edn. Tokyo: Soubunsha.

de Doelder, Hans (1996) 'Criminal liability of corporations – Netherlands', in Hans de Doelder and Klaus Tiedemann, *Criminal Liability of Corporations* (the Fourteenth International Congress of Comparative Law 1994 by the International Academy of Comparative Law). The Hague: Kluwer Law International.

Eser, Albin et al. (eds) (1989) *Old Ways and New Needs in Criminal Litigation*. Freiburg: Max Planck Institute for Foreign and International Criminal Law.

Feuerbach, Paul Johann Anselm Ritter von (1799) *Revision der Grundsätze und Grundbegriff des positiven peinlichen Rechts*, Teil 1. Erfurt (reprinted in 1966 by Scientia Verlag, Aalen).

French, Peter A. (1984) *Collective and Corporate Responsibility*. New York: University of Colombia Press.

Fujiki, Hideo (1972) *Keihou Kakuron* [Criminal Law, Special Part]. Tokyo: Yuhikaku.

Itakura, Hiroshi (1973) 'Kigyoutai-no Keijiseikinin – Kigyou Soshikitai Sekininron-no Teishou' [Criminal Liability of a corporation – a theory of corporate liability of a business organization] *Keihou Zasshi* (Criminal Law Journal), 19 (1 and 2): 21–44.

Kobayashi, Hideyuki (2005) *Sabakareru Mitsubishi Jidousha*. Tokyo: Nihon Hyouronsha.

Maeda, Masahide (1993) 'Gas-bakuhatsu-jiko to Kashitsu-sekinin' [Gas explosion accident and criminal negligence], *Jurist*, 862: 147–149.

Maeda, Masahide (2006) *Keihou Souron Kougi* [Criminal Law, General Part], 4th edn. Tokyo: Tokyo University Press.

Numano, Teruhiko (1979) 'Chisso Keiji Hanketsu to Kigyou Soshikitai Sekininron' [Japan Nitrogen criminal judgment and the theory of a business organization's responsibility], *Jurist*, 690 (5.15): 47.

Pye, Michael (1990) *Emerging from Meditation.* London: Duckworth.

Saeki, Hitoshi (1998) 'Houjin Shobatsu-nikansuru ichi Kousatsu' [Some Thoughts on the Punishment of Juristic Persons] in *Matsuo Hiroya-sensei Koki Shukuga Ronbunshuu*, Vol. 1, Tokyo: Yuhikaku.

Shibahara, Kuniji (1992) 'Le droit japonais de la responsabilité pénale de la personne morale' in A. Eser et al. (eds) *Criminal Responsibility of Legal and Collective Entities*. Freiburg: Max Planck Institute for Foreign and International Criminal Law.

Tiedemann, Klaus (1989), 'Strafbarkeit und Bussgeldhaftung von juristischen Personen und ihren Organen', in A. Eser et al. (eds) *Old ways and New Needs in Criminal Litigaton*. Freiburg: Max Planck Institute for Foreign and International Criminal Law.

Utsuro, Hideo (1984) 'Houjin Shobatsu-no arikata' [On the punishment of juristic persons], in H. Matsuo (ed.) (1984) *Gendai Keibatsu Hou Taikei* [System of modern punishment law], No. 1, in *Gendai Shakai-niokeru Keibatsu-no Riron* [Theories of Punishments in Modern Society]. Tokyo: Nihon Hyouronsha, pp. 181–232.

## Suggestions for further reading

### On Japanese law

Norihisa Kyoto (1996) 'Criminal Liability of Corporations – Japan', in Hans de Doedler and Klaus Tiedemann, *Criminal Liability of Corporations* (The Fourteenth International Congress of Comparative Law 1994 by The International Academy of Comparative Law). The Hague: Kluwer Law International.

Kuniji Shibahara (1992) 'Le droit japonais de la responsabilité pénale, en particulier, la responsabilité pénale de la personne morale', in Albin Eser, Günter Heine and Barbara Huber (eds) (1999) *Criminal Responsibility of Legal and Collective Entities*. Freiburg: Max Planck Institute for Foreign and International Criminal Law.

### On Japanese business culture

Dore, Ronald P. (1973) *British Factory, Japanese Factory: The Origins of National Diversity in Industrial Relations*. London: Allen and Unwin.

Dore, Ronald P. (2001) *Social Evolution, Economic Development and Culture: What it Means to Take Japan Seriously*, in selected writings of Ronald Dore, edited by D. Hugh Whittaker, Cheltenham: Elgar, especially Chapter 14, 'Individualism' (1989) and Chapter 25, 'The firm as community' (1987).

Graham, Fiona (2003) *Inside the Japanese Company*. London: Routledge Curzon.

### On Japanese culture

Pye, Michael (1990) *Emerging from Meditation*. London: Duckworth.

# EIGHT

## Rethinking Occupational Deviance and Crime in the Light of Globalization

*Gerald Mars*

### Introduction

It is now a quarter of a century since the original publication of *Cheats at Work* (Mars, 1982/94), an account of occupational deviance in ordinary jobs, showed how its practices significantly contributed to a 'hidden economy'. The book rejected the approach then common, that classified occupations on the basis of their positions in the class structure and, following from that, considered their fiddles, skimming and sabotage also according to class and linked them to blue-collar and white-collar crime. It rejected too the view that occupational crime could be understood through psychological – that is – personality explanations. *Cheats* showed instead that the form and incidence of occupational deviance derived from the way jobs were organized and that their understanding is best approached through the study of their social organization.

*Cheats* argued that occupational deviance, from 'perks' through 'skimming' to outright sabotage, provides the flexibility that makes many organizations workable in the first place: that such practices are intrinsic to organizations rather than an anomaly. This is a vindication of the model that gives theoretical underpinning to what is a commonplace for many managers and workers *in situ*. Stuart Henry (1978) and Henry and Mars (1978) showed that understanding occupational deviance involves a recognition that its criminal aspects are of a different order than 'ordinary' crime and that blurring their differences seriously negates understanding. Henry later extended the discussion to set the hidden economy of pilfering and fiddling within the wider macro context of the informal and formal economies (Henry, 1987). He showed their essential symbiosis, demonstrated how they mutually support and complement each other, live off each other and mutually adapt and amend each other. These insights, however, were located in an implicitly national and indeed in many respects, a local context.

It is now timely to review how far the analytical model employed in *Cheats* might need amendment. In particular, many aspects of social and economic life have been affected by what we know as globalization. Globalization has become a catchall term for changes in technology, communication and travel and no less so, for changes in geo-politics, economic policies, and modes and means of production. For our purposes globalization has certainly meant an 'intensification of worldwide social relations which link distant localities in such a way that local happenings are shaped by events occurring many miles away and vice versa' (Giddens, 1990: 64). This is especially so in the realm of work. We may, therefore wish to ask if the original terms of reference remain appropriate, if the model or matrix that mapped and treated work relations as largely occurring within unitary, autonomous organizations or occupations is still sufficient. This is especially so when organizations are potently influenced by directives and policies from across the globe, where jobs are no longer 'for life', and when much of western work has shifted from production to services.

## A recap

*Cheats* offered a means of classifying differing forms of deviance and indeed, of classifying occupations. It showed how a whole range of concomitant variations other than just deviance was found to correlate with the way occupations were organized. Among these were differing patterns of recruitment and socialization, the nature of group-determined controls and sanctions as well as distinct variations in the nature of worker–management relations. Such findings related to the micro influences to be found within the workplace. Now, however, macro influences that derive from globalization increasingly affect workplace relations and their associated deviance. These must now be considered and are the prime concern of this chapter. But before attempting to extend the understanding of occupational deviance to a wider transnational context, however, it will first be necessary to outline the approach adopted in *Cheats* in 1982.

The model used in 1982, known then as Grid/Group Analysis, now coming to be known as Dynamic Cultural Theory (DCT), has come a long way in this last quarter century. Derived from work of the anthropologist, Mary Douglas (1970; 1978), it has been extended through a variety of social analyses to a wide range of fields (see Perri and Mars, 2008) and in doing so has developed a theoretical sophistication that has effectively countered critics' accusations that it could not account for change (Thompson et al., 1990: Chapter 4). In its essence though, it remains today much as it was first expounded. I will not dwell here on the theoretical underpinning of the model other than to record that it identifies two dimensions or parameters. These are held to be common in all social situations and therefore also apply to the way any job is organized 'on the ground'.

The first, 'Grid', assesses the relative strength of constraints operating in a job: such constraints might involve the classifying of members by differences in rank, by the requirement to wear uniforms, with controls over an incumbent's occupancy of space or whether there are restrictions over time. In brief, grid is a measure of autonomy where 'Strong Grid' means little autonomy and 'Weak Grid' means a good deal. A high grid job today might be a call centre operative or, as in the example of the 1982 text, a skivvy in a Victorian one-servant family, whereas a self-employed entrepreneur's job would be low grid.

The second dimension, Group, assesses the degree of incorporation in face-to-face groups. An army platoon, for instance, is strong on the group dimension since it is the basis not just of its members' work but also of their leisure and indeed is a potent source of group identity and group controls. An independent management consultant's job would rate weakly on the group dimension. For much of the twentieth century, coal miners would have served as the canonical group example, for the features of 'group' that serve to identify one, *qua* group member, would be the bonds between them and others both outside and/or inside the workplace. Both the dangers of the workplace for miners and their own unique history reinforced group solidarity of the kind we are identifying here.

If we place these two dimensions as continua on a two by two matrix, we can identify four occupational archetypes,[1] as follows (see Figure 8.1):

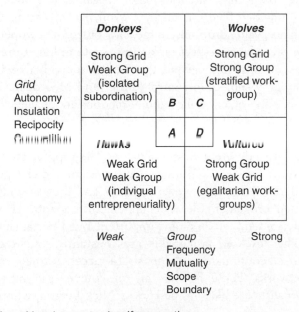

Figure 8.1  Using grid and group to classify occupations

*Weak Grid/Weak Group* (A) jobs are free of group membership and group controls and their members determine their own *modus operandi*. These are the entrepreneurs, fixers and dealers who emphasize autonomy and value competition, since to them, positions are 'up for grabs', not ascribed. These are the networking Hawks.

*Strong Grid/Weak Group* (B) jobs are those strongly constrained by externally set rules and categories and who lack the support of face to face group membership. These are the Donkey[2] jobs whose members lack autonomy and are isolated. 'Work-alone' dial-watchers and unemployed social security claimants are likely to be in this category.

*Strong Grid/Strong Group* (C) jobs have a marked sense of boundary readily demarcating those inside the group from those outside. Here are the stratified and ranked workgroups I term Wolf-packs. They have assertive self-identity and are controlled, disciplined, and strategic in their dealings. They can impose strong constraints on their members.

*Weak Grid/Strong Group* (D) jobs are those having a strong sense of boundary but which impose few constraints on their members. These are groupings of egalitarians as are found in co-operatives and which characteristically 'de-emphasize' distinctions of rank. I call these Vultures – they are co-operative to a degree but their members essentially pursue their own benefit. Driver/Deliverers are likely to be Vultures. So are groups of same-grade waiters as found in low and middle status restaurants while more stratified teams of waiters in top grade restaurants are more Wolf-pack.

The primary significance of DCT is that it relates these categories of job organization to ideology and to appropriate behaviours. Each archetypal form of organization has a distinct and different 'view of the world' – an ideology, a cosmology, a coherent 'cluster' of justifications and values that, to their members, make sense of their situation, their organization and the forms of deviance they practice. The bureaucratic Wolf-packs (Strong Group/Strong Grid), for instance, value order, discipline and control. They operate according to rules, value precedents, respect rank and operate in long time spans – since the group has an existence beyond that of the individuals within it. Their deviance is similarly subject to controls, order and precedents. Amounts and types of deviance are set, controlled and infractions are penalized, according to group set rules.

The competitive, innovative and corner-cutting Hawks (Weak Group/Weak Grid) operate with a different cluster of values. They appreciate independence, autonomy and the freedom to transact. Competition and change are inherent to their worldview. Their time scales are short and they see rules as made to be circumvented, broken or at least bent. Flexibility, adaptation and individual flair are highly valued, networking is important but their alliances shift with expediency. The new and fashionable are constantly sought and exhibited since Hawks need continually to demonstrate success to their ever potentially extending networks. These features are of course, also inherent to their deviance. Journalists are likely to be Hawks. Nick Leeson, who broke Barings

Bank, was a classic Hawk who operated in a traditional Wolf-pack context. Globalization opens an ever expanding arena for Hawks.

The egalitarian, enclavic Vultures (Strong Group/Weak Grid) are groups that tend to be co-operative for some purposes but competitive for others. They are the least consistent or secure of all the categories since, unlike Wolfpacks, they lack the stabilizing influences, and internal arbitrator role derived from stratification and the surety of controls these generate. Their values derive from their structured insecurity and they tend to be suspicious in dealings with outsiders. Compared to Hawks, individual Vultures have less independence and personal power. There are fewer professionals among them, more craftsmen and semi-skilled. 'Fiddle fiefs' – as are common among waiters and driver/deliverers – are likely to be granted through the collusion of managers which often brings competition into Vulture groups and is a frequent cause of dissent and insecurity. In addition, Vultures are reluctant to grant authority and arbitrational functions to any of their members. As a result, dissent tends to be kept under, often to emerge as sudden schism. Lacking internal structure, Vultures cohere by tightening their boundary against what they often perceive as a threatening and dangerous 'outside'. It is against such 'outsides' that they are likely to unify and act in the face of perceived threats. Such behaviours are often seen as 'erratic' (Sayles, 1956).

Donkey job holders, sometimes called Fatalists or Isolates, characterized by both isolation and subordination, are in the paradoxical position of being powerless if they accept the constraints they normally face, or powerful – that is disruptive – if they reject them. At high points of grid where constraints are strongest, individual acts of sabotage are a not infrequent response to alienation – particularly where constraints are mechanized – or as they now more often are – computerized. At weak levels of grid, resentment fiddles come into their own. The number of Donkey jobs have increased where, as we shall see, globalized driven technology imposes constraints on workers – as in call centres and in electronic component assembly plants.

## A previously unexplored aspect of occupational deviance: total institutions

One area of conflict – or of tolerated levels of deviance – the balance can be struck in a variety of ways – is to be found in 'total institutions', a phrase coined by Goffman to define those organizations that combine work, residence and leisure. Here 'like situated individuals are cut off from the wider society for appreciable periods of time' (Goffman, 1961: 4–5). Organizations such as ships, hospitals, prisons, work camps and armies all tend to operate as total institutions. In total institutions, relationships are liable to be 'concentrated' so that their workers have an enhanced opportunity to form groups which, according to the nature of their work encourage either Wolf-packs or Vultures. Because relationships are 'concentrated', attempts at control can be particularly disruptive. Yet this contrast, and the heightened liability to sabotage in total institutions which ensues, have not been recognized. Hodges (1974) gives a hilarious account of life in the peacetime US army, when this anomaly comes to the fore, to show how squaddies, to the applause of their colleagues, would drive tanks over cliffs or into swamps – to assert control and reduce frustration.

## Total reward systems

If we are fully to understand the nature of occupations, we must also appreciate and calculate 'the total rewards' – both 'official' and 'unofficial' – that normally accrue to them together with their sources and the nature of relationships involved in obtaining them. These together comprise an occupation's 'Total Rewards System'. As we shall see, the nature of a Total Rewards System can be radically influenced by factors deriving from globalization.

## Fiddle factors and fiddle proneness: an update

Under this heading in *Cheats* (Ch. 6), I attempted to identify factors that structure and facilitate the regular payment of a significant part of an occupation's total rewards in the form of fiddles. These depend on an imbalance in underlying structural differences of knowledge, control, power and ability held by some groups over others. It paralleled attempts at determining criminogenesis in criminology. Five such areas were identified. How are these likely to have been influenced by macro factors derived from globalization?

The first, 'Passing Trade,' exists where two sides to a transaction typically meet only once, as with tourists in a strange city, unlike say, regular customers to a village shop. Globalization together with Individualism affects the increasing proportions of populations living in urban conurbations while the Technology influencing cheap air travel that underpins the burgeoning travel and tourism industry can all be expected to have increased deviance from Passing Trade. John Adams (2000) points to the 'hypermobility' of Western society which involves increasing distances that its people annually travel. Hypermobility can be said to be fuelling passing trade deviance.

The second, 'Exploiting Expertise', can be expected to have increased with ongoing and incremental additions in technical complexity, as has been discussed – especially as this more fully permeates the market for consumer goods.

'Triadic Occupations', the third 'fiddle-prone' factor, operates where occupations are involved with customers/clients so that there is the opportunity for any two to combine against the interests of a third. The increase of personal services throughout Western society can be expected to have increased Triadic Occupation fiddles.

The fourth fiddle-prone area, focusing on rewards for 'Special Efforts and Special Skills', operates where economic return is directly relatable to individual efforts or skill. It flourishes among employed managers, professionals and tradesmen where formal rewards are bureaucratically, often collectively fixed but where the real market value of such labour is adjusted not through collective means but by individual arrangements (Dalton, 1959: 194–217). It is especially a feature of occupations that demand quick fluid adjustments and where the return to talents and flair vary widely. These then are the fiddles of employed Hawks. Insofar as globalization has increased worldwide competition, where managements are more distant and where technical innovation serially produces new mutually competing products, then Special Efforts and Skills can be expected to increase.

Lastly, 'Gatekeepers' designate a further area that applies where there is unilateral control of an imbalance between supply and demand. This can apply either to information or goods. The widespread permeation of computers and the worldwide web have reduced the efficacy of this factor. This is the only fiddle-prone factor of the original five that does not contribute to increased deviance.

Since it was applied to occupations, the Dynamic Cultural Theory Model has shown it has worn well – despite massive changes that have occurred in the workplace since 1982. This of course, is because the two dimensions are as valid now as they ever were. What *has* altered are the influences that have operated to affect the two dimensions. We must therefore ask what has occurred since 1982 that has weakened or strengthened either Grid or Group characteristics of particular jobs and assess, first, how these influences are manifest in new jobs that have arisen in the interim. Now, in moving from the micro-level of organization to include macro-global influences, I hope therefore to overcome a certain weakness in the initial analysis that largely focused on micro-local influences.[3]

## Globalization and change

Globalization, involving the free movement of capital, labour and ideas across boundaries, is a long-term and accelerating process that has sharpened competition primarily in finance and more lately in production and services. In political and economic fields, it represents the transition from independence, through interdependence, to integration so that many now argue we are seeing an increase in the power of multinational and transnational companies at the expense of the nation-state and its specifically national institutions such as trades unions. Globalization is not new. What is new and important today are the speed, extent and the impact of globalization. It has usefully been described as 'the intensification of worldwide social relations which link localities in such a way that local happenings are shaped by events occurring many miles away and vice versa' (Giddens, 1990: 6) which is why it has to be considered in any contemporary discussion of occupational deviance.

The ability of transnational corporations to move capital and production around the world, on progressively short-term considerations, represents one of the main distancing elements affecting the relationship of management and labour. Such corporations and the decisions their managements make – whether affecting the siting of factories or the human relations policies within them – are made at more and more distant removes from the local communities that supply their labour. This effect works in association with a growing internationally-based cultural homogeneity of managers whose education, life-styles, residence, aspirations and ideologies are also becoming more divorced from the communities in which their working lives are set (Mars, 1981). Given that many manpower policies of transnationals are Stateside-oriented and often demonstrate a more ethnocentric and individualist, short-termist ideology than possessed by workers, from the (usually) more hierarchic, traditional *Gemeinschaft* communities in which they are set, we are, I suggest, due to see a progressive conflict between the two, as the following discussion on call centres in Malaysia and Thailand indicate. Such conflict is liable to increase if Management and Business Schools continue to orient their courses to the conception of organizations as narrowly bounded concerns at the expense of understanding the wider communal orientations of their workforces and the communities in which they are set.

This insulation of managers has developed progressively since the beginnings of the Industrial Revolution but in the relatively recent past its effects were modified and mediated by trades unions. With their currently reduced effectiveness, and the growing differences between managers and the managed in terms of careers, education, residence and aspirations, the gap between them has never been wider. Twenty-five years ago, most managers knew about the social bases of pilferage practised by their workers. Today, for example, managers are mostly unaware of the institutionalized means by which pilfered goods are obtained and distributed and which are a culturally embedded feature of many *Gemeinschaft* communities – as found for instance in many traditional dockland areas (Mars, 2001b: xviii–xix).

One important aspect of globalization is the freer movement of labour across national boundaries. Much of such labour is essentially marginal (in terms of their conditions of employment), and there is considerable evidence to show that marginal workers are more prone (and subject to) deviance than are non-marginal workers (Tucker, 1989). Building on the work of Hollinger and Clark (1983: 69–78), Tucker found a tendency to theft more pronounced among marginal workers such as cosmopolitan and mobile technicians who lack control over their work when compared to 'localized' managers who do not (Gouldner, 1957–8). This, he states, helps explain why the young and 'engineers and computer specialists employed in manufacturing firms [are] more significantly theft-prone than other high status employees' (Tucker, 1989: 71).

Globalization and computer technology together offer an extended arena for Hawks. One of the defining features, particularly of employed Hawks, is their need to insulate their activities, so that parties aware of one set of their concerns are not allowed knowledge of others. Commonly, Hawks need to insulate private and alternative activities when they perform them in the firm's time. Globalization enhances a Hawk's ability to insulate their activities and to fiddle time on a transnational scale. I know one highly regarded computer specialist whose London employers believe he works exclusively for them from home when in reality he lives in the States and works extensively for others. To maintain this deception he has, for the past several years, regularly commuted back to London every Christmas to attend the staff's annual party.

If globalization has one defining characteristic it is that individual enterprises become owned and controlled by ever-larger conglomerates. Size certainly is a factor that encourages deviance: it has long been recognized as related to worker propensity to theft (Smigel, 1956).

## Technical changes and old and new sabotage

An early insight into the effects of globalization, its influence on workplace relations, on sabotage and on 'negotiation by riot', comes from a remarkable case study by Quantaert (1986). He alerts us to the influence of trade cycles and of new technology that led to machine breaking and factory destruction at Usak by Anatolean carpet makers in 1908. Massively increased demand in Europe for 'Turkey carpets' during an economic boom led to the introduction of new artificial dyes under the control of German merchants. They came to dominate the industry and, to rationalize production, attempted to move their workers from a network of domestic manufacture to factory production. The resultant riots occurred in a period of general social unrest and were significant in fomenting the successful political revolution later spearheaded by the 'Young Turks'.

The significance of events at Usak points up the social implications of possibly the most potent contributory cause of industrial unrest in modern society – shifts in trade due to economic cycles whose effects are more readily transmitted – as they are with globalization – when economies are integrated or are at least interdependent. These shifts, often involving sudden disruptions to social life and frequently having political implications, invariably also affect industrial relations. This is so whether, as at Usak, the market increases in boom, or shrinks in slump/recession. It is the disruption to relationships, to trust and to shifts in power and control that are destabilizing, resented, and can lead to the coalescing of previously segmented workforces that leads to increases in occupational deviance.

Since the emergence of concerns about hidden economies in the 1970s and 1980s, economic conditions have been reasonably equable, at least in the West. This, however, is unlikely to continue indefinitely; nor can the same be said of the developing world where the harsher effects of globalization are felt. The high mobility of capital with globalization and the arbitrary relocation of production with its concomitant social effects have increasingly polarized the interests of local producers and their distant controllers. Such 'flexibility' can be extremely disruptive and in the developing world, particularly so. The resulting instability may well have considerable political implications, as Usak suggests.

In their strivings for competitive advantage, multinational and transnational corporations are up-to-date innovators of the latest technologies and especially of computerized production and control systems. It is almost platitudinous to note how computers, especially, have radically affected workplace relations and, I would argue, workplace deviance. While the extension of IT has undoubtedly reduced workers, control in some jobs, it has increased it in others. Increases in the control over strong Grid/Donkey jobs – as in call centres and electronic assembly firms, for example – encourage deviance, particularly resentment fiddles. But IT can also paradoxically increase the power of such workers who, if resentful, can be disruptive and prone to sabotage (Mars, 2001a). I recall a receptionist in a large chain hotel whose job was subject to considerable bureaucratic controls. On his last day with that employer he used the hotels computerized booking system to 'add' 50 extra rooms to its database. These were duly booked out – and generated chaos when expectant guests arrived to claim their non-existent rooms.

Sabotage that involves computers is not necessarily a new form of sabotage – though some, as will be discussed – undoubtedly is. Hollinger (1997: xx) points out that much behaviour involving computers represents merely a 're-tooling' of deviant and criminal activity for the computer age. Many computerized jobs – as in call centres – by closely charting and monitoring performances and comparatively rating them – increase responsibility, even as they simultaneously reduce control – a sure method, if these are sufficiently out of balance, of raising resentment. But in essence such conditions are no different from those that previously had existed among workers operating conveyor belts whose [traditional] response had been to 'throw a spanner in the works' as was often applied to resented Taylorian production methods.

An effective response to such up-gridding is often unable to be mounted by individuals and usually, but not always, needs collective action, as did most of what can be called the 'traditional sabotage' of the past. The form this takes, however, varies and would well repay systematic comparative study. A comparison of responses to coercive technology in Malaysia, and Thailand shows very different responses to similar technical up-Gridding.[4] Throughout Malaysia in the 1980s and 1990s there was a rash of collective disruptions in transnational factories assembling electronic components. Staffed mostly by rural young women, selected for compliance and dexterity, they were closely monitored by computers that fully controlled their pace and mode of work. Responsibility was inherent, errors quickly identified, and penalties imposed. They did not, however, go sick, strike or sabotage their controlling computers. Such responses had no place in their 'culture of complaint', which indigenously had involved intervention in disputes by intermediaries. With no intervening unions that could take on this role, or people so ascribed by kinship, these routes to resolve grievances were blocked. Instead they invoked supernatural intervention: they collectively refused to work because they found their factories to be haunted by malevolent spirits. They collectively refused to return until elaborate, extensive and time-consuming ceremonies by 'Bomo' (spirit mediums who were specialist shamans) had restored their factories to spiritual purity. There is no suggestion that the Malaysian response was not one of genuine fear. It bears comparison with forms of spirit possession found among low-status peasants in a variety of cultures analysed by Joan Lewis (1971: 115) and discussed in Scott (1985: 289). Lewis found that among the Indian Nayar, such spirits functioned as 'consciences of the rich'. The main difference between the Nayar and Malay cases is that the one locates its spirits in its workers, the other in the factory buildings of employers.

In Thailand, similar factories employing the same computerized control systems employed predominantly male workers. There, however, traditional conflict resolution tends to be direct and face-to-face. Factory disruptions involved direct action against products, machinery and premises. More comparative research is needed – if only to further test technically determinist arguments, assumptions of global 'convergence',[5] and to comparatively explore the influence of 'cultures of complaint'. Both responses have in common an activating of the latent collective propensity of culture groups.

These cases represent 're-tooled sabotage'. But the IT revolution has now made possible a qualitatively different and more individualist form of sabotage. First, whereas 're-tooled sabotage' invariably reveals a unifying and collective grievance, a marked imbalance of formal power, and the ability and opportunity to communicate and organize, not all of these factors are now necessary: a saboteur's grievance no longer needs to be localized. Nor does it need to be collective – those with an individual grievance can act unilaterally without the need for any support other than technical support – as did the hotel receptionist who acted on his own. Again, with the increased connectivity IT provides, groups or individuals can act across divergent parts of a dispersed organization that might have little apparent relation to one another. Similarly, the communication and organization required to act in concert no longer require a face-to-face contact locally. These factors make it difficult to locate and to control 'The New Saboteur's.

The second distinctive feature of 'the new sabotage' which hardly existed a quarter century ago, is that instead of disrupting process and products along-side fellow workers, a saboteur's primary, and in most cases individual concern, is now likely to be involved with manipulating information. The most feared and potent forms of information manipulation derive from devices capable of sending radio signals strong enough to disrupt and permanently damage computer systems. No less dramatic is the planting of viruses that have the potential to steal, erase, or modify data and that can travel to all parts of a globally dispersed organization or/and to its customers or suppliers. Among the most common forms of information manipulation are:

- The deletion, addition, modification, adaptation or distortion of information (which can involve the reprogramming of procedures affecting production outputs and quality).
- The unauthorized promulgation or publication of information, as when two staff members broke into IBM's personnel system and widely disseminated confidential information on staff and managerial salaries that informed and empowered personal negotiation. This same scam occurred recently within the BBC.
- 'Denial of service' by which an 'online service' may be overwhelmed by excesses of unwanted data.

These types of information manipulation are most appropriate (but not exclusive) to Donkey job-holders. A fourth form, however, appropriate to Hawks, is the introduction of 'eavesdropping programmes' that allow periodic or continual access to confidential data which can then be sold on to a firm's rivals: the IT generation's version of industrial espionage and a point where the legitimate and illegitimate might be said to meet. It has never been easy to obtain reliable statistical data on the incidence of hidden economy activity and especially to gain access to case material on IT deviance. Employers are understandably reluctant to admit they have been vulnerable to, or victims of, IT scams.

Not all technical complexity, however, has to do with computers. The steady march of technological advance operates throughout the economy and the ever more refined divisions of labour it fosters extends the power of Hawks. As technical complexity increases, there grows an ever widening 'knowledge gap' between specialist experts in these fields and their customers and clients. Twenty-five years ago it was still possible for a reasonably handy amateur mechanic to carry out routine repairs and servicing to an average car. Now one has only to consider the ever more (and to a degree, even here, computerized) complexity of cars, to appreciate the increasing imbalance in the knowledge of their owners compared to that of garage staff on whom they depend and the deviance to which this inevitably leads (O'Brien, 1977). This 'knowledge gap' operates of course, in relationships other than car owners and garage staffs; it is an iconic example of a problem that extends throughout the economy

## Psycho/social change: the growth in individualism

Psycho/social changes that follow from the increasingly competitive tempo of globalization and its marketing emphasis on consumption are an increasing influence affecting occupational deviance. Chief among these is an ongoing acceleration of the trend to low grid/low group individualism – evident in Europe at least since the Renaissance. Individualists are less bound by group incorporation nor by prescribed social roles than are other constituencies. These are the Hawks to whom all boundaries are provisional and subject to negotiation. This trend has been progressively driven by the exponential growth of technology and knowledge, of resultant specialization and increases in the overall divisions of labour that have ensured that access to jobs increasingly depends less on ascription and more on at least some degree of objectively defined merit. Such individualism is most evident, to very broadly generalize, in that most technologically complex country, the United States. Insofar as the States exports its technology, organization and ideology, so it exports individualism.

Individualism's principal manifestations are a gradual shaking off of constraints from, and the respect afforded to, hierarchies (and therefore to employers and indeed all sources of institutionalized authority): a concomitant relaxation or deflection of group controls that flow from and within them, as well as from outside regulatory bodies. In DCT terms, the growth in individualism represents a marked societal move down-grid so that we see an increasing emphasis on the entrepreneurial (Hawk) aspects of work roles with their tendency to rule bending, short-termism, calculated risk-taking and the cultivation of ever shifting networks favouring the individual – often at the expense of the employer or other stakeholders. What is occurring is a shift from the constraints of organizational hierarchies to the freedoms of employee individualism – from concerns with the long-term position of organizations to the short-term interest of the individuals within them: Wolves are morphing into Hawks. This societal shift to low grid individualism applies at all levels of organizations, particularly so as role holders shift from one employing organization to another with increasing frequency. In addition, the increasing tendency of distant managers who 'manage from afar' through targets, bonuses for achievement and penalties for failure, leads to a replication in the West of some of the excesses noted in the Soviet Union where local managers adapt and cheat in a host of imaginative ways to achieve their targets (Mars and Altman, forthcoming).

Global employers too are more prone to deviance. The Enron scandal and others of similar ilk reflect what appear to be the increasingly short-term concerns of some top managements who sacrifice their and their companies' long-term interests to maintain their short-term share prices (and resultant bonuses) by whatever means they can. With globalization, their customers are dispersed and they are less subject to their localized social controls as well as being out of the reach of many national and regional governments.

There is insight to be gained from Shapiro's (1989) explanation for the rise in white-collar crime. The 'flattening' of hierarchies, a marked feature of the efficiency drives of globalized corporations has led to a necessary increase in delegation and discretion – that is, in allocations of responsibility and control – and thus to enhanced individualism. Such delegated relationships involve significant shifts in power – from upper to lower levels of organization – and these entail trust – with all its concomitant opportunities for betrayal. Increased delegation, if allied to increases in personal control, add to a job's autonomy, and together with a loss of the efficacy of group controls, further fuels the down-grid shift to increase the deviance liability of Hawks. Such circumstances increase the opportunities for individualistic, self-serving behaviour, which is in essence the central characteristic of Hawks.

On the other hand, increasing delegation without the trust inherent to also grant control is a sure-fire means of increasing the number of Donkey jobs. Trust is of course, two-way and is consolidated in long-term relationships. Since there has been an accelerating reduction of lifetime employment with one employer – as evident in the increasing propensity to employ via short-term contracts – this further encourages occupational deviance. This growing lack of long-term commitment towards their employees by increasingly individualistic, Hawk-like employers is manifest in changing pension arrangements (at lower levels, though not for the most senior managements). These unsurprisingly generate resentment and a lack of loyalty from workers. The main theme to consider here is the growing disparity between levels of pay on the 'shop floor' and the pay of senior managements. This is a feature of most western economies and the differential has been progressive over the past quarter century. 'Iniquity theorists' such as Tucker (1989), following Adams (1965), demonstrate that such perceived iniquity invariably leads to increases in occupational deviance; though Sieh (1987) found that the likelihood of a recourse to occupational deviance was minimized where strong unions and strong work groups operated. The one institutionalizes effective grievances; the other exerts group controls. But there has been a noted weakening of both unions and group cohesion in the West during the last quarter century.

## Conclusion

In the absence of authoritative statistics there can be no clear answers to the question: 'Has occupational deviance and the hidden economy of occupations increased in the past quarter century?' Consideration of globally derived macro-features – technology and individualism – when projected onto the 1982 micro-analyses, suggest that developments in these areas since then offer a mixed picture, though with the likelihood of an overall increase. While, for instance, technology has made conveyor belts obsolete, together with their liability to sabotage, it has also facilitated computer-based controls in newer kinds of enterprise, whose staff still retain similar tendencies towards sabotage. While it seems likely that IT-derived constraints such as monitoring appear to be increasingly imposed at higher levels of the status hierarchy, IT, as noted, has in some cases increased autonomy – and therefore the fiddle potential – of many staffs at lower organizational levels.

Overall, it appears likely that there has been an increased potential in occupational deviance emanating from globalism and from four of the five fiddle-prone areas – though no attempt has been made to weigh their impacts. Compared to *Cheats* in 1982, much of the discussion on occupational deviance here has been concerned with the illicit obtaining of resources and time – the concerns of Hawks, Wolves and Vultures. It is important, however, to distinguish such deviance from sabotage, the primary province of Donkey jobs which, because of the increasingly organic nature of global production and of technologically derived constraints might be expected to facilitate sabotage.

Globalization with its long-distance managerialism has brought ethnocentrically imposed constraints on some, but it also offers more Hawks yet more facilities to insulate their different activities and the divergence between ever widening arenas and markets and has increased their opportunities for autonomous scams. As individualism encourages the appreciation of autonomy and freedom from constraints for some, it also invariably involves those same individualists imposing constraints on others. As a result, more Hawk activity means that more constrained Donkey jobs have also been created.

As previously noted, DCT analysis applied to occupational deviance has proved remarkably robust over the past quarter century. Whereas then it was exclusively directed at 'ordinary people in ordinary jobs', it would seem worthwhile now, however, to extend it to the activities of extraordinary people in extraordinary jobs – to the distant controllers of multinational corporations whose Hawk-like behaviours benefit from enhanced opportunities to insulate different aspects of their activities with limited constraints from national legal liabilities or the inhibitions of group involvements.

Neither the macro-factors nor the five 'fiddle-prone' areas, considered here are presented as either exhaustive or exclusive: other factors may emerge as of equal or greater significance. Not least is the significance of trade cycles that has been raised earlier. The macro-areas are intuitively derived. But intuition is, after all, the first stage of most scientific enquiry. They are offered here to encourage further and more systematic research as they influence the micro concerns that were originally discussed in *Cheats at Work*. I hope to have suggested some fruitful areas to explore and some effective conceptual frameworks to use on the way. What is needed now is more comparative, systematic, quantitative work and the collection of qualitative data.

## Acknowledgements

Some of the arguments and some of the text of this chapter have appeared in various forms in other of the authors publications: Mars (1982/94; 2001(a); 2001(b); 2006).

## Notes

1  It is important to recognize that these categories are extremes – ideal types: that they describe social categories based on structure. They apply to situations and contexts: they are not psychological categories, nor derived from 'common-sense,' intuitive categorizations as favoured by journalists, valuable as these may be on occasion.

2  I am NOT here referring to the holders of these jobs as 'Donkeys' but to the *structure* of their jobs that determines behaviours appropriate to them. The same applies to the other mnemonic animal categories used.

3  According to C. Wright Mills:

> Only by moving grandly on the macroscopic level can we satisfy our intellectual and human curiosities. But only by moving minutely on the molecular level can our observations and explanations be adequately connected. So, if we would have our cake and eat it too, we must shuttle between macroscopic and molecular levels in instituting the problem *and* in explaining it. (C. Wright Mills, undated c.1963, in an essay, 'Two Styles of Research', p. 563)

4  Much of the discussion of sabotage here is taken from the Introduction to Mars (2001a).

5  I am grateful to Prof. Michael Hitchcock for fruitful discussions on sabotage in Asian communities.

## References

Adams, J. (2000) 'The hypermobility of Western society', *Prospect Magazine*, 50.

Adams, J.S. (1965) 'Iniquity in social exchange', in L. Berkowitz (ed.), *Advances in Experimental Social Psychology, vol. 2*. San Diego: Academic Press, pp. 267–99.

Bank of England Report (1995) *Report of the Board of Banking Supervision Inquiry into the Circumstances of the Collapse of Barings*. London: HMSO.

Dalton, M. (1959) *Men Who Manage*. New York: John Wiley & Sons, Ltd.

Douglas, M. (1970) *Natural Symbols: Explanations in Cosmology*. Harmondsworth: Penguin.

Douglas, M. (1978) *Cultural Bias*. London: Royal Anthropological Institute.

Giddens, A. (1990) *The Consequences of Modernity*. Cambridge: Polity Press.

Goffman, E. (1961) 'On the characteristics of total institutions', in *Asylums: Essays on the Social Situation of Mental Patients and Other Inmates*. New York: Doubleday.

Gouldner, A.W. (1957–8) 'Cosmopolitans and locals', *Administrative Science Quarterly*, 2. 281–300, 444–80.

Henry, S. (1978) *The Hidden Economy: The Context and Control of Borderline Crime*. Oxford: Martin Robertson.

Henry, S. (1987) 'The political economy of informal economies', *The Annals of the American Academy of Political and Social Science* (Special Issue: The Informal Economy), September, 493: 137–53.

Henry, S. and Mars, G. (1978) 'Crime at work: the social construction of amateur property theft', *Sociology*, 12: 245–63.

Hodges, E.J. (1974) 'A sociological analysis of dud behaviour in the United States Army', in C.D. Bryant (ed.) *Deviant Behavior: Occupational and Organisational Bases*. Chicago: Rand McNally Publishing Co.

Hollinger, R.D. (1997) *Crime, Deviance and the Computer*. Aldershot: Dartmouth Publishing.

Hollinger, R.D. and Clark, J.P. (1983) *Theft by Employees*. Lexington, MA: Lexington Books.

Lewis, J.M. (1971) *Ecstatic Religions: An Anthropological Study of Spirit Possession and Shamanism*. Harmondsworth: Penguin.

Mars, G. (1981) 'The anthropology of managers', *RAIN, Royal Anthropological Institute News*, 42, February.

Mars, G. (1982, 1994) *Cheats at Work: An Anthropology of Workplace Crime*. Aldershot: Dartmouth Publishing.

Mars, G. (ed.) (2001a) *Sabotage*. Aldershot: Ashgate.

Mars, G. (ed.) (2001b) *Occupational Crime*. Aldershot: Ashgate.

Mars, G. (2006) 'Changes in occupational deviance: scams, fiddles and sabotage in the twenty-first century', *Crime, Law and Social Change*, 45: 285–96.

Mars, G. and Altman, Y. (forthcoming) 'Managing in Soviet Georgia: an extreme example in comparative management', *European Journal of Management*.

Mills, C. Wright. (undated, c. 1963) *Power Politics and People: The Collected Essays of C. Wright Mills*. New York: Ballantine Books.

O'Brien, D.P. (1977) 'Why you may be dissatisfied with garage servicing', *Motor*, 10 September.

Perri and Mars, G. (2008) *The New Durkheimians: The Institutional Dynamics of Culture*. Aldershot: Ashgate.

Quataert, D. (1986) 'Machine breaking and the changing carpet industry of Western Anatolia, 1880–1908', *Journal of Social History*, 19: 473–89.

Sayles, L.R. (1956) *Behaviour in Industrial Work Groups*. New York: John Wiley & Sons, Ltd.

Scott, J.C. (1985) *Weapons of the Weak: Everyday Forms of Peasant Resistance*. New Haven, CT: Yale University Press.

Shapiro, S. (1989) 'Collaring the crime not the criminal: reconsidering White Collar crime', *American Sociological Review*, 55: 346–65.

Sieh, E.W. (1987) 'Garment workers: perceptions of iniquity and employee theft', *British Journal of Criminology*, 27: 174–90.

Smigel, E.O. (1956) 'Public attitudes towards stealing as related to the size of the victim organisation', *American Sociological Review*, 21(3): 320–7.

Thompson, M., Ellis, R. and Wildavsky, A. (1990) *Cultural Theory*. Boulder, CO: Westview Press.

Tucker, J. (1989) 'Employee theft as social control', *Deviant Behaviour*, 10: 319–34.

## Suggestions for further reading

Ackroyd, S. and Thompson, P. (1999) *Organisational Misbehaviour*. London: Sage.

Dalton, M. (1959) *Men Who Manage*. New York: John Wiley & Sons, Ltd.

Hollinger, R.C. and Clark, J.P. (1983) *Theft by Employees*. Lexington, MA: Lexington Books.

Mars, G. (1982, 1984) *Cheats at Work: An Anthropology of Workplace Crime*. Dartmouth: Allen and Unwin.

Mars, G. (ed.) (2001) *Occupational Crime*. Aldershot: Ashgate.

Punch, M. (1996) *Dirty Business: Exploring Corporate Misconduct*. London: Sage.

# NINE

# Getting Beyond the Moral Drama of Crime
## What We Learn From Studying White-collar Criminal Careers

*David Weisburd, Elin Waring and Nicole Leeper Piquero*

## Introduction

When Edwin Sutherland coined the term 'white collar crime' in his address to the American Sociological Society in 1939, he used the concept to challenge conventional stereotypes and theories.[1] In 1939, crime was generally seen as the work of disadvantaged young men from broken homes and decaying neighborhoods. Through films and books, the criminal was portrayed as a tough guy growing up on the wrong side of town. He was either to be saved by the church or the community or to be condemned to a sad fate determined by the difficult circumstances in which he was raised.

Such stereotypes were not limited to popular images of criminality. In a series of enduring empirical inquiries, sociologists at the University of Chicago in the 1920s and 1930s emphasized the link between social disorganization and poverty in areas within a city and high rates of criminal behavior (e.g. see Thrasher, 1927; Shaw, 1929). Their work, which continues to have an important role in American criminology (e.g. see Reiss and Tonry, 1986), served to focus attention on crimes of the lower classes. When Sutherland gave his ground-breaking speech to the American Sociological Society, scholars and lay people alike saw poverty or conditions associated with poverty as intricately linked to criminality.

Sutherland challenged the traditional image of criminals and the predominant etiological theories of crime of his day. The white-collar criminals he identified were often middle-aged men of respectability and high social status. They lived in affluent neighborhoods and they were well respected in the community. Sutherland was not the first to draw attention to such criminals. In earlier decades, scholars such as W.A. Bonger (1916) and E.A. Ross (1907) and popular writers such as Upton Sinclair (1906) and Lincoln Steffens (1903) pointed out a variety of misdeeds by businessmen and elites. However, such people were seldom considered by those scholars who wrote about or studied crime and were not a major concern of the public or policy-makers when addressing the crime problem.

Sutherland (1940) argued that the predominant conceptions and explanations of crime in his day were 'misleading and incorrect' because they were developed from 'biased samples' of criminals and criminal behavior (see also Sutherland, 1945; 1949). He noted that 'vast areas of criminal behavior of persons not in the lower class' had been neglected in prior studies (1940: 2). In Sutherland's view, poverty and social disorganization could not be seen as the primary causes of crime, if crime could also be found among people who grew up in 'good neighborhoods and good homes' and lived in situations of authority and privilege. He believed that much could be learned about the crime problem by focusing on the category of white-collar crime. He declared that white-collar crime was not an isolated phenomenon, but a significant part of the landscape of criminal behavior.

Despite Sutherland's recognition of the importance of the white-collar crime category, it never achieved the centrality in criminological study that he proposed. White-collar crime has, for the most part, been treated as a deviant case, invoked primarily to provide a contrast to the common crimes and street criminals that continue to dominate research and theory about crime. In our work, we seek to return the white-collar crime category to the mainstream (see Weisburd and Waring, 2001). Our specific focus has been on what criminologists term criminal careers (see Blumstein and Soumy, 1982; Blumstein et al., 1986). Much research on crime has focused on general portraits of crime in the population. The concern of such studies is with aggregate crime rates in communities or regions of the country, or the relative changes in crime rates over time. The criminal career approach, in contrast, 'seeks to analyze the activity – the careers – of the individuals who commit criminal offences' (Blumstein et al., 1986: 1). In this context, the criminal career approach allows scholars and policy-makers to focus directly on the causes of criminality, and potential methods of effective prevention and treatment of crime (Farrington et al., 1986).

Though the study of criminal careers has come to occupy a central place in the study of crime, criminologists have largely overlooked the criminal careers of white-collar offenders (Piquero and Benson, 2004). For study of criminal careers, as with study of other crime and justice problems, the primary focus of researchers has been upon street crimes and common criminals. The fact that white-collar criminals have been assumed to be one-shot offenders (e.g. see Edelhertz and Overcast, 1982; Wheeler et al., 1988) has reinforced this bias. Even though there is a long tradition of scholarship dating back to Sutherland (1949) that recognizes that white-collar criminals, like common criminals, may repeat their involvement in law-violating acts, most scholars (including Sutherland) have assumed that white-collar criminals are unlikely to have multiple contacts with the criminal justice system. Since such contacts have formed an important part of the study of criminal careers (Blumstein et al., 1986), white-collar crime has not been seen as a fruitful area of concern for criminal career researchers.

Our research contradicts this common assumption about white-collar criminals (see Weisburd et al., 1990; Weisburd and Waring, 2001; see also Benson and Moore, 1992). We have found that a substantial number of offenders who are convicted under white-collar crime statutes in the United States federal courts have multiple contacts with the criminal justice system. This fact led us to explore the problem of white-collar criminal careers, allowing us to examine white-collar crimes and criminals using a different approach than has traditionally been applied by other white-collar crime scholars. It also provides us with an opportunity to critically examine assumptions about criminality and criminal careers that have been developed primarily in the context of studies of street criminals.

In taking this approach, we are led to a portrait of crimes and criminals that is very different from that which has traditionally dominated criminology. Criminologists have generally focused on the ways in which criminals differ from those not involved in crime. As Thomas Gabor writes:

> Traditionally, criminologists have attempted to explain why some people become criminals and others do not. Some have attributed the apparent differences between criminals and the law-abiding to innate or genetic factors, others to personality differences, and still others to social circumstances. Whatever their persuasion, these traditionalists shared the assumption that there were clear differences between criminals and the rest of society. The traditional goal of research and theory in criminology, therefore has been to identify these differences as precisely as possible. (1994: 14)

Our examination of white-collar crime and criminal careers suggests an understanding of crime that relies less on identifying characteristics of criminality than on understanding the circumstances surrounding crime situations. The emphasis that traditional scholarship has placed on distinguishing between criminals and non-criminals adds little to understanding the involvement in crime of many of those we study. Rather, our data suggest the importance of the immediate context of crime and its role in leading otherwise conventional people to violate the law. In this chapter, we want to focus directly on two main areas where our work has raised new concerns or intriguing questions. By necessity we begin by describing the study upon which our observations are based, and the main findings of our work on white-collar criminal careers. We then examine the ways in which our description of criminal careers in a white-collar crime sample challenges traditional stereotypes of criminals and criminality, and discuss the implications of our study for understanding involvement in crime more generally. We focus particular attention on the importance of situational, as contrasted with historical, explanations for criminal behavior. In concluding, we turn to our thoughts about the policy implications of our work.

## White-collar crime and criminal careers

Prior to the 1980s, very little was known about white-collar offenders. The dearth of quantitative data required that descriptions of white-collar offenders be derived from case studies which usually depicted highly publicized, egregious offenders and offences. Two data collection efforts in the 1980s, one effort led by Stanton Wheeler, David Weisburd and Nancy Bode (1988; see also Weisburd et al., 1991) and the other by Brian Forst and William Rhodes (n.d.), changed the portrait of white-collar offenders by providing information that detailed both offender and offence characteristics. The sample from both data collection efforts was based upon individual offenders who were convicted in US federal courts of a white-collar crime. Two notable findings emerged: (1) most of those convicted of white-collar crimes came from the middle class of society; that is, they were average citizens with moderate incomes (see Weisburd et al., 1991); and (2) a substantial proportion of convicted white-collar offenders had at least one prior arrest (Piquero and Benson, 2004; Weisburd et al., 1990). These conclusions challenged existing assumptions about the characteristics of white-collar criminals, and suggested that study of white-collar crime was relevant to criminal career research.

Building upon the Wheeler et al. data collection effort, our study of white-collar criminal careers (see Weisburd and Waring, 2001) gathered additional longitudinal data tracking the criminal records of the white-collar offenders for more than ten years. White-collar crime was defined by Wheeler, Weisburd and Bode as 'economic offences committed through the use of some combination of fraud, deception, or collusion' (1982: 642; see also Shapiro, 1981). They examined eight federal crimes that fit, in their statutory descriptions, this broad definition: antitrust offences, securities fraud, mail and wire fraud, false claims and statements, credit and lending institution fraud, bank embezzlement, income tax fraud, and bribery. Recognizing that many of those who committed these crimes were repeat criminals, we set out to examine how the officially recorded criminal careers of white-collar offenders were similar to or different from those of common crime offenders.

Their data allowed us to focus upon five specific dimensions of offending employed in criminal career research (see Blumstein et al., 1986): onset, frequency, specialization, duration, and desistance. In terms of offence frequency, we found that that approximately one-third of the repeat offenders in the sample had one additional arrest beyond the criterion white-collar crime with a similar proportion having been arrested between two and four additional times. Twenty percent of the sample had been arrested between five and nine times while 13 percent of the sample had ten or more additional arrests since the original white-collar crime offence.

Important differences were identified between the criminal careers of white-collar offenders and those of common crime offenders. We found that white-collar offenders were much older at the time of their first and last arrest with the average age of onset at 35 and the average age of last recorded arrest was 43. Additionally, we identified a substantial number of offenders who were arrested much later in life with some (though relatively few) offenders arrested in their late sixties or early seventies. At the same time, as is generally the case in common crime samples, the sample indicated a decline in the likelihood of offending as the subjects age. As such, we found that like common crime samples, the white-collar offenders also age out of crime, though these offenders appeared to desist *much* later in life.

Whatever the age at which the white-collar offenders have their last recorded arrest, the duration of their criminal histories seemed to be very long. We found a mean duration of criminal career length of about 14 years. However, while the length of time between age of onset and last arrest is very long, the number of offences on average, committed in this time period is comparatively small. By examining the mix of offences reflected in the rap sheets, we found evidence of only moderate specialization, a finding similar to the criminal histories of common offenders.

In order to study the criminal careers of white-collar offenders in more detail, we examined the social histories of their offenders as well as the factors which appear to lead to their involvement. Of first concern was the difference between low-frequency offenders, those with one or two arrests in their criminal histories, and the chronic offenders, those with three or more arrests. We found that low frequency offenders were significantly more likely to: own their own homes, be steadily employed, have marital stability, evidence high educational achievement, and were less likely to be defined as a substance or alcohol abuser.

In a qualitative review of the pre-sentence investigation reports from the criterion offence, we identified three main criminal career patterns for white-collar criminals. The first included the low-frequency offenders, those whose criminal histories were marked with one or two arrests. For this group of offenders, criminal activities appear to be an aberration in an otherwise conventional social record. Other than the instances of criminality, these offenders' lives were virtually indistinguishable from those of other people in similar social and economic circumstances. Overall, this group corresponded to images of respectability and conformity rather than instability and deviance.

Some subtle differences did emerge within the 'crime as an aberration' group and two categories of offenders appeared. One group, the 'crisis responders', engaged in criminality in response to some type of perceived crisis in their professional or personal lives. Although the nature of the crisis varied considerably, in general, these individuals responded by taking advantage of a position of trust that they occupied (see also Cressey, 1980; Zietz, 1981). Most members of this group had been in positions of trust for extended periods without, as far as is known, violating that trust. Describing one such offender, Weisburd and Waring observe:

> One construction contractor, for example, had participated in a straw bidding process that resulted in the government paying artificially high prices for repairs to repossessed homes. The probation officer noted that family and friends described the defendant as 'being hard-working,' a 'self-made man' who was 'successful in his endeavors in the field of construction.' The probation officer also noted that the defendant's financial condition just before the commencement of the offence was 'very bleak and very desperate.' While the defendant had been married three times, his most recent marriage was still intact and had lasted for more than 20 years. Though he never earned a college degree, he had attended college for two years, and had been honorably discharged from the army. The probation officer argued that the sentence should be mitigated by 'the defendant's lack of a prior criminal record and by the positive elements of his past social history.' (2001: 59)

The criminality of the second group, the 'opportunity takers', appeared to be linked strongly to some unusual or special set of opportunities that suddenly materialized for the offender. These appeared to be offenders who led otherwise conventional lives and took advantage of a set of specific opportunities despite their understanding that the behaviors involved were criminal. The crimes are usually defined as part of the normal procedures at their families' businesses or in their business networks. Taking advantage of this opportunity does not appear to be consistent with other aspects of their lives or indicative of a tendency toward instability or deviance. In general, they entered into a situation without a plan to engage in criminal activity; but as they become aware of the opportunity for a particular offence, they took it. One securities violator, who otherwise had no criminal record, explained:

> Business on Wall Street was in one of the biggest booms ever. People were making money hand over fist. I had never in my life seen anything like it. It was like a dream or something that I had read about in fiction novels. People around me kept telling me to jump on the so-called band wagon – how easy it was to make money quickly. 'Buy new issues' they told me. 'Trade in any name'; they said ... After working so many years and putting in 16–20 hour days, six and seven days per week, and seeing how people around me were making money so easily, I succumbed to their advice ... All I knew was that for the first time in my whole life I was finally making money for my family. (Weisburd and Waring, 2001: 64–65)

By examining the pre-sentence investigation reports of chronic offenders, two main types of criminals were identified: opportunity seekers and stereotypical criminals. The 'opportunity seekers' seemed to seek out opportunities to commit crime or, at times, create a situation amenable to committing a specific type of offence. Many of these offenders exhibited characteristics of conventionality and stability with large gaps in time between their arrests. Therefore, people in this category did not fit traditional stereotypes of criminality, but nonetheless, turned more than once or twice to criminal behavior. More generally, there appears to be a defined pattern of offending which suggests a willingness to seek out specific types of situational opportunities for crime. For this group, there is strong evidence of propensity to crime early on in life. But there is also evidence that offenders are influenced and strongly affected by events and situations in the life course. As Weisburd and Waring write, regarding a defendant whose criterion offence was false claims to a bank:

> [He] contended [in explaining his crime] that he was 'in a financial bind and needed money desperately.' He noted that 'I was about to lose my house and everything. I am sorry for what I have done but at the time, I saw no other way out.' To get the loan that he needed he and his wife listed false accounts and then had their credit report changed to list the non-existent assets.
>
> In contrast to the defendant's representation of the situation, the probation officer argued that the '[D]efendant is not prone to criminal behavior but is miserably lacking in scruples and moral values and not above committing criminal acts to perpetuate his life style.' Like many of those who fall in this category, he fulfills neither images of respectability and success on the one hand, nor those of a life which is defined by low self-control, disorganization, and deviance on the other. While the defendant dropped out of high school after performing poorly, he was honorably discharged as a corporal from the marines. After his discharge he completed two years of college as an average student. He was born out of wedlock, did not know his father, and was raised by a great-aunt. Nonetheless, the defendant had a stable marriage of nine years at the time of the criterion offence, although it should be noted that his wife played a key role in the criterion offence by making the first contact with the person who changed their credit report.
>
> This offender held ten different jobs in just ten years, but his employer at the time the PSI report was completed, a home shopping service, considered his performance to be above average. Although his FBI rap sheet shows no arrest prior to the criterion event, the probation officer identified four prior instances of contact with the criminal justice system: speeding and running a red light; use of a fictitious name to secure a driver's license; issuance of bad checks; and illegal use of a credit card. (2001: 78–9)

The second category of chronic offenders, the 'stereotypical criminals', evinced prior criminal histories indicating a strong commitment to breaking the law, as well as instability and low self-control in their lives more generally. The white-collar crime prosecutions for these offenders were often only one part of a mixed bag of criminal conduct. While they intermittently exhibited conventional lives, their personal histories more often included difficult childhoods, substance abuse, disruptions of divorce, unsteady unemployment and educational failure. In this sense, they fit a model in which criminality is just one part of a more complete portrait of the offender which reaches deep into his or her personal history and is reflective of a wide group of behaviors beyond criminality itself. A typical description of such stereotypical criminals is given by Weisburd and Waring:

> [He] had been arrested ten times between 1966 and 1988. The arrests ranged from white collar related crimes such as fraud, forgery and theft of securities, to aggravated arson, a weapons offence, and, finally, distribution of cocaine. In his brief periods of employment he reportedly had two different hourly jobs and was fired from them both. The defendant's mother was institutionalized when he was young, and he was raised by his father and a housekeeper whom his father eventually married. The defendant was divorced once and was separated at the time of the criterion offence and waiting to marry a woman with whom he was living. While the defendant admitted no addictions, his family revealed a serious drinking problem. The probation officer remarked that the defendant was 'an unsettled, poorly adjusted young man of low normal intelligence'. (2001: 84)

## Implications for traditional understandings of criminality

We believe that our identification of different patterns of criminal careers among white-collar offenders has important implications for our understanding of criminality more generally. When lay people use the term criminality, or when they call people criminals, they are not simply referring to the fact that someone has come into contact with the criminal justice system. Criminality has a much broader meaning. Like nationality, culture or religion, the criminal label is intended to convey a great deal about those to whom it is applied. Criminals are generally viewed as dangerous to society, as products of bad genes or bad parenting or broken communities. Crime is not merely an incident in such people's lives. The criminal label summarizes a vast array of behaviors and activities, and communicates something very meaningful about who such people are and where they are going. Most importantly, criminals are different.[2] This is a very comfortable moral position, and one that helps the rest of us to define what we have in common with each other.

The lay view of criminality is reflected in the interests of professional criminologists. Almost from the outset, scholars concerned with crime and justice have sought to identify those characteristics of offenders that set them apart from ordinary law-abiding citizens (Gabor, 1994). Of course, in searching for the characteristics that make criminals different, criminologists have accepted, in some sense, the view that criminals are indeed different in the first place. The choice of subject reflects the basic theoretical assumptions of this approach. In looking to identify the factors that distinguish criminals from non-criminals, criminologists have begun with theories that locate the causes of crime in the biological, personal, or social histories of offenders.

Many of the predominant themes in this criminological perspective can be traced to the founding generations of criminology in the nineteenth century. Lombroso (1911), for example, looked for the origins of criminality in the physical characteristics of the criminals he studied. He stressed that the 'anti-social tendencies of criminals are the result of their physical and psychic organization, which differs essentially from that of normal individuals' (ibid.: 5). A series of other nineteenth-century scholars concerned with crime noted differences in the economic, social, and religious characteristics of geographic areas, and the relationship of these factors to official crime rates (e.g. see Durkheim, [1897] 1951; Guerry, 1833; Quetelet, 1835). In one sense, this view of the correlates of crime was not so much focused on the factors that differentiate offenders from others as with identifying areas where crime is more common. However, criminologists have generally used these broader social characteristics to identify factors that lead individuals to crime.

For example, the important insights related to crime and social disorganization brought by University of Chicago sociologists in the 1920s and 1930s (e.g. Thrasher, 1927; Shaw and McKay, 1931; 1942) are often translated into correlates of individual criminality. The idea that areas where social control is weak are breeding grounds for crime became part of a more general theory of criminality in which criminals are regarded as the products of broken neighborhoods and broken families. They are different from others because of the defects found in their upbringings and circumstances, not in their genes. Still, criminals continued to be considered different from others, and these differences were identified as the keys to understanding criminality.

In distinguishing elements of the prior experiences, social backgrounds, and development of offenders that produce criminality, criminologists have advanced a diverse group of theories and perspectives that are too numerous to mention here. But it is fair to say that whether the focus has been on factors such as anomie (Merton, 1938; see also Adler and Laufer, 1995; Passas and Agnew, 1997), social control (e.g. Hirschi, 1969), social learning (e.g. Akers, 1996, 1998; Sutherland and Cressey, 1960), or culture (e.g. Miller, 1958), there is a common theme in much criminological theory that looks to the offender and his or her past to gain an understanding of involvement in crime. The idea of criminality is one of process and history, in which specific characteristics of offenders and their environments lead them almost inevitably to criminality. Its portrait of offending, moreover, many times fits a morality play, in which the first acts, representing the first years of an offender's life, lead to an inevitable decline into deviance and criminality.

Even more recent perspectives which recognize that offenders, like others, will change and develop as a response to life course events and experiences begin with an assumption that there is something unique to the development of offenders that explains their participation in crime. Robert Sampson and John Laub (1993), for example, in their book, *Crime in the Making*, look to develop a comprehensive theory to explain the varied pathways to crime that are found in childhood, adolescence and adulthood. They argue that some offenders will evidence continuity in deviant and anti-social behavior throughout the life course. Others will end their criminal careers as a result of 'salient life events and socialization experiences in adulthood' (ibid.: 246). Still others will initiate involvement in crime in adulthood as a consequence of weak social bonds, such as weak labor force or marital attachments. But even while recognizing that paths to crime may begin at different stages of an offender's life, scholars taking this approach identify in every stage specific influences that increase (or decrease) the propensity of offenders to participate in crime and other deviant behaviors in the future. The causes of crime remain rooted in the factors that differentiate offenders from others.

One challenge to the traditional idea of criminality was brought by advocates of the societal reaction approach to deviance (e.g. Becker, 1963; Erikson, 1962; Kitsuse, 1962). These scholars began with a radical critique of conventional theories. In explaining the causes of crime, they emphasized the reactions of society rather than the nature of offenders themselves. Again, this approach may be traced to nineteenth-century criminology, especially to Emile Durkheim's ([1895] 1958) theories of the functionality of deviance for society. Societal reaction theorists did not assume that criminals began as different from others. Indeed, building on self-report studies which showed a very broad range of offending among people without criminal records (e.g. see Short and Nye, 1958; Wallerstein and Wyle, 1947), they argued that what differentiated criminals from others was simply the fact that they were labeled as such (e.g. see Erikson, 1962).

But this fact once again becomes a very important part of defining the ways in which criminals are different from non-criminals. Even if the fault lies with the societal reaction, once caught, the criminal is seen to fall into a spiral of deviance and related social problems (Wilkins, 1965). The criminal in this case begins much like others, but becomes different once labeled, fulfilling society's image of what the criminal should be like.

Another challenge to the moralistic view of criminals and criminality was initiated by crime prevention scholars in England (Clarke, 1980; 1983; Clarke and Cornish, 1985). In part, because of the seeming failures of offender-centered crime prevention strategies (e.g. see Lipton et al., 1975; Martinson, 1974; Sechrest et al., 1979), these theorists began to explore the importance of situational opportunities in the development of crime. They called for a more crime-specific and situational approach to crime, focusing less on the offender than on the opportunities available in specific situations. Many advocates of this approach adopted a perspective on crime which emphasized rational choice in the identification of criminal targets and the decision to commit crimes (e.g. see Cornish and Clarke, 1986).

Nonetheless, situational crime prevention advocates did not stake out a clear position on the idea of criminality, and the implications of their approach for the traditional distinctions made between offenders and non-offenders (Clarke, 1999). They sought more generally to offset the imbalance in criminological theory, which had neglected the crime situation and the importance of opportunities for crime in favor of asking 'why certain people might be more criminally inclined or less so' (Felson and Clarke, 1998: 1). Their approach did not demand a radical restructuring of traditional images of criminality, but rather that situational opportunities be given greater weight in understanding and preventing crime. Moreover, in their efforts to reorient crime prevention policies, situational prevention scholars naturally placed the question of criminality in the background, and focused their primary interest on the problem of how opportunities for crime may be blocked in specific situations (Weisburd, 2002).

Even the emphasis on rational choice that is often part of situational crime prevention approaches does not necessarily require that perspectives that emphasize distinctions between criminals and non-criminals be abandoned. Offenders' assessments of the costs and benefits of criminal behavior are often considered to be different from those of ordinary people (Cornish and Clarke, 1986). Their particular commitment to crime may lead them to weigh costs and benefits differently. Weak social bonds, social instability, and inability to delay gratification, may in this context also be seen as impacting upon the processes that underlie the rational choices of offenders to take advantage of criminal opportunities (Hirschi and Gottfredson, 1986). In theory, situational prevention does not require that offenders differ at all from non-offenders. In practice, however, many situational crime prevention researchers continue to accept traditional assumptions about criminality.

A major goal of our research was to examine the extent to which offenders convicted of white collar crimes would challenge this comfortable view of criminals as different from others in society. While theorists concerned with crime have more often than not ignored white-collar criminals, those who have taken this category into account have typically assumed that these offenders have pathways to crime that are similar to other criminals, even if their circumstances are very different (e.g. see Sutherland, 1940; Hirschi and Gottfredson, 1987). For example, Gottfredson and Hirschi argue in their *A General Theory of Crime* (1990) that the characteristics of individuals committing crime are similar regardless of the types of crimes they commit. They assert that 'crime in the street and crime in the suite is an offence rather than an offender distinction,' and that 'offenders in both cases are likely to share similar characteristics' (1990: 200). For Hirschi and Gottfredson, as well as many other criminologists, those characteristics set the offender apart from the rest of us:

> [C]riminality is the tendency of individuals to pursue short-term gratification in the most direct way with little consideration for the long term consequences of their acts (Indicators of such a tendency include impulsivity, aggression, activity level, and lack of concern for the opinion of others) ... (P)eople high on this tendency are relatively indifferent to punishment and to the interests of others. As a consequence, they tend to be impulsive, active and risk taking. (1987: 959–60)

Do convicted white-collar crime offenders exhibit traits that are associated with more traditional criminal populations? While of higher social class, do white-collar criminals evidence significant degrees of social instability, short-sightedness, inability to delay gratification, impulsiveness, and a series of other characteristics often associated with criminality? Or can we say that for white-collar crime, criminals are not very different from other people in similar social and economic circumstances who do not have contact with the criminal justice system?

Our research on white-collar crime does not provide a single answer to these questions. We do identify offenders in our study, those we define as 'stereotypical criminals', who fit traditional stereotypes of criminality. Their social and criminal records are consistent with common images of the criminal. However, most of those we study do not fit easily into conventional understandings. Irrespective of their involvement in crime, their lives do not appear to be very different from those of law-abiding citizens. For those termed opportunity-takers and crisis responders, the notion of a progression into crime and deviance belies what is most important about their involvement in the criminal justice system: such involvement is often an aberration on a record that is otherwise characterized by conventionality and not by deviance.

Even many of those in our sample who have more serious criminal records depart markedly from common stereotypes of criminality. These offenders were labeled opportunity seekers. On the one hand, their social and criminal records suggest that their crimes are not aberrations on unblemished records. Instead, they are part of a pattern of behavior often reaching into childhood, and sometimes leading to a lifetime of scheming and fraud. On the other hand, these criminals still evidence many characteristics of conformity and stability that are generally not associated with criminality.

Some scholars would argue that white-collar crime is interesting precisely because it is a deviant case. In this sense, our findings might be regarded as a reinforcement of what is conventionally believed about white-collar criminals: they are so different from other offenders that little can be learned from their experiences about the more general problem of crime. Study of white-collar crime, in this context, represents an interesting though esoteric enterprise.

While our results are gained from a sample of convicted white-collar criminals, we believe that they have broader implications for the study of crime. In the most basic sense, many individuals who are convicted for common crimes are similar to white-collar criminals in that they do not show evidence of a criminal career. Although the study of criminal careers has largely focused on chronic offenders, it has long been recognized that lower frequency offenders comprise a large part of the criminal population (e.g. see Blumstein et al., 1986). Petersilia (1980), for example, observes that more than half of all offenders with one official contact with the police will never have another (see also Tillman, 1987). While re-arrest rates are much higher for those who are convicted of crimes, and even higher for those who have served prison sentences (e.g. see Maltz, 1984; Schmidt and Witte, 1988), a substantial portion of those who experience arrest, conviction and even imprisonment will have only one or a very small number of contacts with the criminal justice system.

It is possible that infrequent contacts with the criminal justice system belie otherwise deviant and unconventional life styles. These offenders may conform to many of the stereotypes of criminality that we have discussed. However, we suspect that in common crime samples, as in our sample, many such people do not differ very much from others in their communities who are not identified and processed by the criminal justice system.[3]

Our decision to examine criminal careers in a white-collar crime sample led us to a focus on types of offenders that are often ignored in other studies. This approach leads us to abandon, at least in part, the moralistic view of criminality that has drawn the public's imagination and is reflected in much criminological theory. Criminals may often be just like others in the community. Their criminality may reveal little more than that they have committed a crime. This may be a less satisfying position for some than perspectives that attempt to distinguish offenders from non-offenders, but it is relevant to large numbers of people who participate in crime.

### The relevance of situational attitudes and opportunities

Having argued that traditional distinctions made between offenders and non-offenders are often more reflective of society's moralistic approach to the crime problem than the reality of crimes and criminals, we are led to the second major theme of our work. For many criminals, the key to understanding involvement in crime is not found in their distant pasts, or in the complexities of human development. Rather, it lies in the immediate context of the crimes that they commit.

Situation plays a central role in explaining participation in crime for most offenders in this sample.[4] The lives of those we have termed opportunity-takers and crisis responders do not seem to be characterized by instability and deviance, and there was little in their records that indicated a predisposition to criminality. Indeed, there was frequently evidence to the contrary. A specific crisis or special opportunity appears to have drawn otherwise conventional people across the line to crime. Even for those described as opportunity-seekers, situational opportunities play an important role in defining why offenders commit crimes at specific junctures.

While theorists concerned with the personal attributes associated with criminality have sometimes recognized the relevance of situational characteristics of crime (e.g. see Gottfredson and Hirschi, 1990), they are primarily interested in the offender and not the crime situation. For our sample, however, understanding criminality best begins not with the characteristics of individuals but rather with the situations in which crimes occur. But how we can such criminality be understood? Is it plausible to suggest that individuals will suddenly become involved in crime, and then, just as suddenly, return to conventional life styles and careers?

Many of these white-collar criminals maintain positive attitudes toward conventionality and legality even while participating in crime. Many of those labeled crisis responders are, by and large, conformists, but, in a specific situation, they feel the need to do something they define as wrong in order to deal with some perceived crisis that threatens them, their families, or their companies. Even when committing crime, they accept the fact that they should conform to legal norms, but believe they cannot.

People we have defined as opportunity-takers also accept more generally legal and conventional norms. Arguably, such people would not have violated the law in the first place if a specific opportunity had not confronted them. Although they do not seek out such criminal opportunities, once they appear, opportunity-takers decide that conventional norms are holding them up in a specific circumstance. Thus even when becoming involved in crime, both crisis responders and opportunity-takers maintain their commitment to conventionality. The crimes they commit appear as aberrations on otherwise law abiding records.

Of course, it is still the case that these criminals have made the decision at that situational juncture to become involved in crime. They might, in contrast, have decided not to take advantage of a specific criminal opportunity and responded with conventional rather than criminal behavior to a specific crisis in their lives. This line of reasoning implies that there is a specific moral decision that is made before each criminal act. Clearly, different people might respond differently in such circumstances, and individual personality traits are likely to influence the decisions made.

The question for criminologists and others interested in understanding crime is whether it is possible to identify these traits systematically. If they are peculiar to each individual's development, then they offer little assistance in the prediction of criminal involvement. For many criminals in our sample it is very difficult to identify characteristics that help to unravel their choice to become involved in crime. Such causes may be so individualistic and varied, and found in such different places over the life course, that it is virtually impossible for scholars to identify them or for public policy makers to use them to develop crime prevention policies. The causes of criminality in this context may be similar to the causes of changes in our weather or other phenomena for which long range forecasts are difficult. The chain of causal events involves so many factors that can have such varied effects that long-term prediction at the individual level becomes virtually impossible.

It need not be assumed, however, that the white-collar criminals we study are distinguishable from those who do not commit crime by the ways in which they make situational choices about criminal involvement. It may be that, at some point, most people allow deviations from what is otherwise considered acceptable behavior. This position is taken, for example, by Thomas Gabor (1994), in his provocative book, *Everybody Does It!* (see also Felson, 1998). He argues 'that most, if not all, of us break laws, formal rules, and other social conventions at some point' (1994: 12). In this context, we might speculate that many people would make similar decisions to those of the offenders we study when confronted with similar circumstances.

Mordechai Nisan, a scholar concerned with moral development, has coined the term 'limited morality', to recognize that most people will, under specific circumstances, allow themselves to violate norms that they accept as legitimate (Nisan, 1985; 1991; Nisan and Horenczyk, 1990):

> when faced with a moral conflict, people do not aspire to be saints but rather allow themselves a measure of deviation from what they consider proper behavior. Such deviation would not stem, therefore, from lack of knowledge or a distorted view of the right behavior (e.g. neutralization of the deviation: Sykes and Matza, 1957), nor would it stem from weakness of will or an inability to resist temptation. The leeway a person gives him/herself to deviate from the right course may be a considered decision guided by principal. (Nisan and Horenczyk, 1990: 29)

To explain the decision to deviate, Nisan proposes a model of 'moral balance', in which individuals weigh moral considerations against 'non moral considerations' in deciding whether to violate a specific rule. Financial pressures, personal crises, or unusual opportunities all fall within the boundaries of non-moral considerations. Violation of norms in this context does not imply that the individual has been improperly socialized or has a predisposition to rule breaking. This model appears particularly appropriate for those in our sample who argue that a specific crisis or opportunity has led them to violate the law.

Our emphasis on the situational components of criminal careers is consistent with data drawn from a sample of convicted white-collar criminals. However, the notion that situations play a central role in the development of crime is not unique to white-collar offenders. Indeed, the situational crime prevention approach discussed earlier in the chapter, has been applied primarily to common crimes such as burglary, prostitution, auto theft, and robbery (Poyner, 1993; Clarke, 1992; 1995). But our approach, does not simply recognize the importance of the crime situation in explaining a criminal event, we argue that for many criminals situational components of crisis and opportunity are in fact the main explanations for their involvement in crime. While this issue is not generally addressed in situational prevention studies, a similar approach is suggested by Felson and Clarke (1998) in an article entitled 'Opportunity makes the thief'.[5]

Finally, we think it important to recognize that the situational causes of crime we observe in our sample, may not be relevant for other crime samples. For common crime offenders, other considerations may have more significance. For example, Donald Black (1983: 34) contends that much common crime is a form of social control:

> There is a sense in which conduct regarded as criminal is often quite the opposite. Far from being an intentional violation of a prohibition, much crime is moralistic and involves the pursuit of justice. It is a mode of conflict management, possibly a form of punishment, even capital punishment ... To the degree that it defines or responds to the conduct of someone else – the victim – as deviant, crime is social control.

Crimes that involve retribution for offences against family members, which result from disputes over property or rights, or that are aimed to punish others would all fall under this general rubric. Black argues, as we have here, that it is often not useful to try to identify 'how criminals differ from other people' (ibid.: 42). His approach, like ours for white-collar crime, suggests that more is often learned by examining how specific situations lead otherwise law abiding people to participate in crime.

## Implications for policy and practice

In drawing policy implications from an empirical study it is important to recognize the difficulty of making generalizations about broad societal concerns from data that are limited to specific settings and circumstances. Nonetheless, in our study, as in others, the findings do not simply reflect on academic debate and scientific concerns. Our observations regarding the nature of offenders, in particular, raise questions about criminal justice policies, and suggest directions for criminal justice practice.

Our study emphasizes that offenders are often not very different from others in similar social and economic circumstances. This view of criminals is very much at odds with the underlying assumptions that are behind much recent criminal justice policy. The public and many policy makers remain committed to an idea of criminality which separates saints from sinners, and places a clear boundary between criminals and the rest of us (Gabor, 1994). This view of criminality has, as discussed above, been reinforced by many scholars who have tried to identify what distinguishes criminals from others.

Of course, one implication of what we have defined as the moral drama of criminality, is that criminals are defined by the public as outsiders. They are not simply neutral outsiders, they are outsiders who threaten the community and its values. Deviance theorists have long pointed out the functions of the criminal for reinforcing community solidarity, and clarifying community norms (e.g. see Becker, 1963; Durkheim, [1895] 1958; Erikson, 1962). In defining the criminal we reinforce what the rest of us have in common with each other. As in other forms of conflict, in the common threat that criminals represent, we are all brought closer together (Coser, 1967; Simmel, 1964).

The threat of crime and the perception that criminals are easily distinguished from the rest of us combine to create a powerful justification for ever increasing criminal justice punishments. Such policies often begin with the offender in the community, and what the community and the police can do to prevent crime. There is for example a growing focus on quality of life offences in most American cities (e.g. see Kelling and Coles, 1996). Such policies often test the constitutional boundaries of how police may restrict the movements and activities of citizens. While many such policies are justified by recent crime prevention theory and are attempts to empower communities in their efforts to control crime, they reflect, in a broader sense, a willingness on the part of Americans to tighten their control over offenders, even when such actions may limit traditional American freedoms. As one commentator on controlling crime in New York has observed, recent tough crime control policies sometimes appear to be a 'zero sum game in which more safety for some means more oppression for others' (Weisberg, 1999: 18). Of course, it is assumed that limits on freedom will apply only to the class of Americans that are defined as criminals.

Recent American imprisonment policies reflect in even starker terms the new punitive policies of crime control. In the 1990s prison populations increased more than 100 percent (Gilliard, 1999). By the twenty-first century about 2,000,000 Americans were held in prisons or jails on an average day (Walmsley, 2003), and some states were spending more on prisons than on colleges (Ambrosio and Schiraldi, 1997). Many states in the US, and the federal government have instituted so-called 'three strikes and you're out' laws, which demand that offenders be given long-term sentences after a set number of arrests, irrespective of the nature of the offender or the circumstances of his or her crimes (Shichor, 1997; Vitiello, 1997).

While the moral idea of criminality is not the only cause of such punitive punishment policies, we believe that common assumptions about the criminal have allowed Americans to support such policies. Would it be so easy to call for more intrusive surveillance and control policies if such policies were directed at those we see as part of our communities? If criminals are just like us, would we be so quick to imprison them? Would ever increasing punishment policies receive such support, if we believed that people like us, could in specific circumstances also become offenders?

We suspect that the answer to these questions is no. And in this sense, our data have particular importance for rethinking recent punitive crime control policies. We recognize that many offenders do in fact fit common stereotypes. However, many other people who commit crime are not very different from people who do not. This is true for white-collar crime, and as noted above, we suspect also true for much common crime. Recognition of this fact would we believe lead policy-makers and the public to think more cautiously before developing more intrusive strategies for cracking down on offenders in the streets, and raise important concerns about present imprisonment policies.

## Conclusion

Our work has centered both on descriptions of the criminal careers of white-collar offenders and on the implications that study of white-collar criminal careers has for understanding criminality more generally. We believe that this perspective is very much in the tradition that Edwin Sutherland began more than half a century ago. When Edwin Sutherland first introduced the concept of white-collar crime, he sought to add complexity and generality to theories of crime that were all too often focused on a particular type of offender and circumstance. Certainly, he argued, it is incorrect to see crime as a problem unique to the poor and disadvantaged if it can be found in well-off neighborhoods and among those who live in situations of authority and privilege. Obviously, the harms of major stock frauds and the creation of illegal trusts have more long term impact than the petty offences of most street criminals. But Sutherland hoped to do more than debunk what had seemed certain about the origins or characteristics of criminality. For Sutherland, the identification of white-collar crime was meant to provide substantive contributions to our understanding of crime, criminality and the criminal justice system.

In studying the criminal careers of convicted white-collar offenders we have taken an approach consistent with Sutherland's original intention of using the white-collar crime category to explore more general questions in the study of crime and justice (see Weisburd and Waring, 2001). When Edwin Sutherland raised the problem of white-collar crime, he sought to inform our general understanding of crime and criminality. Our approach has followed this tradition. In examining white-collar crime and criminal careers we have sought to raise broader questions related to crimes, criminals and the criminal justice system. Our work has focused our attention on a part of the criminal population that is often overlooked in studies of criminal careers. Studying these offenders has led us to think much more carefully about stereotypes of criminality, and situational factors in the development of crime.

Both lay people and criminologists often ask why others become involved in criminality. This seems a natural approach when the criminal population is defined as different from the rest of the community. However, our data suggest that to understand many of those who commit crime the view of criminality that sets offenders and non-offenders apart must be abandoned. This position may be unfamiliar, and less comfortable than the moral drama that ordinarily focuses attention on crimes and criminals. Nonetheless, it is consistent with a significant proportion of the crime and criminals in our society.

## Acknowledgements

We draw heavily in this chapter on material published in David Weisburd and Elin Waring with Ellen F. Chayet, *White-Collar Crime and Criminal Careers*, 2001, © Cambridge University Press, reproduced with permission. We wish to thank Gali Weissmann for her help in preparing this chapter for publication.

## Notes

1   The address was published the following year in the *American Sociological Review* under the title 'White Collar Criminality' (Sutherland, 1940).
2   Marcus Felson refers to this perspective as the 'not-me fallacy', arguing that most people would like to believe that they are 'fundamentally' different from serious offenders (1998: 10).
3   Support for our position comes in part from street crime studies that have contrasted offenders with less and more serious criminal records. In general, it is reported that less chronic offenders are less likely to evidence traits of instability and deviance than are chronic offenders. Of course, this does not directly address the question of whether such offenders are similar to non-offenders in comparable social and economic circumstances.
4   It is important to note that our study also supports specific elements of perspectives that emphasize the importance of life course events in understanding crime. For example, the emphasis on adult development and informal social controls in the workplace of Sampson and Laub (1995) is confirmed in our finding of the consistent importance of marital status in understanding criminal histories. Nonetheless, what is most striking in our work is the degree to which attributes of the offender's prior social record fail to provide very much insight into his or her involvement in crime.
5   It is interesting to note that Felson and Clarke use similar language to Nisan in discussing the idea 'that opportunities cause crime' (1998: 2). They note in discussing 'experiments in temptation', the findings indicate 'that a person makes a *considered decision* whether to respond to temptation'.

# References

Adler, Freda and Laufer, William S. (eds) (1995) 'The legacy of anomie theory', *Advances in Criminological Theory,* Vol. 6. New Brunswick, NJ: Transaction Publishers.

Akers, Ronald R. (1996) 'Is differential association/social learning cultural deviance theory?', *Criminology,* 34(2): 229–47.

Akers, Ronald R. (1998) *Social Learning and Social Structure: A General Theory of Crime and Deviance.* Boston: Northeastern University Press.

Ambrosio, Tara-Jen and Schiraldi, Vincent (1997) 'Executive summary', in *From Classrooms to Cell Blocks.* Washington, DC: The Justice Policy Institute.

Becker, Howard S. (1963) *Outsiders: Studies in the Sociology of Deviance.* New York: Free Press of Glencoe.

Benson, Michael and Moore, Elizabeth (1992) 'Are white-collar and common offenders the same? An empirical and theoretical critique of a recently proposed general theory of crime', *Journal of Research in Crime and Delinquency,* 29(3): 251–72.

Black, Donald (1983) 'Crime and social control', *American Sociological Review,* 48(1): 34–45.

Blumstein, Alfred, Cohen, Jacqueline, Roth, Jeffrey A. and Visher, Christy A. (eds) (1986) *Criminal Careers and 'Career Criminals'.* Washington, DC: National Academy Press.

Blumstein, Alfred and Soumyo, Moitra (1982) *Analysis of Trends in Offence Seriousness over a Criminal Career.* Washington, DC: National Institute of Justice.

Bonger, Wilhelm, A. (1916). *Criminality and Economic Conditions.* Boston: Little, Brown.

Clarke, Ronald V. (1980) 'Situational crime prevention: theory and practice', *British Journal of Criminology,* 20(2): 136–47.

Clarke, Ronald V. (1983) 'Situational crime prevention: its theoretical basis and practical scope', in Michael Tonry and Norval Morris, (eds) *Crime and Justice: An Annual Review of Research,* vol. 4, Chicago: University of Chicago Press, pp. 225–56.

Clarke, Ronald V. (ed.) (1992) *Situational Crime Prevention: Successful Case Studies.* Albany, NY: Harrow and Heston.

Clarke, Ronald V. (1995) 'Situational crime prevention', in Michael Tonry and David P. Farrington (eds) *Building a Safer Society: Strategic Approaches to Crime Prevention.* Chicago: University of Chicago Press, pp. 91–150.

Clarke, Ronald V. (1999). Personal correspondence to David Weisburd.

Clarke, Ronald V. and Cornish, Derek B. (1985) 'Modeling offenders' decisions: a framework for research and policy', in Michael Tonry and Norval Morris (eds) *Crime and Justice: An Annual Review of Research,* vol. 6, Chicago: University of Chicago Press, pp. 145–85.

Cornish, Derek B. and Clarke, Ronald V. (eds) (1986) *The Reasoning Criminal: Rational Choice Perspectives on Offending.* New York: Springer-Verlag.

Coser, Louis. (1967) *Continuities in the Study of Social Conflict.* New York: Free Press.

Cressey, D.R. (1980) 'Employee theft: the reasons why', *Security World,* (Oct.): 31–36.

Durkheim, Emile ([1895] 1958) *The Rules of Sociological Method.* New York: The Free Press.

Durkheim, Emile ([1897] 1951) *Suicide.* Glencoe, IL: The Free Press.

Edelhertz, Herbert and Overcast, Thomas D. (eds) (1982) *White Collar Crime: An Agenda for Research.* Lexington, MA: Lexington Books.

Erikson, Kai T. (1962) 'Notes on the sociology of deviance', *Social Problems* 9: 307–14.

Farrington, David P., Ohlin, Lloyd E. and Wilson, James Q. (1986) *Understanding and Controlling Crime.* New York: Springer-Velag.

Felson, Marcus (1998) *Crime and Everyday Life*. Thousand Oaks, CA: Pine Forge Press.

Felson, Marcus, and Clarke, Ronald V. (1998) 'Opportunity makes the thief: practical theory for crime prevention', *Police Research Series*, Paper 98.

Forst, Brian and Rhodes, William (n.d.) *Sentencing in Eight U.S. District Courts, 1973–1978. Codebook* (Interuniversity Consortium for Political and Social Research Study No. 8622). Ann Arbor, MI: University of Michigan Press.

Gabor, Thomas (1994) *Everybody Does It! Crime by the Public*. Toronto: University of Toronto Press.

Gilliard, Darrell, K. (1999) *Prison and Jail Inmates at Midyear 1998*. Washington, DC: Bureau of Justice Statistics.

Gottfredson, Michael and Hirschi, Travis (1990) *A General Theory of Crime*. Stanford, CA: Stanford University Press.

Guerry, A.M. (1833) *Essai sur la Statistique de la France*. Paris: Crochard.

Hirschi, Travis (1969) *Causes of Delinquency*. Berkeley, CA: University of California Press.

Hirschi, Travis and Gottfredson, Michael (1986) 'The distinction between crime and delinquency', in Timothy F. Hartnagel and Robert A. Silverman (eds) *Critique and Explanation: Essays in Honor of Gwynne Nettler*. New Brunswick, NJ: Transaction Books, pp. 55–69.

Hirschi, Travis and Gottfredson, Michael (1987) 'Causes of White Collar Crime', *Criminology*, 25(4): 949–74.

Kelling, George and Coles, Catherine M. (1996) *Fixing Broken Windows: Restoring Order and Reducing Crime in Our Communities*. New York: Free Press.

Kitsuse, John J. (1962) 'Social reaction to deviant behavior: problems of theory and method', *Social Problems*, 9: 247–56.

Lipton, Douglas, Martinson, Robert and Wilks, Judith (1975) *The Effectiveness of Correctional Treatment: A Survey of Treatment Evaluation*. New York: Praeger.

Lombroso, Cesare (1911) *Criminal Man*. Montclair, NJ: Patterson Smith.

Maltz, Michael D. (1984) *Recidivism*. Orlando, FL: Academic Press.

Martinson, Robert (1974) 'What works? Questions and answers about prison reform', *Public Interest*, 35: 22–54.

Merton, Robert K. (1938) 'Social structure and anomie', *American Sociological Review*, 3: 672–82.

Miller, Walter B. (1958) 'Lower class culture as a generating milieu of gang delinquency', *Journal of Social Issues*, 14(3): 5–19.

Nisan, Mordechai (1985) 'Limited morality – a concept and its educational implications', in M. Berkowitz and F. Oser, (eds) *Moral Education: Theory and Practice*. Hillsdale, NJ: Erlbaum, pp. 403–20.

Nisan, Mordechai (1991) 'The moral balance model: theory and research extending our understanding of moral choice and deviation', in W. Kurtines and J. Gewirtz (eds) *Handbook of Moral Behavior and Development*, vol. 3. Hillsdale, NJ: Erlbaum.

Nisan, Mordechai and Horenczyk, Gaby (1990) 'Moral balance: the effect of prior behavior on decision in moral conflict', *British Journal of Social Psychology*, 29: 29–42.

Passas, Nikos and Agnew, Robert (eds) (1997) *The Future of Anomie Theory*. Boston: Northeastern University Press.

Petersilia, Joan (1980) 'Criminal career research: a review of recent evidence', in Norval Morris and Michael Tonry (eds) *Crime and Justice: An Annual Review of Research,* vol. 2. Chicago: The University of Chicago Press, pp. 321–79.

Piquero, Nicole L. and Benson Michael L. (2004) 'White-collar crime and criminal careers: specifying a trajectory of punctuated situational offending', *Journal of Contemporary Criminal Justice*, 20(2): 148–65.

Poyner, Barry (1993) 'What works in crime prevention: an overview of evaluations', in Ronald V. Clarke (ed.) *Crime Prevention Studies*, vol. 1. Monsey: Criminal Justice Press, pp. 7–34.

Quetelet, A. (1835) *Sur l'Homme et le développement de ses Facultés, ou Essai de Physique Sociale*. Paris: Bachelier.

Reiss, Albert J. and Tonry, Michael (eds) (1986) *Communities and Crime*. Chicago: The University of Chicago Press.

Ross, E.A. (1907) *Sin and Society: An Analysis of Latter-Day Iniquity*. Boston: Houghton Mifflin.

Sampson, Robert J. and Laub, John J. (1993) *Crime in the Making: Pathways and Turning Points Through Life*. Cambridge, MA: Harvard University Press.

Schmidt, Peter and Dryden Witte, Ann (1988) *Predicting Recidivism Using Survival Models*. New York: Springer-Verlag.

Sechrest, Lee, White, O. Susan, and Brown, Elizabeth D. (1979) *The Rehabilitation of Criminal Offenders: Problems and Prospects*. Washington, DC: National Institute of Justice.

Shapiro, Susan P. (1981) *Thinking about White Collar Crime: Matters of Conceptualization and Research*. Washington, DC: National Institute of Justice.

Shaw, Clifford R. (1929) *Delinquency Areas*. Chicago: The University of Chicago Press.

Shaw, Clifford R. and McKay, Henry D. (1931) 'Social factors in juvenile delinquency', in *Report on the Causes of Crime,* vol. 2. Washington, DC: National Commission on Law Observance and Enforcement.

Shaw, Clifford R. and McKay, Henry D. (1942) *Juvenile Delinquency and Urban Areas*. Chicago: The University of Chicago Press.

Shichor, David (1997) 'Three strikes as a public policy: the convergence of the new penology and the McDonaldization of punishment', *Crime and Delinquency* 43(3): 470–92.

Short, James F. and Nye F. Ivan (1958) 'Extent of unrecorded juvenile delinquency, tentative conclusions', *Journal of Criminal Law, Criminology, and Police Science*, 49: 296–302.

Simmel, Georg (1964) *Conflict and the Web of Group Affiliations*. New York: Free Press.

Sinclair, Upton (1906) *The Jungle*. New York: Doubleday.

Steffens, Lincoln (1903) *The Struggle for Self-Government: Being an Attempt to Trace American Political Corruption to Its Sources in Six States of the United States*. New York: Phillips McClure.

Sutherland, Edwin H. (1940) 'White Collar Criminality', *American Sociological Review*, 5: 1–12.

Sutherland, Edwin H. (1945) 'Is White Collar a Crime?', *American Sociological Review*, 10: 132–9.

Sutherland, Edwin H. (1949) *White Collar Crime*. New York: Dryden Press.

Sutherland, Edwin H. and Cressey, Donald R. (1960) *The Principles of Criminology*. Chicago: J. B. Lippincott.

Sykes, Gresham M. and Matza, David (1957) 'Techniques of neutralization: a theory of delinquency', *American Sociological Review*, 22: 664–70.

Thrasher, Frederic (1927) *The Gang*. Chicago: The University of Chicago Press.

Tillman, Robert (1987) 'The size of the "Criminal population": the prevalence and incidence of adult arrests', *Criminology*, 25(3): 561–79.

Vitiello, Michael (1997) 'Three strikes: can we return to rationality?', *Journal of Criminal Law and Criminology*, 87(2): 395–481.

Wallerstein, J.A. and Wyle, C.E. (1947) 'Our law-abiding law-breakers', *Probation*, 25: 107–12.

Walmsley, Roy (2003) 'World prison population list', 4th edn, in *Findings*. London: Home Office Research, Development and Statistics Directorate.

Weisberg, Jacob (1999) 'The way we live now: 8-15-99; body count', *New York Times Magazine*, 15 August, p. 17.

Weisburd, David (2002) 'From criminals to criminal contexts: reorienting criminal justice research and policy', *Advances in Criminological Theory*, 10: 197–216.

Weisburd, David, Chayet, Ellen F. and Waring, Elin (1990) 'White-collar crime and criminal careers: some preliminary findings', *Crime & Delinquency*, 3: 342–55.

Weisburd, David and Waring, Elin (with Ellen F. Chayet) (2001) *White-Collar Crime and Criminal Careers*. Cambridge: Cambridge University Press.

Weisburd, David, Wheeler, Stanton, Waring, Elin and Bode, Nancy (1991) *Crimes of the Middle Classes*. New Haven, CT: Yale University Press.

Wheeler, Stanton, Mann, Kenneth and Sarat, Austin (1988) *Sitting in Judgment: The Sentencing of White Collar Offenders*. New Haven, CT: Yale University Press.

Wheeler, Stanton, Weisburd, David and Bode, Nancy (1982) 'Sentencing the White Collar offender: rhetoric and reality', *American Sociological Review*, 47(5): 641–59.

Wheeler, Stanton, Weisburd, David and Bode, Nancy (1988) *Study of Convicted Federal White-Collar Crime Defendants*. National Archives of Criminal Justice Data. The Inter-University Consortium for Political and Social Research. Ann Arbor, MI: University of Michigan Press.

Wilkins, Leslie T. (1965) *Social Deviance: Social Policy, Action, and Research*. Englewood Cliffs, NJ: Prentice-Hall.

Zietz, Dorothy (1981) *Women Who Embezzle or Defraud: A Study of Convicted Felons*. New York: Praeger Publishers.

## Suggestions for further reading

Benson, M. and Moore, E. (1992) 'Are white-collar and common offenders the same? An empirical and theoretical critique of a recently proposed general theory of crime.' *Journal of Research in Crime and Delinquency*, 29(3): 251–72.

Benson, M.L. and Kerley, K.R. (2000) 'Lifecourse theory and white collar crime', in H.N. Pontell and D. Shichor (eds) *Contemporary Issues in Crime and Criminal Justice: Essays in Honor of Gilbert Geis*. Upper Saddle River, NJ: Prentice Hall, pp. 121–36.

Piquero, A.R., Farrington, D.P. and Blumstein, A. (2003) 'The criminal career paradigm', in M. Tonry (ed.) *Crime and Justice: A Review of Research*. Chicago: The University of Chicago Press, pp. 359–506.

Weisburd, D., Chayet E.F. and Waring, E. (1990) 'White-collar crime and criminal careers: some preliminary findings', *Crime & Delinquency*, 3: 342–55.

Weisburd, D. and Waring, E. (with E.F. Chayet) (2001) *White-Collar Crime and Criminal Careers*. Cambridge: Cambridge University Press.

Weisburd, D., Wheeler, S., Waring, E. and Bode, N. (1991) *Crimes of the Middle Classes*, New Haven, CT: Yale University Press.

# TEN

## Concluding Comments

*John Minkes and Leonard Minkes*

This book, as we pointed out in the Introduction, has been designed to enable the individual contributors to set out their analyses of corporate and white-collar crime without seeking to establish one uniform explanation of the subject. There are, nevertheless, a number of unifying themes:

1   Corporate and white-collar crime is a significant feature in modern societies and is a major subject for study.
2   The questions it raises should engage, not only criminologists, but also economists and students of organization and management, ethics, law and public policy.
3   It is useful to establish an international perspective and to have regard to the possible influence on corporate behaviour of cultural characteristics of different societies.

Readers will have observed, as the Editors themselves have found, that while the individual chapters have each been drawn from different disciplines, there are parallel interests in a number of areas. One distinctive example can be found in the references to ethical characteristics and behaviour in general terms and in relation to corporate social responsibility. Another major instance can be found in the question of systemic malpractice and the view expressed in several chapters that corporations governed by a rational profit-maximizing goal in a market economy are inherently disposed to malpractice. In other words, that corporate crime is both systemic and endemic.

These are among the most significant matters to be considered and they especially cross the boundaries of disciplines. The debate about whether the business corporation is inherently criminogenic, for example, crosses the boundaries of criminology and could involve the analysis of corporations which commit crimes and corporations which do not. What, for instance, governs the differing responses to the pressures and attitudes which can lead to unlawful or unethical behaviour?

The debate should not be restricted to commercial corporations. Problems have also arisen in public organizations, both those which operate within a generally commercial environment and those which are publicly funded. The implications for the National Coal Board of the Aberfan disaster of 1966 are a case in point, as are those of the *Challenger* and *Columbia* disasters of 1986 and 2003 for NASA. Similarly, in centrally-planned and controlled systems, there have been serious problems, of which the Chernobyl breakdown of 1986 is a major instance.

A fuller understanding of questions of this kind requires understanding of what organizations are, how they function and what the lines of accountability in management are. It also demands consideration of how we view acts of omission and negligence as opposed to deliberate commission and how far we may hold individuals responsible for harms caused by mistakes and misjudgements or unintended consequences of managerial action. This links with the notion we raised in the Introduction of multi-causality and multi-responsibility.

The study of organizations has drawn attention also to questions of uncertainty and ambiguity and problems of control. To set this together with the study of corporate crime demonstrates the importance of motivation, standards of behaviour, and the cultural climate within the organization. It also highlights the role of law in society and the extent to which behaviour, legal or conventional, derives from ethical principles.

Ultimately, the study of corporate and white-collar crime raises questions of fairness and justice in our societies. If our criminal justice systems concentrate on the misdeeds of the poor and disadvantaged, we cannot claim to provide equality before the law and protection from crime for all our citizens; we must also confront the wrongdoing of the wealthy and powerful. It is our contention that a transdisciplinary approach offers the best means of understanding and responding to the latter crimes.

# Glossary

*Actus reus*   the conduct of the accused and its results.

**Bounded rationality**   intendedly rational but limited by inherent limits to knowledge.

**Bull market**   market in which investors buy stocks and shares in the hope and expectation of rising prices so that they can sell later at a profit. The reverse is a bear market; bears expect falling prices so there is an incentive to sell before they drop.

**Cartel**   an agreement between different firms to fix prices or market shares rather than compete. Cartels usually result in customers paying higher prices and are illegal in most jurisdictions under laws intended to promote competition.

**Cognition**   the process of knowing, acquiring information and understanding.

**Cognitive dissonance**   unwillingness or inability to believe evidence that conflicts with existing beliefs.

**Corporate culture**   complex term relating generally to accepted patterns of behaviour, both formal and informal, in an organization, whether established through formal rules or regulations, or by 'understood' habits or conventions.

**Criminogenic**   inherently tending to produce crime.

**Decision cycle**   processes of deciding, including implementation.

**Deregulation**   reduction in the controls placed by government regulations on the conduct of business; a marked feature of British and American policy during the 1980s and 1990s.

**Differential association**   general theory of crime put forward by Sutherland among others which argues that criminal behaviour is learned from others and the likelihood of an individual becoming a criminal depends on whether his or her associates view crime favourably or unfavourably.

**Economies of scale**   reduction in unit costs as size of enterprise grows.

**Estoppel**   a rule of evidence which states that a witness cannot deny the truth of a statement he or she has previously made or the existence of facts which he has led another to believe.

**Framing device**   the way in which facts or a typically complex situation are presented i.e. 'framed'; this may influence attitudes towards them so that the same facts may thus evoke different responses.

**Group think**   tendency for individuals to conform to the group view rather than make an individual decision.

**Hermeneutic**   relating to interpretation.

**Iatrogenic regulation**   from iatrogenic meaning illness caused by medical treatment e.g. as side-effects. In matters of, say, economic or social policy, the term could apply to the risk of unintended or contradictory effects and the need to deal with them. For example, rent control to benefit tenants was held by critics to reduce landlords' incentive to spend on property maintenance.

**Identification principle**   in English law, the principle that a corporation cannot be convicted of a criminal offence unless an individual officer of that company, senior enough to be identified as the 'controlling mind' is also convicted.

**Induction**   reasoning from the facts.

**Insider trading**   using knowledge gained as an insider to one's advantage in share dealings; a criminal offence in some jurisdictions.

*Mens rea*   guilty mind or criminal intention.

**Methodological individualism**   attempting to explain societal phenomena by focusing on the decisions and actions of individuals.

**Micro-, macro-**   as in micro-economics relating to the theory of the firm, or the individual consumer; macro-economics relating to the economy as a whole.

**Neo-liberalism**   political movement that views economic liberalism and deregulation as the key to economic and social development, widely regarded as the dominant philosophy in the West in the 1980s and the 1990s.

**Organisational culture**   see corporate culture.

**Oxymoron**   juxtaposition of seemingly contradictory terms e.g. bitter laughter; gentle tyrant.

**Paradigm**   a model or pattern of thought, particularly one that defines the parameters of an academic discipline.

**Positivism**   the theory that human behaviour can be understood by scientific observation; *individual positivism* focuses on explaining the behaviour of individuals and *sociological positivism* on understanding the behaviour of groups or societies.

**Rational Choice theory**   assumption that individuals and organizations make choices based on rational consideration of the advantages and disadvantages.

**Satisficing**   accepting choices and solutions which are satisfactory (i.e. good enough) rather than perfect, since we cannot know all possible choices and outcomes.

**Schumpeterian**   following the doctrines of J.A. Schumpeter (1880–1953), noted Austro-American economist, who wrote on many topics, e.g. entrepreneurship, innovation, business cycles.

**Self-regulation**   the practice of allowing industries or professions to regulate the conduct of their members rather than establishing an external body to regulate them. The British Medical Association is an example of self-regulation; in contrast, the Health and Safety Executive is a statutory regulatory agency external to the industries it regulates.

**Strain theory**   the theory that crime is caused by strain between people's legitimate aspirations and the opportunities available to them to achieve them; crime is one of a number of possible responses (the others include e.g. withdrawal from society).

**Synergy**   a situation where the effects of combining two or more items or units are greater than the sum of the individual parts, e.g. two individuals or departments working together might have ideas which would not occur to either of them working separately.

**Techniques of neutralization**   the means of minimizing or denying the impact of one's crimes, such as blaming the victim or claiming that no harm was caused.

**Transactions costs**   the costs of making (market) transactions, e.g. of finding suitable suppliers; of making contracts; of collecting information.

# Index

Entries in the Glossary are highlighted in **bold**